Data Visualization and Storytelling with Tableau

Tableau, one of the most widely used visualization tools, helps in illustrating the ideas of data visualization and storytelling. Through Tableau's Data Visualization and Storytelling feature, aspiring data scientists and analysts can develop their visual analytics skills and use them in both academic and business contexts.

Data Visualization and Storytelling with Tableau enables budding data analysts and data scientists to develop and sharpen their skills in the field of visual analytics and apply them in business scenarios as well as in academic contexts. This book approaches the Data Visualization workflow from a practical point of view, emphasizing the steps involved and the outcomes attained. A major focus of this book is the application and deployment of real-time case studies. Later chapters in this book provide comprehensive coverage for advanced topics such as data storytelling, data insights, color selection in graphs, publishing in tableau public, and misleading visualizations. Thus, this book emphasizes the need to visually examine and evaluate data through stories and interactive dashboards that are made up of appropriate graphs and charts. The case studies covered in this book are a natural extension of the visualization topics that are covered in each chapter. The intention is to empower readers to generate various dashboards, stories, graphs, charts, and maps to visualize and analyze data and support decision-making in business. Advanced charts that are pertinent to project management operations are also thoroughly explored, including comparison charts, distribution charts, composition charts, and maps. All these concepts will lay a solid foundation for data visualization applications in the minds of readers.

This book is meant for data analysts, computer scientists/engineers, and industry professionals who are interested in creating different types of visualization graphs for a given data problem and drawing interesting insights from the plotted trends in order to make better business decisions in the future.

Features:

- Introduces the world of Business Intelligence to readers through visualizations in Tableau.
- Discusses the need and relevance of each business graph with the help of a corresponding real-time case study.
- Explores the art of picking a suitable graph with an appropriate color scheme for a given scenario.
- Establishes the process of gaining relevant insights from the analysis of visualizations created.
- Provides guidance in creating innovative dashboards and driving the readers through the process of innovative storytelling with data in Tableau.
- Implements the concept of Exploratory Data Analysis (EDA) in Tableau.

Innovations in Multimedia, Virtual Reality and Augmentation

Series Editors:

Rashmi Agrawal, Professor, Manav Racna International Institute of Research and Studies

Lalit Mohan Goyal, J.C. Bose Univ. of Sci. and Tech.

Multimedia Data Processing and Computing
Edited By Suman Swarnkar, J P Patra, Tien Anh Tran, Bharat Bhushan, Santosh Biswas

Artificial Intelligence in Telemedicine: Processing of Biosignals and Medical Images
Edited By S. N. Kumar, Sherin Zafar, Eduard Babulak, M. Afshar Alam, Farheen Siddiqui

Multimedia Computing Systems and Virtual Reality
Edited By Rajeev Tiwari, Neelam Duhan, Mamta Mittal, Abhineet Anand, Muhammad Attique Khan

Advanced Sensing in Image Processing and IoT
Edited By Rashmi Gupta, Arun Kumar Rana, Sachin Dhawan, Korhan Cengiz

Data Visualization and Storytelling with Tableau
Mamta Mittal and Nidhi Grover Raheja

For more information about this series, please visit: https://www.routledge.com/ Innovations-in-Multimedia-Virtual-Reality-and-Augmentation/book-series/IMVRA

Data Visualization and Storytelling with Tableau

Mamta Mittal and Nidhi Grover Raheja

CRC Press
Taylor & Francis Group
Boca Raton London New York

CRC Press is an imprint of the
Taylor & Francis Group, an **informa** business

Designed cover image: © Shutterstock Images

First edition published 2024
by CRC Press
2385 NW Executive Center Drive, Suite 320, Boca Raton FL 33431

and by CRC Press
4 Park Square, Milton Park, Abingdon, Oxon, OX14 4RN

CRC Press is an imprint of Taylor & Francis Group, LLC

© 2024 Mamta Mittal and Nidhi Grover Raheja

ISBN: 9781032552224 (hbk)
ISBN: 9781032547916 (pbk)
ISBN: 9781003429593 (ebk)

DOI: 10.1201/9781003429593

Typeset in Times
by codeMantra

Contents

Preface

OVERVIEW

Emerging data scientists and analysts may sharpen their visual analytics skills with Tableau's Data Visualization and Storytelling feature and use them in academic and business contexts. The case studies in this book are an extension of the subjects covered in each chapter and serve as a complement. The goal is to include key advanced charts pertinent to project management operations, including maps, graphs, distribution charts, composition charts, and comparison charts. Using Tableau, one of the most widely used visualization tools, the data visualization and narrative ideas are presented.

AUDIENCE

The book is appropriate for any undergraduate or postgraduate students and working professionals who want to develop and upgrade their careers in the fields of data visualization and analysis. Each chapter covers the basic to advanced knowledge of every topic in simple language along with easy-to-understand examples.

CHAPTER OUTLINE

CHAPTER 1: GETTING STARTED WITH DATA VISUALIZATION

This chapter focuses on data visualization basics, data types, significance, and the data analysis life cycle. It provides an in-depth understanding of the phases of converting raw data into valuable insights, laying a solid foundation for the core concepts of data visualization.

CHAPTER 2: TABLEAU FOR VISUALIZATION

This chapter introduces the Tableau visualization tool, covering its components, data types, and file types. It provides a detailed explanation of analytical applications created in Tableau. The chapter also provides a step-by-step guide on downloading and installing Tableau on a system, with screenshots provided. Later, it introduces users to Tableau Public and the process of online publishing a workbook created on Tableau Desktop.

CHAPTER 3: CONNECTING DATA IN TABLEAU

This chapter expands on previous knowledge, assisting users in connecting various data sources like MS Excel, CSV, Oracle, and SQL Server to Tableau. It also discusses data extraction in Tableau and covers various Relational Database Management System (RDBMS) concepts like Keys, Data Joins, and Data Blending. The goal is to equip readers with the ability to connect and use various Tableau data sources effectively.

CHAPTER 4: TABLE CALCULATIONS AND LEVEL OF DETAIL

This chapter covers Tableau table computations and Level of Detail (LOD) ideas, providing examples and explanations of calculation components like functions, fields, operators, and expressions. Tableau offers various functions like logical, aggregate, date, string, and numeric functions, as well as general, arithmetic, relational, and logical operators. LOD expressions, which allow users to compute values at both data source and display levels, are covered separately in the chapter.

CHAPTER 5: SORTING AND FILTERS IN TABLEAU

This chapter discusses the sorting process and various filters in Tableau, including Dimension Filter, Measure Filter, Dates, Context, Extract, Condition, Quick, and Table Calculation Filters. It also covers various sorting techniques, such as Toolbar Sorting, Axis Sorting, Manual Sorting, Nested Sorting, and Custom Sorting using Parameter. The chapter aims to help readers manipulate, sort, and filter data from a Tableau data source.

CHAPTER 6: CHARTS IN TABLEAU

This chapter delves into Tableau's diverse chart and graph types, including 24 types like Text Tables, Heat Maps, Bar Charts, Box Plots, etc. It also discusses advanced combination charts and dual-axis charts. The chapter explains the use cases and color schemes for each chart, aiming to help users understand the importance of different charts and their applications.

CHAPTER 7: COMPARISON CHARTS IN TABLEAU

This chapter covers Tableau comparison charts, including Text Table, Bar Chart, Column Chart, Lollipop Chart, Line Chart, Time Series, and Trendlines. It provides examples using Tableau Desktop and Tableau Public; discusses different types of trend lines and their mathematical basics, equations, and examples; and discusses assessing their significance using P-value and R-squared statistics. The chapter concludes by explaining their usage for future forecasting and stakeholder decision-making.

CHAPTER 8: DISTRIBUTION CHARTS

This chapter explores various distribution charts in Tableau, including Histograms, Scatter plots, Bubble charts, Radar charts, Heat maps, and Box plots. These charts provide a deeper understanding and insights for intelligent investigation, especially when compared to average numbers like sales and revenue. Each chart is discussed in separate sections, with a case study provided. The chapter aims to help users understand the need for distribution charts and their structure, advantages, and disadvantages.

CHAPTER 9: PART-TO-WHOLE RELATIONSHIP: COMPOSITION CHARTS

Composition charts are covered in this chapter in several ways. Charts that display the data's static composition and charts that depict compositional changes over time are the two main types of Composition charts that Tableau supports. Pie charts, donut charts, waterfall charts, and tree maps are among the static composition charts. Stacked charts, however, show how the composition has changed over time. Each of these charts is covered separately along with useful case examples that will aid users in understanding these charts.

Chapter 10: Project Management with Evaluation Charts

This chapter introduces project management and visualization graphs, detailing the phases of software project conceptualization and development. It provides detailed insights into evaluation graphs, which help project managers coordinate team members, schedule tasks, and track progress. The final section focuses on advanced project management activities essential for project progression.

Chapter 11: Maps in Tableau

This chapter introduces the concept of Maps in Tableau, which are useful for efficiently and visually presenting geographical information. It covers six types of maps and their techniques for presenting demographic data. Through real-time case studies using various datasets, users learn about the benefits of maps over other graphs when working with latitude and longitude-based location data.

Chapter 12: Designing Stories through Data

This chapter explores the concept of creating interactive business stories to enhance audience impact. It provides examples and case studies to understand different types of stories, their components, and the progression of storytelling. The chapter also discusses the decision-making process in the storytelling framework and the insights that can be derived from interactive stories. It also provides a detailed discussion of the types of insights that can be derived from these stories.

Chapter 13: Exploratory Data Analysis (EDA) in Tableau

This chapter provides a comprehensive understanding of Exploratory Data Analysis (EDA) in Tableau, examining various graphical and non-graphical approaches, and comparing exploratory and explanatory data analysis practices. It also introduces the concept of data storytelling, which arises from the interaction between exploratory and explanatory data analysis procedures.

Chapter 14: Misleading Visualizations

This chapter discusses misleading visualizations, which can be confusing and deceptive when the format is not suitable for the data being examined. It provides examples of misleading graphics and their impact on decision-makers, influencing business decisions. The chapter also highlights mistakes users must avoid when creating accurate and effective visuals.

Acknowledgments

Dr. Mamta Mittal

Writing a book is harder than we think and more rewarding than we could have ever imagined. I want to thank my family and friends from the bottom of my heart for their continuous support and encouragement while I wrote this book. Writing a book from a concept is not as easy as it seems. It is a rewarding and internally demanding experience. I am also appreciative of CRC Press/Taylor & Francis Group for their advice and knowledge in making this book possible. This book took a long time to revise, and editors, technical specialists, and reviewers all contributed significantly. I want to convey special thanks to my co-author Ms. Nidhi Grover Raheja who has always stood by my side during the journey of writing this book. Lastly, I want to express my gratitude to every reader for showing interest in my work and helping to make it a reality.

Mrs. Nidhi Grover Raheja

In writing this book, I want to thank my family and friends from the bottom of my heart for their constant support and encouragement, especially my parents and family, Mr. Rakesh Kumar Grover, Mrs. Saroj Grover, Isha Grover, Mr. Ashok Kumar Raheja, and Mrs. Renu Raheja. I want to convey special thanks to my husband Mr. Sameer Raheja and my daughter Cherika Raheja for their unconditional love and support. I also acknowledge the help and support of CRC Press/Taylor & Francis Group in making this book a reality. I want to convey my deepest gratitude to Dr. Mamta Mittal for her guidance and expertise in conceptualizing the idea. Editorial staff, technical experts, and reviewers all contributed greatly to the extensive and laborious process of book revision. I would also like to acknowledge all my coworkers and colleagues for their support. Finally, I want to thank God most of all because without God I would not be able to do any of this.

Authors' Biography

Dr. Mamta Mittal is working as Associate Professor and Programme Anchor for Data Analytics and Data Science at Delhi Skill and Entrepreneur University, New Delhi (under the Government of NCT Delhi). She has received a PhD in Computer Science and Engineering from Thapar University, Patiala; a MTech (Honors) in Computer Science & Engineering from YMCA, Faridabad; and a BTech in Computer Science & Engineering from Kurukshetra University, Kurukshetra. She has been teaching for the last 21 years with an emphasis on Data Mining, Machine Learning, DBMS, and Data Structure. Dr. Mittal is a lifetime member of CSI and has published more than 110 research papers in SCI, SCIE, and Scopus-indexed journals. She holds five patents and two copyrights in the area of artificial intelligence, IoT, and deep learning. Dr. Mittal is working on the DST-approved project "Development of IoT based hybrid navigation module for midsized autonomous vehicles" with a research grant of 25 lakhs. Currently, she is guiding PhD scholars in the field of Machine Learning and Deep Learning. She is the editor of the book series Edge AI in Future Computing with CRC Press, Taylor & Francis, USA.

Mrs. Nidhi Grover Raheja is actively working as a Technical Trainer in the domains of Python Programming, Data Analytics, and Visualization Tools. She is currently associated as Guest Faculty in the Data Analytics Department, Bhai Parmanand DSEU Shakarpur Campus-II, New Delhi (under Govt. of NCT Delhi). She has over a decade of experience and is associated with numerous reputed educational and training institutions in the role of Technical Trainer and Guest Lecturer. She qualified UGC-NET (Lectureship) and GATE in Computer Science. After completing her MCA from GGSIPU, Delhi, she accomplished MTech (CSE) from DCRUST, Sonipat, with distinction. Her interest areas include Python programming with machine learning, deep learning, natural language processing, statistical analysis, and visualization tools, including Tableau and Microsoft Power BI. She not only endeavors to train students with an experiential learning approach but also continuously tries to shape up their careers with the best of skills and knowledge as per standards.

1 Getting Started with Data Visualization

1.1 INTRODUCTION TO DATA AND ITS TYPES

Data, a collection of facts and figures, is prevalent in various industries like technology, medicine, retail, business, and social network data. British mathematician and data science entrepreneur Clive Humby believes that data is valuable but must be refined before use [1]. To create useful entities, data must be transformed into gas, plastic, or chemicals. For data to be useful, it must be separated and analyzed. For example, open-ended questions require more pre-processing than multiple-choice questions, as the group may answer differently and leave some answers blank. Therefore, it is essential to refine and clean data before data analysis, creating reports, and discovering valuable trends for future decision-making [2].

1.1.1 CATEGORIES OF DATA

Data falls into one of two primary groups: qualitative data and quantitative data. Below is the flowchart showing different types of data with examples (Figure 1.1).

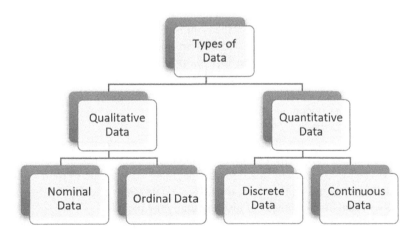

FIGURE 1.1   Different types of data.

A. Qualitative or Categorical Data

Qualitative or categorical data is non-quantifiable information organized by category rather than number. It allows market researchers to understand their target market's preferences and develop effective tactics and products.

DOI: 10.1201/9781003429593-1   1

Examples of qualitative data include language spoken by clients, popular vacation spots, opinions, and customer color preferences. This type of data helps in understanding the preferences of consumers and enhancing marketing strategies. The qualitative data are further classified into two categories:

1. Nominal Data

Nominal data are variables lacking a numerical value or order. Nomen, which means "name" in Latin, is the source of the word "nominal." Since the values of nominal data are dispersed among many categories, we are unable to do any mathematical operations with them or provide any direction for sorting the data. Nominal data includes, for instance:

- Hair color, such as red, brown, black, or blonde;
- Relationship status (single, widowed, or married);
- Nationality (American, Indian, or German);
- Gender (female, male, other);
- Eye color, which can be black, brown, etc.

2. Ordinal Data

Ordinal data, which have a natural ordering based on scale position, is useful for observations like customer satisfaction and feedback ratings but cannot be used for statistical analysis due to its lack of order compared to nominal data. Ordinal data includes, among other things:

- A scale of 1–10 for rating customer feedback.
- Exam grade outcomes (A, B, C, D, etc.).
- Positioning of competitors (first, second, third, etc.).
- Financial well-being (high, medium, and low).
- Level of education (schooling, graduation, post-graduation, etc.).

B. Quantitative Data

Quantitative data, which includes numerical values, is countable and enables statistical analysis. It responds to queries like "how much," "how many," and "how often." Statistical manipulation can be done on quantitative data, such as height, weight, cost, RAM, temperature, and student scores. Examples include 59, 80, 60, and time duration. The quantitative data are then divided into two groups:

1. Discrete Data

Discrete denotes uniqueness or distinction. Discrete data contains values that are categorized as whole numbers or integers. These data cannot be used to extract any fractional or decimal values. Due to their countable nature and finite values, the discrete data cannot be divided further. Representative instances of discrete data may include:

- Overall count of students attending the class.
- Net price of a cell phone.
- Department-wise count of employees in a company.
- Number of participants in a competition.
- Number of working days per week.

2. Continuous Data

Continuous data, which can be subdivided into smaller levels, is represented by fractional numbers like an Android phone's version or an object's size. It can hold any value within a range, unlike discrete data which includes integers or whole numbers. However, continuous data preserves fractional values to capture various forms of data, including temperature, height, width, time, speed, etc. Several instances of continuous data are:

- Height of students in a class
- Vehicle speed
- Time taken for task completion
- Wi-Fi speed or frequency
- Stock prices of a company

1.2 DATA ANALYSIS LIFECYCLE

Data analytics is the act of examining and analyzing massive databases to spot hidden patterns and unobserved trends, establish correlations, and derive insightful knowledge for business forecasting. It increases the speed and effectiveness of business operations. To execute data analytics, businesses use a variety of contemporary tools and technology. The acronym CRISP-DM, or cross-industry standard process for data mining, is a tried-and-true way to guide your data mining efforts. A data analytics project's execution is outlined by the data analytics lifecycle, which has six primary components and is based on the CRISP-DM methodology. The data analytics lifecycle entails six phases, which are:

I. Identify the business issues
II. Understand the dataset
III. Prepare the data
IV. Perform exploratory analysis and modeling
V. Validate your data
VI. Visualize and present your findings

Figure 1.2 gives an overview of each phase in the data analytics life cycle.

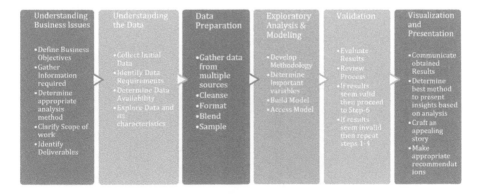

FIGURE 1.2 Data analytics lifecycle phases.

1.3   DATA VISUALIZATION IN DATA ANALYSIS

Data visualization is a way to visually represent information and data using charts, graphs, and maps. It helps to identify trends, patterns, and outliers in the data, making it easier to analyze large volumes of data and make data-driven decisions [3]. Data visualization enhances the usability, accessibility, and comprehension of complex data and can uncover unknown insights and patterns. Consider the following examples to understand the importance of visualization in different scenarios:

- As an illustration, consider how line charts might be used to visualize change over time in product sales, profit earned, stock price variations, etc.
- Bar and column charts are helpful for comparing data and identifying relationships such as comparative analysis of yearly sales, monthly units sold, etc.
- Pie charts are a fantastic method to display portions of a whole such as viewing category-wise share of total product sales made in a year.
- The most effective method for disseminating geographic information is through maps such as depicting state-wise distribution of sales across a country.

1.3.1   NEED FOR DATA VISUALIZATION

Data visualization is crucial in the data analysis lifecycle, aiding in understanding consumer behavior, improving customer ratings, and forecasting sales volumes. Better judgment results from improved perceptions and market analysis [4, 5]. With the help of sophisticated visualization technologies, users and viewers can see data presented in a variety of formats, including pie charts, heat maps, dials, gauges, maps, and fever charts. Data visualization can be used for the following scenarios:

- Data visualization helps in making data interesting and easy to understand by using graphics, charts, descriptive text, and appealing design. It allows for the grouping and arrangement of data according to groups and themes, making it easier to divide into digestible portions (Figure 1.3).

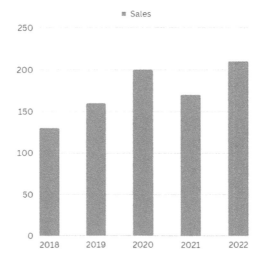

FIGURE 1.3   Bar chart showing 5-year sales of products from 2018 to 2022.

- Data visualization tools like charts can quickly evaluate and sort large amounts of data, enabling quicker identification of patterns and trends, compared to manual data analysis that may take months or years. Take the "sanitizer" search trend on Google Trends as an example (Figure 1.4).

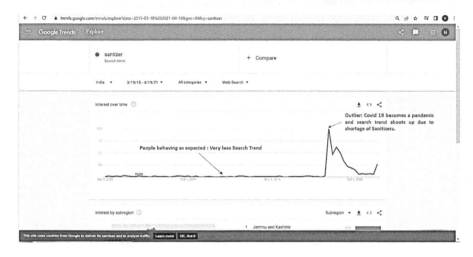

FIGURE 1.4   Google trends for the keyword "Sanitizer."

- Charts also make it much easier for us to spot trends than manually browsing through data. Here is a straightforward chart produced by Google Search Console as an illustration of how Google searches for "Python" have changed over time. As you can see, searches for "Python" significantly increased in March 2022 (Figure 1.5):

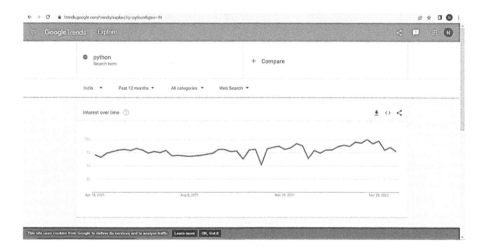

FIGURE 1.5   Google trends for the keyword "Python."

- When insights from a dataset are effectively communicated through tales and visualizations, it is known as data storytelling. This technique puts the findings into context, gives the data a strong sense of relevance, and inspires action from the audience.
- Supporting an argument or opinion: People frequently need to observe something to accept it as true or to be convinced that it is true. A strong infographic or chart can strengthen your case and highlight your originality. The following situations may benefit from infographics:
    1. Visualize advantages and disadvantages to promote wise decision-making
    2. Compare items to draw attention to characteristics and influence consumers
    3. Use information that is easy to understand through visuals
    4. Compare facts and figures for better decision-making (Figure 1.6)

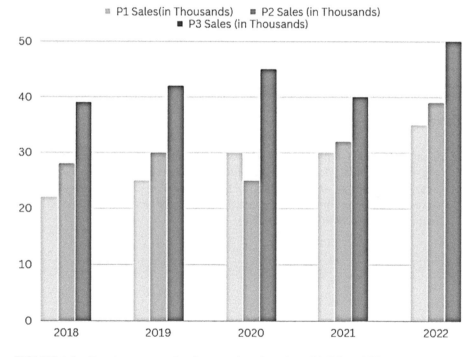

FIGURE 1.6   Bar chart comparing 5-year sales of products P1, P2, and P3.

- **Emphasizing the key elements of a set of data:** Readers can more easily study the data and draw their own conclusions with the help of data visualizations. Data visualizations are frequently used to tell a story, support a point of view, or influence readers to reach a particular conclusion. Designers use graphic hints to direct the viewer's attention to different areas of a page. Visual cues in data visualization are shapes, symbols, and colors that indicate or highlight specific areas of the visualization (Figure 1.7).

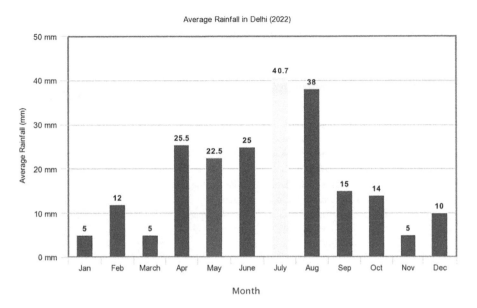

FIGURE 1.7 Bar chart highlighting the highest rainfall in Delhi in July month. (Based on hypothetical data.)

1.3.2 PROS AND CONS OF DATA VISUALIZATION

The following benefits and drawbacks of visual data representation should be considered:

Benefits of Data Visualization

- A larger audience can easily access it.
- It packs a lot of information into a little area.
- It improves the aesthetic appeal of your report.

Drawbacks of Data Visualization

- If an improper visual representation is made, it may misrepresent information.
- If the visual information is misinterpreted or distorted excessively, it may be distracting for the audience.

1.4 POPULAR TOOLS FOR DATA VISUALIZATION

For businesses to handle massive volumes of data, make critical decisions, and draw in audiences, data visualization technologies like Google Charts, Tableau, Grafana, Chartist.js, FusionCharts, Datawrapper, Infogram, Qlik, Microsoft Power BI, and ChartBlocks are indispensable. These tools offer unique features, allowing users to

TABLE 1.1

Comparison of Tableau, Power BI, and Qlik

Feature	Tableau	Power BI	Qlik Sense
Visualization feature	Perfect graphics and visualization features	Easy to use and quick to learn	Self-service analytics tool
Analytics capability	Complete integration with R and Python	Supports R language-based visualization	Does not support R or Python-based objects
Cloud support	Support for cloud platforms like Azure, AWS, etc.	Support for Microsoft Azure	Support for SaaS cloud product
Big data integration	Enables data integration with almost any data repository from MS Excel to Hadoop clusters	Better support	Allows data management within a single environment
Storage capacity	100 GB cloud storage	10 GB cloud storage	500 GB cloud storage

add datasets and visually display them, making data visualization a crucial aspect of decision-making. Let us explore the most common visualization software:

1. **Tableau:** Due to its superior visualization capabilities, front-end graphical user interface, integrated analytics modules, online report interchange, and flexibility in customizing dynamic visuals and app features, Tableau is the most widely used and effective business intelligence (BI) solution.
2. **Qlik Sense:** While QlikView, a possible rival, can interact with numerous data sources at once, Qlik Sense is an intuitive data visualization tool that lets users import and aggregate data from multiple big data sources.
3. **Microsoft Power BI**: It is the preferred data visualization tool due to its seamless integration with Microsoft Azure and its ability to create personalized dashboards by linking to Excel.

Table 1.1 shows a comparative analysis of the three most popular visualization tools nowadays namely, Tableau, Power BI, and Qlik.

KEY NOTES

- Observations, measurements, words, numbers, and specific item descriptions are examples of facts and figures that make up data.
- The two primary types of data are qualitative and quantitative.
- Category data, sometimes referred to as qualitative data, is information that cannot be measured or totaled numerically.
- Statistical data analysis and counting are both made possible by the quantitative data's capacity to be expressed numerically.
- Your audience and you can both benefit from data visualization as you interpret and understand the information.

- Chartist.js, FusionCharts, Datawrapper, Infogram, Tableau, ChartBlocks, and Google Charts are some of the greatest tools available for data visualization.
- Large data volumes, several graphical styles, and ease of use are all requirements for these products.

TEST YOUR SKILLS

1. Differentiate between data and information. Elaborate with relevant business examples.
2. Discuss the different categories of data and their use cases.
3. How data analysis is different from data analytics?
4. Establish various phases involved in the process of data analysis.
5. Discuss the need of data visualization with respect to a restaurant chain business. Here, multiple outlets of the restaurant are open across the city with dine-in, takeaway, and home delivery options. The business stakeholders want to analyze the present business scenario and compare it with their competitors for future forecasting and decision-making for growth.
6. Compare the features of Tableau with Power BI and Qlik.

REFERENCES

[1] Sadiku, Matthew, Shadare, Adebowale, Musa, Sarhan, Akujuobi, Cajetan, and Perry, Roy. Data visualization. *International Journal of Engineering Research and Advanced Technology (IJERAT)*, 12, 2454–6135, 2016.
[2] Eigner, W. "Current work practice and users' perspectives on visualization and interactivity in business intelligence." *2013 17th International Conference on Information Visualisation,* London, 2013, 299–306, doi: 10.1109/IV.2013.38
[3] Manyika, J., Chui, M., Brown, B., Bughin, J., Dobbs, R., Roxburgh, C., and Byers, A.H. *Big Data: The next Frontier for Innovation, Competition, and Productivity.* 2011. https://www.mckinsey.com/insights/business_technology/big_data_the_next_frontier_for_innovation.
[4] Negash, S. Business intelligence. *Communications of the Association for Information Systems*, 13, 177–195, 2004.
[5] Zhu, Weiming, and Ni, Tongguang. A study of big-data-driven data visualization and visual communication design patterns, 2021, 1058–9244, Article ID 6704937. https://doi.org/10.1155/2021/6704937.

2 Tableau for Visualization

2.1 INTRODUCING TABLEAU

Tableau Software is an interactive data visualization software supplier based in the United States specializing in corporate information [1,2]. Seattle, Washington, serves as its present headquarters. It was initially founded by Pat Hanrahan, Christian Chabot, and Chris Stolte in Mountain View, California, in 2003, but Salesforce acquired the company in 2019. Tableau is one of the most powerful and quickly evolving data visualization tools within the business intelligence space [1] (Figure 2.1).

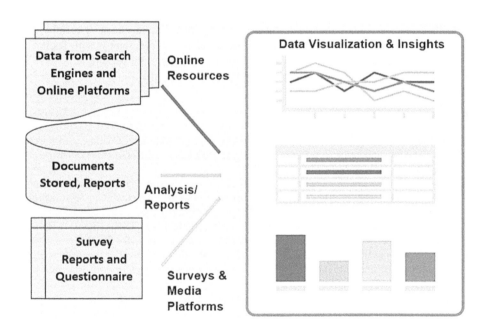

FIGURE 2.1 Data binding from multiple sources for visualization.

Tableau facilitates the conversion of unprocessed data into a comprehensible and readable manner. Data created with Tableau's help is interpreted by experts at any level of a company. It also enables non-techies to design unique dashboards [3,4]. The Tableau program allows for quick data analysis and generates worksheets and dashboards that serve as visuals.

DOI: 10.1201/9781003429593-2

2.1.1 CHARACTERISTIC FEATURES OF TABLEAU

Tableau offers solutions for various departments, industries, and data settings. The following special attributes allow Tableau to handle a variety of scenarios (Figure 2.2):

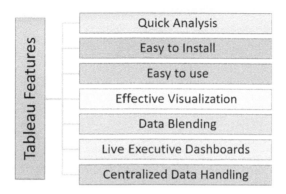

FIGURE 2.2 An overview of Tableau characteristics.

- **Quick Analysis:** Anyone with access to data can start using Tableau to extract value from the data because it does not require sophisticated programming experience.
- **Simple Installation and Use:** No sophisticated software setup is necessary to use Tableau. Installing the desktop version is the simplest and provides all the necessary tools to initiate and finish data analysis.
- **Effective Visualization:** Colors, trend lines, charts, and graphs are examples of visual tools that allow the user to explore and interpret data. Almost everything is done with drag and drop, therefore there is not much script to write.
- **Blend Numerous Datasets:** Tableau enables you to quickly merge various relational, semi-structured, and unstructured data sources without incurring expensive upfront integration costs.
- **Live Executive Dashboards:** Live executive dashboards allow for the quick filtering, sorting, and debating of data in portals like Salesforce or a SharePoint site.
- **Centralized Data Handling:** All of the organization's public data sources can be managed from one central location, thanks to the Tableau Server. Schedules can be added, modified, deleted, and permissions changed all in one handy place.

Example of sales data analysis: Assume that we have Excel sheets with the sales data and the sales target data. To gain access, we must now contrast real sales with the sales we had hoped to achieve. Data blending incorporates two sorts of data sources: primary and secondary. The primary and secondary data sources will be joined on the left, using all of the primary data source's rows and any matching rows from the secondary data source.

2.2 DIFFERENT TABLEAU PRODUCTS

Tableau offers a wide range of products, which are divided into groups according to how they perform. The various categories of tools include the Data Preparation tools, the Viewer tools, the Server tools, and the Developer tools (Figure 2.3).

FIGURE 2.3   A view of the Tableau product suite.

Let us discuss each category in detail:

A. Tableau Server Tools
 1. **Tableau Server:** On a Windows or Linux server, Tableau Server must be installed as a paid server application. This is commonly utilized in the business sector. A specialized admin team or individual would typically oversee the tasks of managing the server's memory, users, data sources, folders, and other server-related tasks.
 2. **Tableau Online:** There is no need to install Tableau Online on any Windows servers because it is already hosted by Tableau Software and is a paid server program. When you need to have access to your Tableau dashboards from anywhere, this is preferable. Nearly all of Tableau Server's functionality are included here, just online. Tableau Desktop workbooks are necessary for publishing on Tableau Online and Server. Data streaming from web applications like Google Analytics and Salesforce.com is supported by Tableau Server and Tableau Online.

B. Tableau Developer Tools

1. **Tableau Desktop:** The premium and sophisticated desktop program for application development is known as Tableau Desktop or Tableau Desktop Professional Edition. The developers may create a wide variety of charts, calculations with formulas, attractive dashboards, etc. here. The trial period is 14 days after which users need to buy for paid services. Any of the servers mentioned above can receive the dashboards created here, and it is easily accessible using Tableau Reader.

2. **Tableau Public:** This particular version of Tableau was developed with cost-effectiveness in mind. When workbooks are marked as "Public," it means that they cannot be stored locally; instead, they must be saved to Tableau's publicly available cloud. People publish their thoughts and visualizations here for free. It has no features for managing users or folders. It can only have an extract as a data source instead of a live one. This is the ideal Tableau version for those who want to study Tableau and share their data with the world.

C. Tableau Viewer Tools

1. **Tableau Reader:** The free desktop viewer called Tableau Reader allows us to see the Tableau dashboards produced by Tableau Desktop. Only extracted connection files are supported. Purchasing one Tableau Desktop license and installing Tableau Reader as a free program on the end user's computer might make it easier for new users to experience Tableau. It can access the dashboards and do operations on them, including filtering, tooltips, and parameters. However, the charts and formulas cannot be changed using Reader.

2. **Tableau Mobile:** An app for mobile devices is known as Tableau Mobile. Both iOS and Android have access to it. It functions similarly to Tableau Reader and can connect to Tableau Online or Tableau Server. An interactive dashboard published to the Tableau Server or Tableau online can be seen and interacted with using Tableau Mobile on a smartphone.

D. Data Preparation Tool

1. **Tableau Prep Builder:** A recent release from Tableau is the Tableau Prep Builder. It assists programmers in blending, cleaning, and managing the raw data. It is a small-scale ETL (extraction, transformation, and loading) tool that connects to several databases, joins data, transforms data, and outputs a file. It is automatable and can save developers from needless manual data processing.

2.3   TABLEAU SERVER ARCHITECTURE

Tableau's n-tier, highly scalable client-server architecture works with desktop-installed programs, web clients, and mobile clients. For producing shared views on Tableau Server, utilize the writing and publishing tool Tableau Desktop. The Tableau Server component provides an enterprise-class business analytics platform to thousands of clients. It uses organizational data strategy and security protocols to provide robust analytics for mobile and browser-based devices. It is a multi-process, multi-user, and multi-threaded system overall. A strong architecture is necessary to provide all these prevalent unique traits. The following architectural diagram lists the several layers that are utilized by Tableau Server (Figure 2.4).

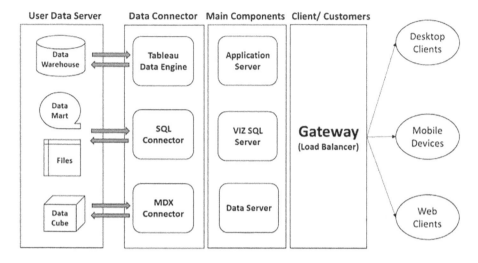

FIGURE 2.4   The Tableau server architecture components.

Let us discuss each layer in the Tableau architecture in detail:

1. **Data Server Layer:** The data sources that can connect to Tableau are its main building blocks. Multiple data sources can be connected to Tableau. It may combine data from several data resources. It may simultaneously connect to an Excel file, a database, a departmental data mart, an organizational Datawarehouse, and a web application. Additionally, it can alter how several data sources relate to one another.

2. **Data Connector Layer:** The data connectors offer a means of launching a connection between external data sources and the Tableau Data Server. SQL/ODBC connectivity is built into Tableau. Any database can be connected to using the ODBC connector instead of the native connector for that database. Both extract and live data can be chosen in the Tableau Desktop. Live data and extracted data can both be simply swapped depending on the usage.

   a. **Live or Real-Time Data:** By directly linking to the external database, Tableau can connect to real data. Also, by transmitting dynamic multi-dimensional expressions (MDX) and SQL statements, it makes use of the infrastructure's existing database. Rather than importing the data, you can utilize this capability to attach the live data to Tableau. The subsequent database system is quick and highly optimized. The database size is massive, and it is updated frequently, mostly in different companies. Tableau connects with the live data in these situations to function as a front-end visualization tool.

b. **Data Extracts:** Tableau has the option to extract data from other data sources, either in-memory or extracted. Using a Tableau extract file, we create a local copy. With only one click, it is possible to remove millions of records from the Tableau data engine. Tableau's data engine uses memory types like ROM, RAM, and cache to process and store data. Tableau enables the use of filters to pull a small sample of data from a larger dataset. This improves performance, especially when working with huge datasets. Without establishing a live connection to the data source, data extracts allow for offline data visualization.

3. **Server Components:** The third layer in the architecture deals with major components doing unique tasks in the Tableau Server. These components are:

a. **Application Server Component:** The application server provides permission and authentication security services. It handles the management and authorization for mobile and internet interfaces. Every Tableau Server session ID is tracked, providing a security guarantee. By default, the server's session timeout is configured by the administrator.

b. **VizQL Server Component:** The VizQL server converts the data source's requests into visual representations. The query is sent to the data source as soon as the VizQL process receives the client request to retrieve the information as images. This graphic or illustration is shown to the users. Tableau Server caches visualizations to speed up loading. The cache can be shared by many authorized users who are permitted to access the visualization.

c. **Data Server Component:** A data server stores and oversees the management of data from external data sources. A centralized system is used to manage data. It provides driver specifications, data storage, metadata management, and data communication. It maintains track of all pertinent data associated with a dataset, including calculated fields, metadata, groups, sets, and parameters. In addition to extracting data, the data server also generates a real-time or live connection to external data sources.

4. **Gateway:** Requests from users are routed through the gateway to Tableau components. The external load balancer receives requests sent by clients and processes them. These processing tasks are distributed to other components through the gateway. The gateway additionally operates as an external load balancer in the absence of one. All processes in a system with a single server are managed by the gateway, often known as the primary server. Consequently, in a Tableau Server arrangement, the primary server is just one machine. However, in multi-server configurations, one physical machine acts as the main server, while other systems function as worker servers.

5. **Data Clients:** Different clients can be used to update and view the Tableau Server's dashboards and visualizations. Web browsers, smartphone applications, and Tableau Desktop are examples of clients.

2.4 TABLEAU DOWNLOAD AND INSTALLATION

To download and install any product from Tableau Suite, we can visit the Tableau official website, www.tableau.com, and navigate to its Products page where we can find the download link for our choice of product. Here, we will focus our discussion mainly on Tableau Desktop. We can download the trial version of the product for learning purposes or buy the license for the professional edition. The steps to download the trial version are as follows:

Step 1. The trial version for Tableau Desktop Professional Edition can be downloaded from the following link: https://www.tableau.com/products/desktop website. Users can explore the latest version from the official website.

Step 2. The next step is to click on the "Try Now" button or "Start a free Trial" button. Both these options redirect to a user registration form to start the download.

Step 3. Fill out and submit the form to start downloading. Click the .exe file downloaded.

Step 4. The installation wizard starts. Click on the Install button (Figure 2.5).

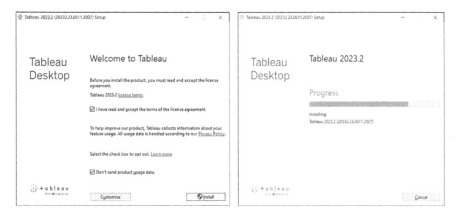

FIGURE 2.5   Installation steps of Tableau Desktop Professional Edition trial version.

Step 5. The installation progress starts. Now, select as per your requirement (Figure 2.6).

FIGURE 2.6   Installation steps of Tableau Desktop Professional Edition (cont.).

Step 6. Here, we select the option Start trial now. Now, we can see the Tableau Desktop product launched on our system. We observe that Connect, Open, and Discover are the three panes that make up the start page (Figure 2.7).

FIGURE 2.7   Start Page of Tableau Desktop Professional Edition.

From the start page in Tableau Desktop, you may perform the following tasks:

- Link to your data.
- Open the worksheets you most recently used.
- Find and look through material created by the Tableau community.

Step 7. From the start page's connect pane, we may establish a connection to any data source from the provided list. We can also open a previously saved data source (Figure 2.8).

FIGURE 2.8   List of installed connectors for supported data sources.

Step 8. Go to the start page, click on File Menu, and select New to open a new Tableau Workspace (or Workbook) for working (Figure 2.9).

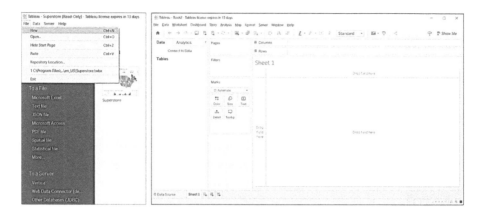

FIGURE 2.9   Open a new workbook in Tableau Desktop.

Several menu options, a toolbar, a Data pane, cards, shelves, and one or more sheets make up the Tableau workspace. In the Tableau workspace, examples of sheets include stories, dashboards, and worksheets.

Following a connection to the default Sample-Superstore data source, the Tableau workspace and all its components are seen in Figure 2.10.

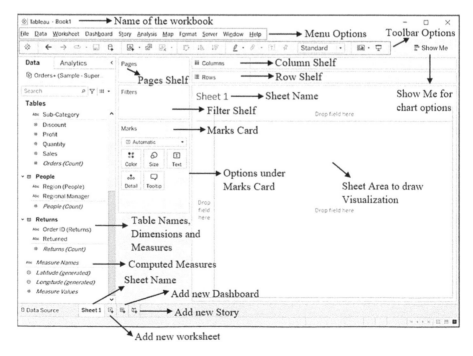

FIGURE 2.10   Various components in Tableau workspace.

The options present in the Toolbar as depicted in Figure 2.11.

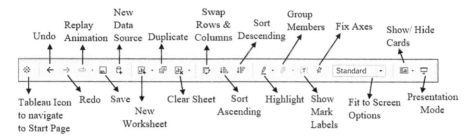

FIGURE 2.11   Different options in the toolbar.

2.5   TABLEAU DATA TYPES

Tableau separates data into two extra sophisticated categories, Geographical Location and Cluster group, or one of four groups: string, number, Boolean, and datetime. Tableau automatically allocates the data types once the data has been loaded from the source. Table 2.1 displays the range of data types supported by Tableau.

TABLE 2.1
Tableau Data Types with Icons and Examples

Data Type	Icons	Description	Example
String	Abc	With zero or more characters, the string data type indicates that it is a text data form. A value is considered to be a string if its characters are surrounded by single or double quotations.	"James Wing" "Hello users" "Good Job!"
Number	#	Numbers are represented by integers or floating-point real values. In order to use floating-point numbers in calculations effectively, they must be rounded off.	35 167.29
Boolean	T|F	Boolean values are the logical values representing True or False.	True False
Date & datetime		Tableau recognizes almost all date formats. If it's necessary to make Tableau interpret a string as a date, the # symbol is inserted before the data.	"05/04/2023" "#5 April 2023"
Geographic values		Geographic data types encompass all values used in maps. Names of countries, states, cities, regions, postal codes, etc. are some examples of geographic data values.	Name of a country, state, etc. a valid geographical location
Cluster group		Values with a variety of data types can occasionally be found in datasets. These values are also referred to as mixed data values or cluster group values.	Cluster-player, team, year

2.6 TABLEAU FILE TYPES

Tableau offers a wide variety of file formats in which the results of data analysis can be stored and shared among users. The numerous file types, also referred to as the various formats, are distinguished by different file extensions [5]. Depending on how these files are made and used, their formats will vary. Each one of these files is kept in an open and editable XML file. The details for each file type are discussed in Table 2.2.

One of the automated folders created in the Documents folder after installing Tableau on a computer is called "My Tableau Repository." This directory contains the files that are stored there. The following steps, however, can also be used to save these files in different folder locations.

Step 1. Select the File Menu option and navigate to the Repository Location option.

Step 2. Select the folder that you want to set as the updated repository in the dialog box.

TABLE 2.2
Different File Types Supported in Tableau

File Type	Extension	Purpose
Tableau Workbook	.twb	Within a Tableau workbook, there could be one or more worksheets in addition to dashboards and stories.
Tableau Packaged Workbook	.twbx	When local file data and backdrop pictures are needed, a Tableau Packaged Workbook is presented as a zip file that includes the workbook and all necessary files. It offers the most effective means of presenting our work to people who are unable to access the original data.
Tableau Data Source	.tds	Information about the connection that was used to generate the Tableau report is contained in this file. The source type (SAP, relational tables, Excel files, etc.) and column data types are also described in the connection metadata.
Tableau Packaged Data source	.tdsx	This file includes data and connection information in addition to being similar to the .tds data source file.
Tableau Data Extract	.tde	A local copy of the whole data collection, called a Tableau Data Extract. If you worked offline and wanted to boost performance, you might utilize it to exchange data with others.
Tableau Bookmark	.tbm	A single worksheet that may be shared and pasted into other workbooks and can be stored in a Tableau Bookmark.
Tableau preferences	.tps	The color preferences used across all workbooks are saved in this file. It mostly serves to maintain a uniform look and feel for all users.

Step 3. To set new repository as the destination location, restart Tableau (Figure 2.12).

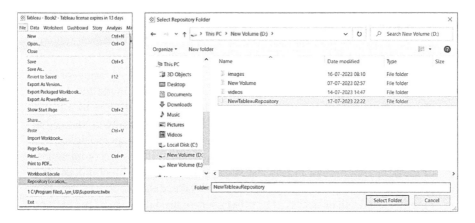

FIGURE 2.12   Setting the new repository location.

2.7   DATA PREPARATION TASKS

Ensuring the accuracy and consistency of the raw data being processed and analyzed is crucial for the validity of the outputs from business intelligence and analytics systems. Before integration, remote datasets must be aligned because they typically take different forms. When data are formed, errors, inconsistencies, and other problems are frequently present. Data preparation procedures may include merging datasets, guaranteeing data quality, and fixing data issues [6]. Finding appropriate data is a further step in the data preparation process that makes it possible for analytics tools to provide useful information and insightful analyses. By combining internal and external sources, the data is continuously enhanced and updated to increase its utility and applicability (Figure 2.13).

FIGURE 2.13   Various stages in data preparation.

The key steps of the data preparation task are as follows:

1. **Data Collection:** Operational systems, data lakes, warehouses, and other data sources are used to collect good quality pertinent data.
2. **Data Discovery and Profiling:** The collected information must then be further reviewed to ascertain what is contained in it and what must be done to make it appropriate for the intended use. Data profiling can assist with this by spotting patterns, correlations, and other features in the data as well as anomalies, imbalances, missing information, and other issues that need to be fixed.

3. **Data Cleaning:** Cleaning up the data is usually the stage that takes the longest, but it is crucial for getting rid of erroneous data and filling in any gaps. The following are numerous essential tasks:
   a. Eliminating pointless data and outliers
   b. Substituting values for missing values
   c. Standardizing data formats
   d. Masking sensitive or private data entries
4. **Transform and Enrich Data:** Changes to the format or value of data entries are known as data transformation, and they are made to obtain a clearly stated conclusion or to make the data more intelligible to a larger audience. Data must be supplemented and improved by being connected to and combined with other pertinent information to give deeper insights.
5. **Validate and Store Data:** The correctness, reliability, and completeness of the data are checked in this last stage using automated techniques. The produced data is subsequently kept in a data lake, data warehouse, or other repository and can be accessed by other users or used directly by the creator.

2.7.1 TABLEAU PREP FOR DATA PREPARATION

A data preparation tool called *Tableau Prep* is intended for analysts and business users who attempt to prepare data on their own but may run into difficulties due to a lack of traditional ETL knowledge [6, 7]. Users can integrate, shape, and purify data with the tool before using it for analysis in Tableau. Tableau Prep tool is as convenient to use as Tableau Desktop. An enhanced understanding of users' data is provided by the user interface's visual experience. The combination of innovative features, easy data preparation, and interaction with Tableau results in a quicker time to insight [8]. Let us discuss the installation steps of Tableau Prep below:

Step 1. To install the Tableau Prep Builder software, we can visit the Tableau website at https://www.tableau.com/products and explore in the product section or visit the link: https://www.tableau.com/products/prep

Step 2. As soon as the .exe file is downloaded, click it to start the installation process (Figure 2.14).

FIGURE 2.14 Installation of Tableau Prep Builder.

Step 3. When we launch Tableau Prep Builder, the home screen or landing page opens, which shows options for Creating a new flow and Connecting to Data (Figure 2.15).

FIGURE 2.15   Interface of Tableau Prep Builder.

We will discuss the further details of data preparation using Tableau Prep Builder in Chapter 3. Let us continue discussing other basic concepts of getting started with Tableau.

2.8   PUBLISHING IN TABLEAU PUBLIC

Users have the option to save their workbook's contents to Tableau Public, a cost-free cloud service, if they wish to share their data results with individuals both inside and outside their organization [8, 9]. Everyone has access to all the data sources, workbooks, and views published on Tableau Public and can interact with them. As its name suggests, it is a freely available public platform meant for knowledge-sharing purpose.

Step 1. To sign up and getting started with Tableau Public, users can view the following web link: https://public.tableau.com/app/discover

Step 2. Once we successfully register and sign-in to Tableau Public, we can easily download the Tableau Desktop Public Edition and begin working on Tableau Public in a single click (Figures 2.16 and 2.17).

FIGURE 2.16   Download and installation of Tableau Desktop Public Edition.

FIGURE 2.17   Interface of Tableau Desktop Public Edition.

Step 3. The interface of Tableau Desktop public edition is like the interface of Tableau Enterprise edition that we installed earlier. Once we create a workbook in Tableau Public, we can directly save it to public server by navigating to the File Menu and selecting the option to save to Tableau Public (Figure 2.18).

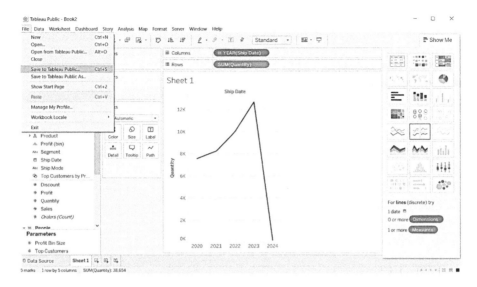

FIGURE 2.18   Saving a workbook from Tableau Desktop Public Edition to the public server.

The desired workbook must first be opened in Tableau Desktop, where we must select the Server Menu option, choose Tableau Public, and then click "Save to Tableau Public" if we wish to publish a workbook from the Enterprise edition. Note that the presence of at least one field in our visualization is a must for this option to be applied. (Figure 2.19).

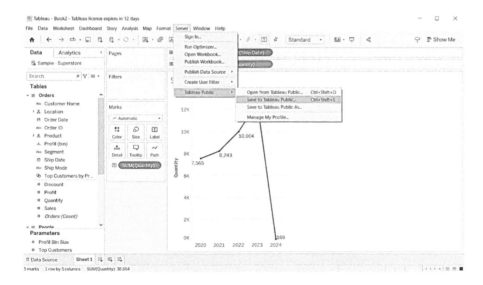

FIGURE 2.19   Saving a workbook from the Enterprise edition to the public server.

Step 4. Now, we need to log in to the Tableau Public account. If one does not possess an account, then the user must select the link to create a new account. After login, click on Create Data Extract and select desired tables. Then, click OK (Figure 2.20).

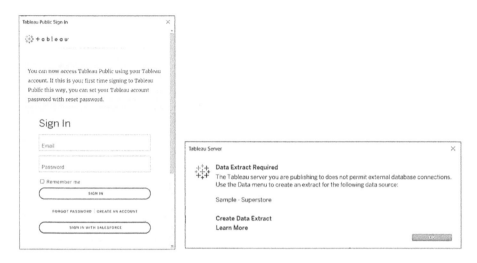

FIGURE 2.20   Create data extract in Tableau.

Step 5. Click "Save" when the workbook has been named. After a worksheet is saved to Tableau Public, the publishing process generates an extract of the data connection (Figure 2.21).

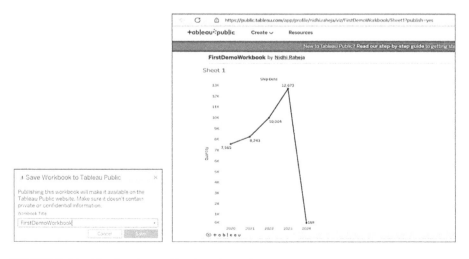

FIGURE 2.21   Naming the workbook and creating an extract.

This opens our saved workbook in Tableau Public as we can observe in the figure above. This is how we can create and publish workbooks in Tableau.

KEY NOTES

- Tableau is an engaging data visualization software company located in the US that specializes in business information. Some of Tableau's features include quick analysis, simple to use and install, effective visualization, combining several datasets, real-time executive dashboards, and centralized data management.
- The various categories of the Tableau product suite include the Data Preparation tools, Viewer tools, Server tools, and Developer tools.
- The n-tier, highly scalable client-server architecture of Tableau supports desktop-installed applications, online clients, and mobile clients as well.
- To download and install any product from Tableau Suite, we can visit the Tableau official website www.tableau.com and navigate to its Products page where we can find the download link for our choice of product.
- Tableau supports the following data types: String, Number, Boolean, and datetime or other two complex types such as Geographical Location and Cluster group.
- A data preparation tool called *Tableau Prep* is intended for analysts and business users.
- To share data discoveries with individuals inside or outside the business organization, users can publish the workbook to Tableau Public, a free cloud service.

TEST YOUR SKILLS

1. Describe data visualization in Tableau?
2. List some of the advantages of using Tableau for data visualization?
3. Describe the various components of Tableau product suite.
4. What are the different file types and extensions supported in Tableau.
5. Install Tableau Desktop and Tableau Public on your system.
6. Discuss data preparation tasks in Tableau.
7. How is the visualization created in Tableau Desktop published on Public.

REFERENCES

[1] Munroe, Kirk. *Data Modeling with Tableau: A Practical Guide to Building Data Models Using Tableau Prep and Tableau Desktop.* United Kingdom, Packt Publishing, 2022.
[2] Hwang, Jaejin, and Yoon, Youngjin. *Data Analytics and Visualization in Quality Analysis Using Tableau.* United Kingdom, CRC Press, 2021.
[3] Sarsfield, Patrick, et al. *Maximizing Tableau Server: A Beginner's Guide to Accessing, Sharing, and Managing Content on Tableau Server.* United Kingdom, Packt Publishing, 2021.

[4] Milligan, Joshua N. *Learning Tableau 2019: Tools for Business Intelligence, Data Prep, and Visual Analytics*, 3rd Edition. India, Packt Publishing, 2019.

[5] Loth, Alexander. *Visual Analytics with Tableau*. United States, Wiley, 2019.

[6] Costello, Tim, and Blackshear, Lori. *Prepare Your Data for Tableau: A Practical Guide to the Tableau Data Prep Tool*. Germany, Apress, 2019.

[7] Sleeper, Ryan. *Practical Tableau: 100 Tips, Tutorials, and Strategies from a Tableau Zen Master*. United States, O'Reilly Media, 2018.

[8] Khan, Arshad. *Jumpstart Tableau: A Step-By-Step Guide to Better Data Visualization*. United States, Apress, 2016.

[9] Acharya, Seema, and Chellappan, Subhashini. *Pro Tableau: A Step-by-Step Guide*. United States, Apress, 2016.

3 Connecting Data in Tableau

3.1 DIFFERENT DATA SOURCES IN TABLEAU

All readily available and widely used data sources can be connected to using Tableau. It can connect to Excel files, text files, JSON files, PDF files, and many more. Using its Open Database Connectivity (ODBC) connector, it can also establish connections to various databases as well as it can connect to different servers and web connectors [1,2]. The following categories of data sources can be accessed using Tableaus native connectors:

- File systems: Examples include CSV, Microsoft Excel, etc.
- Relational system: Examples include DB2, Oracle, Microsoft SQL Server, etc.
- Cloud systems: Examples include Windows Azure, Google BigQuery, etc.
- Additional data sources using ODBC.

Figure 3.1 displays a glimpse of various data sources supported in Tableau Desktop as visible on the desktop homepage.

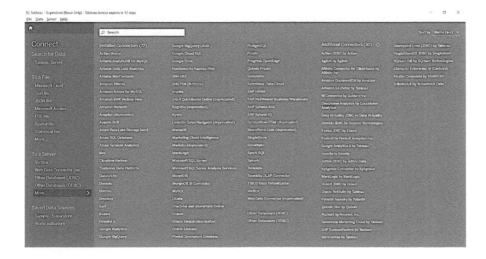

FIGURE 3.1   Data sources supported in Tableau.

Tableau can simultaneously connect to several data sources. For instance, by specifying numerous connections, we can connect to both a relational source and a flat file in the same workbook [3]. This is utilized very well in the technique of data blending, a particularly special Tableau feature. We will discuss data blending in a later section in this chapter. Let us first learn to establish a connection to a text file (.csv) in Tableau using the following steps:

Step 1. In the Tableau Desktop homepage, click on the option Text File present in the category—To a File. Now, navigate to select the desired text file in .csv format. Here, we select the file "Supersore2023.csv" for demo purposes (Figure 3.2).

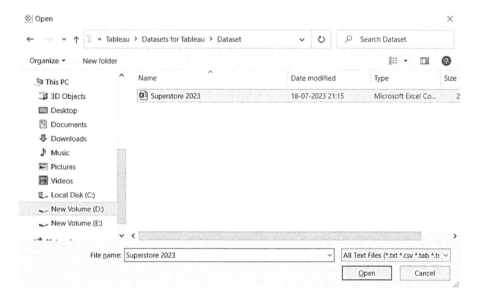

FIGURE 3.2   Output.

Step 2. Once the file is connected, the desktop interface looks as follows (Figure 3.3).

FIGURE 3.3   Output.

Step 3. Now, click the icon <<un03_1.tif>> present at the bottom of the work-space interface to insert a new worksheet. Here, we can create another visualization graph using the tables connected through the data source (Figure 3.4).

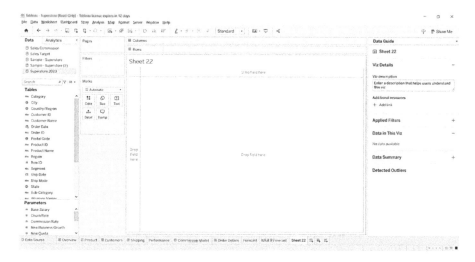

FIGURE 3.4   Output.

In the same way, we can connect to an Excel file, a PDF file, etc. any supported data source files.

Step 4. Let us connect to an Excel file. Here, we use the default sample-super-store.xls file to connect. Now, click on the open option (Figure 3.5).

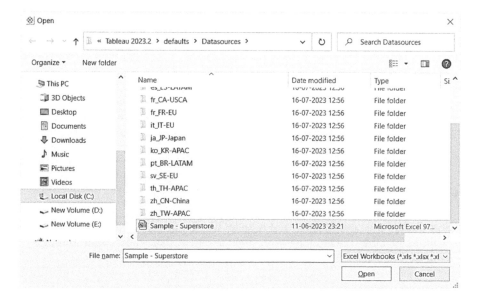

FIGURE 3.5   Output.

Step 5. Once we open the Excel file, the spreadsheets included in the MS Excel file are displayed as icons under the Sheets tab. Now, click and drag one or more sheets (representing tables) in the drag area and establish connections between them (Figure 3.6).

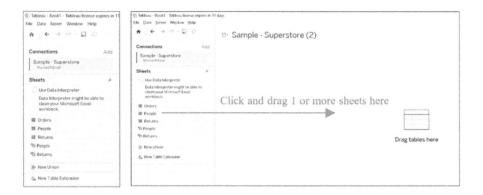

FIGURE 3.6 Output.

Step 6. Suppose we select and drag the Orders sheet in the drag area in Figure 3.7.

FIGURE 3.7 Output.

Step 7. Add a new worksheet and it looks like Figure 3.8. It displays the columns of Order table along with their assigned datatypes visible through datatype icons.

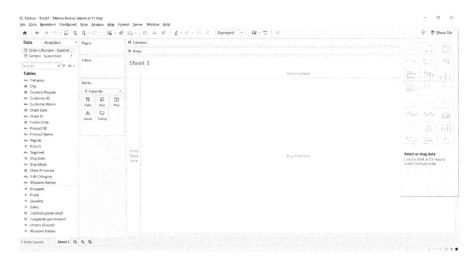

FIGURE 3.8   Output.

3.2   EXTRACTING DATA IN TABLEAU

Data Extracts, which are preserved subsets of data, can be used to improve performance and take benefit of Tableau features that were previously unavailable or not
supported in the original data source. Applying filters and limiting other configuration
parameters can help reduce the number of data when an extract is generated [4]. Once
constructed, the extract can be updated once more using information from the original
data source. Either a full refresh can be used to replace all the data in the extract, or
an incremental refresh can be used to add only the new rows from the source since
the last refresh [5].

3.2.1   CREATING AN EXTRACT

To produce a data extract for the Sample-Superstore data source, follow the
below-given steps:

   Step 1. Go to the new worksheet, click on the menu option "Data," and select
      the connected data source. Next, click on the option to "Extract Data"
      (Figure 3.9).

FIGURE 3.9 Output.

Step 2. Now, an *Extract Data* dialog box opens where we can configure and add filters. For this, click on the *Add...* button to open an *Add Filter* box as shown above to select the desired field.

Step 3. Now, select the *Sub-Category* field as a data filter. In the next step, we can select the desired values from the list of values presented. Then, click OK (Figure 3.10).

FIGURE 3.10 Output.

Step 4. In the above figure, we can observe the new data extract created with 7 out of 17 data values that we chose in the previous step. Now, click on the "Extract" button to create and store the extract (Figure 3.11).

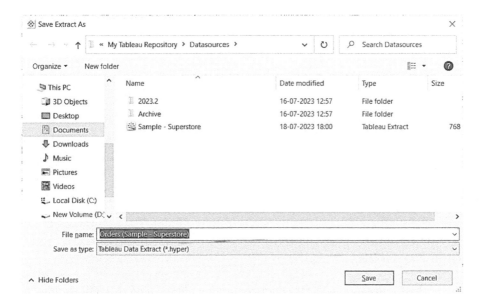

FIGURE 3.11   Output.

Step 5. We can also add more data in a previously created extract. For this, we can choose the menu option Data and Select the data source. Now, click the Extract option. Finally, select the option to Append Data from the File option (Figure 3.12).

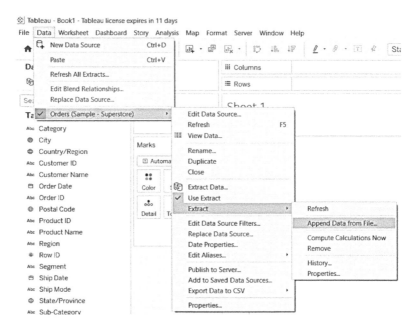

FIGURE 3.12 Output.

In this instance, select the data-containing file and then click OK to complete. Remember that the extracted data should match the existing columns in the file in terms of both number and datatype.

Step 6. To confirm how frequently and when an extract has occurred, we can check the history of data extracts. For this, go to Data Menu → Click Extract → Select History (Figure 3.13).

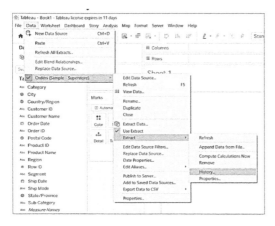

FIGURE 3.13 Output.

3.3 RDBMS BASICS AND TYPES OF KEYS

The most popular type of database is a relational database or more specifically a Relational Database Management System (RDBMS). It has several tables, each with a unique primary key. Data may be accessible quickly in RDBMS because of a collection of a well-organized set of tables. Some terms associated with RDBMS are as follows:

1. **Relation (Table):** A relational database stores everything as relations. Tables are used by the RDBMS database to hold data values. A table is a collection of related data items arranged in rows and columns. Each table denotes a distinct real-world entity for which the data is being gathered, such as a person, place, or event.
2. **Tuple:** Another term for a database row is a record or tuple. It is a horizontal component of the table. For each entry in the table, it contains the specific information.
3. **Attribute:** A column, sometimes referred to as an attribute, in a table is a vertical element that contains all the information associated with a single field.
4. **Data Item:** The individual data item is the smallest piece of data in the table. It is kept when tuples and attributes meet.
5. **Degree:** The degree of a table denotes the total count of attributes (or columns) that together make up a relation.
6. **Cardinality:** The total number of tuples contained in a relation at any given time is referred to as the table's cardinality. A relation with a cardinality of 0 is an empty table. A table with five rows has a cardinality of five, for instance.
7. **NULL:** The table's NULL value indicates that the field was left empty when the record was created. It differs from a value that is blank or a field with nothing in it.

Let us consider an example of an Employee table and understand the terms discussed above (Figure 3.14).

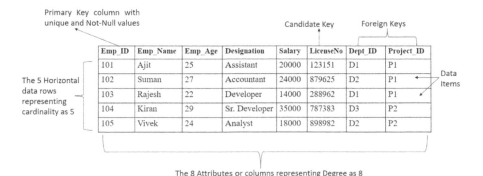

FIGURE 3.14 A simple Table with its components.

The different keys that can exist in a relational model are as follows:

1. **Primary Key:** It is the most important column that can sufficiently identify each row in a table uniquely such as *Emp_ID* in Employee table. A relational table may have multiple keys but the one which best identifies records uniquely is set as primary key.
2. **Candidate Key:** A candidate key is any column that can uniquely identify a tuple as well such as *LicenseNo* in the Employee table and is a good candidate to become the primary key. It is as strong as the primary key. From among these candidate keys, one key is selected as the primary key, and the last remaining key, if any, is referred to as the alternate key.
3. **Super Key:** A super key in a dataset represents a group of attributes that can uniquely identify each record. It can be considered as a superset of all candidate keys. For example, in the Employee table, the set *(Emp_ID, Emp_Name, LicenseNo)* represents the super key.
4. **Foreign Key:** Foreign key is a data column or a set of columns in a table that links one table to another by referencing the primary key of the second table. This helps to create relationships between different tables. For example: In the Employee table, each row represents an employee who works in a particular department in a specific project. The columns *Dept_ID* and *Project_ID* are the foreign keys that link the Employee table to the Department and Project tables, respectively.

3.4   DATA JOINS IN TABLEAU

Any data analysis usually calls for data combining. At times, it may be necessary to combine data from multiple tables that may be present in a common data source or in different data sources [6]. A "Join" refers to the process of merging columns from one or more relational database tables. Additionally, a set is produced that can either be utilized directly or stored as a table. The different forms of joins supported in Tableau are as follows:

- **Inner Join**: An inner join only retrieves the matched rows from the linked tables (Figure 3.15).

FIGURE 3.15   Inner join.

- **Outer Join**: The outside join is a more extensive form of an inner join. For the tables being joined, it returns rows that match and those that don't match. Some instances of outside joins are as follows:
- **Left Outer Join:** This join sets NULL values in the attributes that come from the right table and returns matched rows from the connected tables together with non-matching rows from the left table.

- **Right Outer Join:** This operation returns matching rows from the tables being joined along with non-matching rows from the right table, and it sets NULL values in the attributes derived from the left table.
- **Full Outer Join:** A full outer join is used to connect tables. As a consequence, it contains every value from both tables. When the value in one table does not match the value in another, a NULL value is returned in the resulting data grid (Figure 3.16).

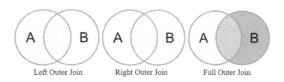

FIGURE 3.16   Different types of outer joins.

Let us implement joins in Tableau now. The steps are as follows:

Step 1. Let us consider the default data source called Sample-Superstore to create a join between the Orders and Returns tables.

Step 2. Select the Microsoft Excel option under Connect from the Data menu. Now, click the Open button after selecting Sample-Superstore as the data source (Figure 3.17).

FIGURE 3.17   Output.

Step 3. Drag and move the Orders and Returns tables from the sheets pane to the space in the middle. Tableau automatically establishes a link between both tables. For this, first drag the Orders table and double-click to open Orders (Figure 3.18).

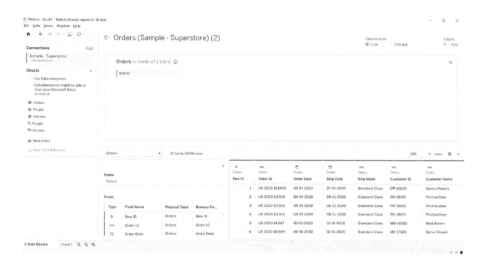

FIGURE 3.18　Output.

Step 4. Now, drag the Returns table to establish default Inner join between the two tables (Figure 3.19).

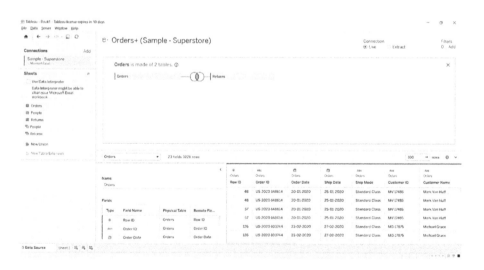

FIGURE 3.19　Output.

Step 5. To modify the type of join, click on the join symbol and select the desired join type (Figure 3.20).

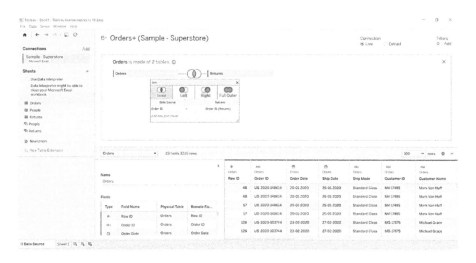

FIGURE 3.20   Output.

Step 6. Please note the joining fields of two tables for establishing any join condition. Here, OrderID column (Primary Key) from the Orders table refers to the OrderID (Foreign Key) in the Returns table. We can select different fields as well for join purposes.

3.5   DATA IMPORT AND BLENDING IN TABLEAU

Data Blending or mixing is one of Tableau's most beneficial features. It is used to examine data from numerous connected data sources in a single perspective [6,7]. Consider this scenario: Assume that a relational database has yearly sales data of a business organization. Also, there is an Excel spreadsheet that contains the target sales data. Data in both databases must be combined based on mutual dimensions such as SalesIDs to compare the actual sales records with the target sales values.

A primary source and a secondary data source are always present when blending in Tableau. Knowing the primary source is crucial because it affects the way data is viewed [8]. Secondary sources have an orange check mark, whereas the primary source has a blue check. Since it is a left join, therefore, all fields from the primary dataset along only with relevant fields from the secondary will be included. The field that first gets added to a worksheet identifies the primary source. Thus, the first field's data source is now the primary data source, with all other data sources being secondary. Please note that we must create a new worksheet and start over in case we want to alter the worksheet's primary data source.

Let us implement blending data using two datasets namely, Sample-Superstore and Sample Coffee Chain in Tableau. We can download the Coffee chain dataset from the below link: https://community.tableau.com/s/question/0D54T00000C5cTzSAJ/sample-coffee-chain

Step 1. To begin, open Tableau and import the coffee chain sample data (Figure 3.21).

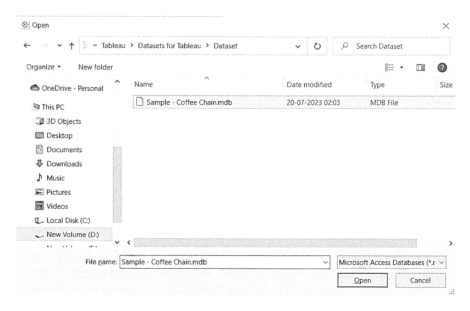

FIGURE 3.21   Output.

Step 2. Browse and select MS Access file to load in data source (Figure 3.22).

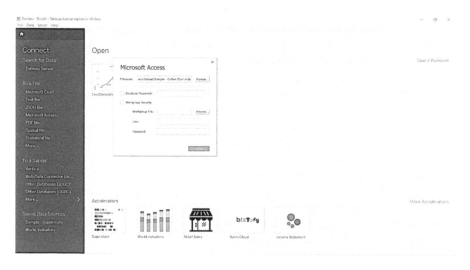

FIGURE 3.22   Output.

Step 3. The data tables loaded look like as shown in Figure 3.23.

FIGURE 3.23 Output.

Step 4. Below is a screenshot showcasing the different tables and joins implemented in the Coffee Chain data source (Figure 3.24).

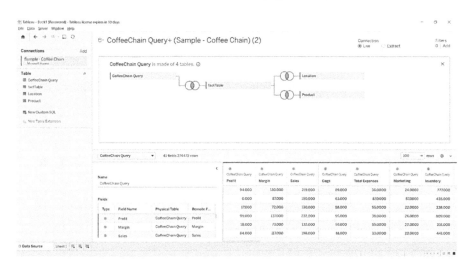

FIGURE 3.24 Output.

Step 5. Now, we need to add a secondary data source named Sample-superstore. xls. The following steps should be followed:

a. First, select the "Data" option in the menu and then click "New Data Source" (Figure 3.25).

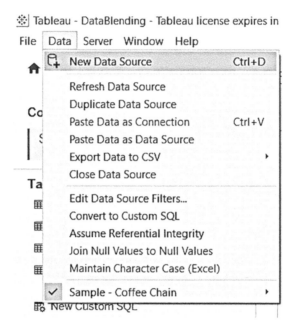

FIGURE 3.25 Output of step 5(a).

b. To get started, select a data source, such as Microsoft Excel (Figure 3.26).

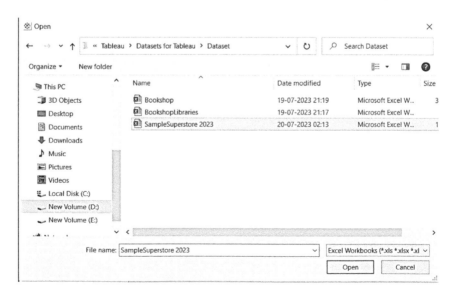

FIGURE 3.26 Output of step 5(b).

c. Both data sources are now displayed in the Data window of the new sheet (see the screenshot below) (Figure 3.27).

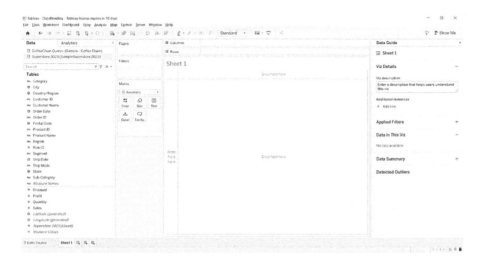

FIGURE 3.27 Output of step 5(c).

Step 6. Using a common dimension, we can combine the data from the Sample-Superstore and the Sample Coffee Chain sources.

a. Consider the State dimension field. It shows the shared dimension between the Sample-Superstore and Sample Coffee Chain data sources.

b. Bring the State field into the rows shelf from Sample-Coffee Chain, the primary data source. From the Secondary Data Source (Sample-Superstore), drag the Profit field into the Columns shelf.

c. To get the graphical visualization, choose the horizontal bar from Show Me.

d. The graph illustrates the differences in profit between each State for the Sample Coffee Chain and the Sample-Superstore data sources as seen in Figure 3.28.

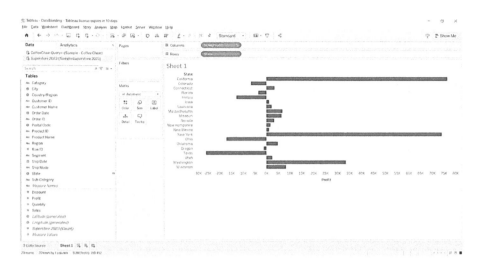

FIGURE 3.28   Output.

Step 7. The dimension *State* is marked with a little chain icon, showing that it is shared by the two data sources (Figure 3.29).

⊕   State   ∞

FIGURE 3.29   State dimension with chain icon.

Now, let us discuss a few differentiating points between data blending and data joins (Table 3.1).

TABLE 3.1
Data Blending vs Data Joins

Data Blending	Data Joins
Data blending can integrate data from various data sources.	Joins can integrate data from the same source only.
Data blending only supports left-join operations.	All four types of joins can be used in an execution.
Different levels of granularity are available for data through data blending.	When employing joins, the granularity of the data must remain at one level throughout the process.
Data blending in Tableau involves querying separate datasets, aggregating data, and then blending it.	Data joins can perform join operations only at the row level.

3.6 DATA SORTING IN TABLEAU

According to user needs, data is saved in the data source and sorted in alphabetically ascending or descending order. The Sort Fields option is used to sort the data once it has been connected to Tableau. In the Data Source tab, there is a Sort Fields option (Figure 3.30).

FIGURE 3.30 A glimpse of the connected data source.

In Tableau worksheets, we can sort the data in two different ways:

1. **Manual Sorting:** Users can manually reorder the order of dimension fields or values by shifting them up or down when using the manual sorting method.
2. **Calculated Sorting:** The calculated sorting uses the sort dialog to be applied straight to the axis.

For example, let us consider the data blending workbook that we created in the above section and try to implement sorting on its worksheet by both ways. For this, we select the State dimension under the rows header and click on the Sort option (Figure 3.31).

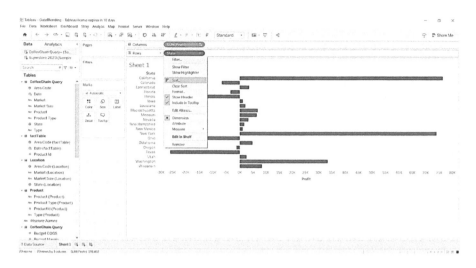

FIGURE 3.31   Sorting option in Tableau.

This will open a Sort dialog box to choose the order for sorting. In the Sort By combo box, the option Data Source Order is selected. This enables automatic sorting of the selected field (Figure 3.32).

FIGURE 3.32   Manual sorting technique in Tableau.

Alternatively, we can choose for the option of Manual Sorting also. Here, manually we drag and shift the state Florida at first position. The output after sorting is shown in Figure 3.33.

FIGURE 3.33 Result of manual sorting.

3.7 DATA PRE-PROCESSING USING TABLEAU PREP

Tableau Prep is a data preparation solution made for analysts and business users who attempt to prepare data on their own but may encounter difficulties since they lack typical Extract, Transform, and Load (ETL) experience [6]. The tool allows users to combine, shape, and clean data in preparation for analysis in Tableau. The interface of Tableau Prep is straightforward and appealing. The design resembles the data source panel in Tableau Desktop in its ultimate version. An image of a Sample-Superstore "flow" in Tableau Prep is shown above. There are some crucial panels to be aware of:

1. **Connections Pane:** In the "Connections Window," we can view all the databases and files we are currently connected to. After adding connections to one or more databases, just drag the required tables and place them into the flow pane.
2. **Flow Pane:** Steps or tasks will show up in the flows as we clean, shape, and merge our data. Hence, the user will be able to see an overview of their applied changes.
3. **Profile Pane:** Users may view the structure of their data in the profile pane, which summarizes each data field and helps to detect any anomalies present in the data.
4. **Changes Pane:** Tableau Prep logs and tracks changes in the order they are made for easy review and updating.
5. **Data Grid:** Enables row-level detail viewing and individual record verification.

Let us perform several operations on data in Tableau Prep.

3.7.1 DATA CLEANING

We must establish a connection to a data source before we can create a flow and start cleaning up our data [8]. Tableau supports a large variety of internal and cloud-based data sources. In order to establish a flow, we will connect to three text files. We can execute all the cleaning, filtering, calculations, and aggregates in a flow, which is a set of operations users perform on the data. Tableau Prep includes several sophisticated cleaning tools that we may use, as well as calculated fields, data splitting, and other capabilities.

> **Step 1.** The orders dataset files such as Orders_Central, Orders_West, and Orders_East and all the files that will used in our example can be downloaded from the following link: https://help.tableau.com/current/prep/en-us/prep_get_started.htm
>
> Please note that Orders_south 2015..2016..2017 and 2018 files are to be saved in a new folder named Orders South.
>
> **Step 2.** Open the Tableau Prep interface (Figure 3.34).

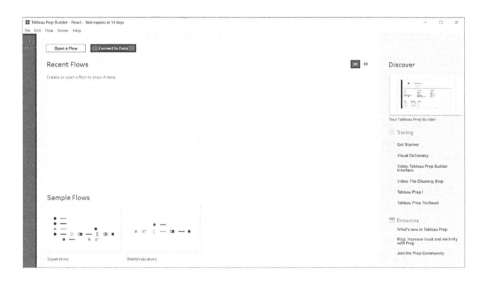

FIGURE 3.34   Tableau Prep Interface.

> **Step 3.** Click on Connections to connect with the.csv files downloaded in Step 1 (Figure 3.35).

FIGURE 3.35 Output.

Step 4. Select the files needed by browsing through their original directory
location. To add the first file, orders_south_2015.csv, to your flow, choose it
from the Orders South subdirectory and click Open (Figure 3.36).

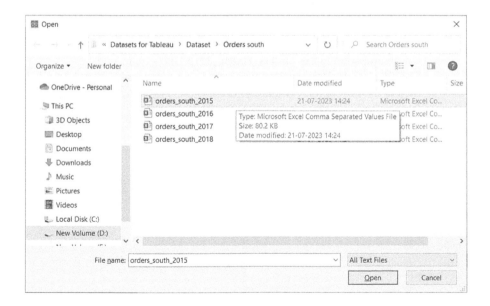

FIGURE 3.36 Output.

The prep interface loads and displays files as visible in the following screen-shot. For orders in the South, there are three other files, and how you combine them depends on your area of work. In Tableau Prep Builder:

- Each file can be added one by one or you can combine all the files into one Input step; to do so, click the Tables tab in the Input pane.
- Select the option for Union multiple tables (Figure 3.37).

FIGURE 3.37   Union of tables option.

- Click on the "Apply" button to include the data after performing the Union operation to the "orders_south_2015" file's input step.
- The files of other regions are composed as a single table file. Add all files to the flow at once (Figure 3.38).

FIGURE 3.38   Output.

Step 5. Add connections to the remaining files namely, Orders_Central.csv, Orders_East.xlsx, and Orders_West.csv by clicking on the + symbol adjacent to the Connections pane (Figure 3.39).

FIGURE 3.39 Output.

Step 6. Now, it is wise to first examine the added data files to see if we can find any potential problems before merging them.

Step 7. Select the Orders_West Input step. We observe numerous fields that begin with "Right,_" representing that these are duplicates of the other fields. To avoid adding redundant fields in the flow, select the "X" button present in front of these fields (Figure 3.40).

FIGURE 3.40 Output.

Step 8. Tableau Prep adds an annotation (a tiny icon) to the Flow pane so that users can monitor their actions while cleaning the data for example— removing fields, etc. Tableau Prep maintains the log of all modifications made by the user in the Changes pane (Figure 3.41).

FIGURE 3.41   Output.

Step 9. In the Flow pane, select the Orders_Central Input step and go to the Input pane where we can identify the following issues:
- Different fields are used for the month, day, and year in the order and shipping dates.
- Some fields have inconsistent data types in comparison to other files.
- There is no Region field.
  Let us solve these issues one by one.

Step 10. To align with other datasets, combine separate order and ship date fields into a single Order Date and Ship Date field, respectively. Use a calculated field for a one-step solution.
- Click the plus icon in the flow, select Add, and click on Clean Step (Figure 3.42).

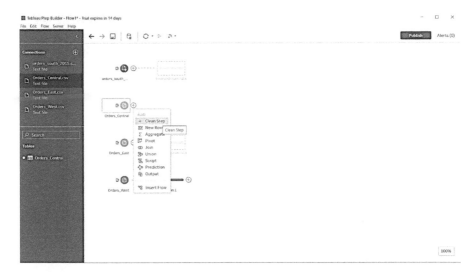

FIGURE 3.42 Adding a cleaning step in flow.

- Select the "Create Calculated Field" option in the toolbar to create a single field with the format "MM/DD/YYYY" that contains the Order Year, Month, and Day fields combined (Figure 3.43).

FIGURE 3.43 Calculated field option in Prep.

- Create a calculated field called Order Date in the Calculation editor and then enter the following calculation in it. When done, click "Save": MAKEDATE ([Order Year], [Order Month], [Order Day]) (Figure 3.44).

FIGURE 3.44   Calculated field to create the "Order Date" field.

- In a similar manner, make another calculated field called Ship Date and enter the following formula. Then, click Save. MAKEDATE([Ship Year], [Ship Month], [Ship Day]) (Figure 3.45).

FIGURE 3.45   Calculated field to create the "Ship Date" field.

- Now, we can see the new calculated fields so created and the changes applied (Figure 3.46).

FIGURE 3.46 Calculated field visible in the Changes pane.

- The fields for Ship Year, Ship Month, Ship Day, Order Year, Order Month, and Order Day as are no longer required. So, we can remove them (Figure 3.47).

FIGURE 3.47 Remove redundant fields.

Step 11. As we can see in Figure 3.48, there are still some issues with the Discounts field that need to be resolved.

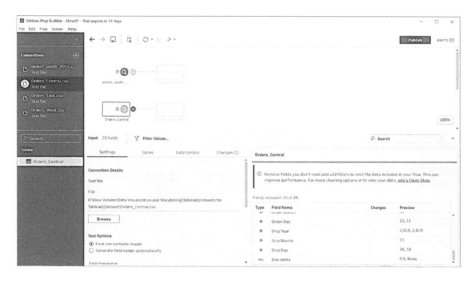

FIGURE 3.48 Resulting data fields after cleaning process.

- Instead of being assigned to a Number (decimal) data type, the variable is being assigned to a String data type.
- "None" is entered in the field for no discount instead of a numerical value.

  Fixing these issues is important before combining files.

Step 12. Select the Discounts field, double-click on None, and change to 0 (Figure 3.49).

FIGURE 3.49 Output.

Click the ABC symbol and choose Number (decimal) from the drop-down list of options to change the data type of the Discount field (Figure 3.50).

FIGURE 3.50 Output.

Step 13. Double-click Clean 1 the step in the Flow pane and change it to Fix dates/field names (Figure 3.51).

FIGURE 3.51 Output.

Step 14. Start by choosing the Orders_East Input step. Even though the fields in this file appear to be consistent with the other files, the Sales values contain the currency code.

Step 15. Choose Orders_East in the Flow pane and add a clean step using the plus + icon.

Step 16. Examining the Sales field, we notice that the sales numbers have the USD currency code included, and Tableau Prep treated these values as a string. To get precise sales data, this field's currency code must be removed and its data type changed. Select the Sales field and click the three dots to open more options and select option Clean > Remove Letters (Figure 3.52).

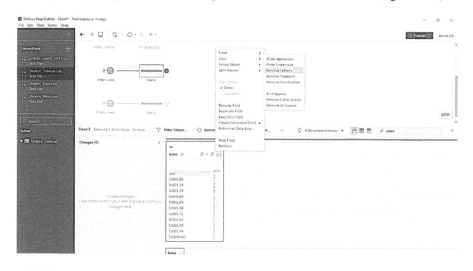

FIGURE 3.52   Output.

The output is displayed as follows (Figure 3.53).

FIGURE 3.53   Remove letters cleaning step visible in the Changes pane.

Step 17. Click the Sales field and select Number (decimal) from the drop-down menu to change the data type (Figure 3.54).

FIGURE 3.54 Output.

Step 18. While reviewing the Orders_West file, it was noticed The States field in the Orders_West file contained abbreviations rather than the state name as it was spelled out in the other files. To merge this file with the others, a cleaning step is added to the Orders_West Input step. Select Orders_West in the Flow window and then add a clean step by clicking the addition (+) symbol (Figure 3.55).

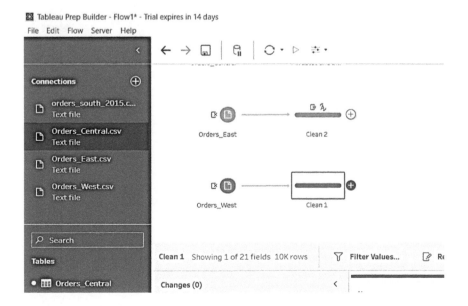

FIGURE 3.55 Output.

Step 19. Next, choose the State field and select the option to "Group Values" by opening more options drop-down. Now, select "Manual Selection" to open the editor (Figure 3.56).

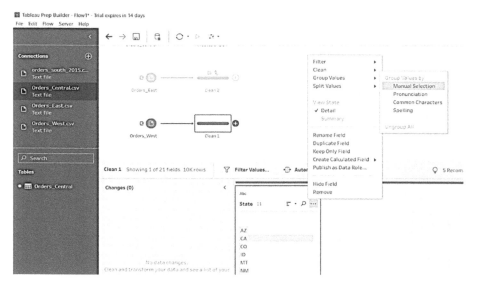

FIGURE 3.56   Output.

Step 20. In the Group Values editor, double-click an abbreviation to select a value and overwrite with its complete value. Press the "Enter" key to reflect the change (Figure 3.57).

FIGURE 3.57   Output.

Step 21. After all the files have been cleaned up, drag the cleaning step for state renaming toward the cleaning step for data type change and drop it onto the Union option that is displayed in the Flow pane to merge the files (Figure 3.58).

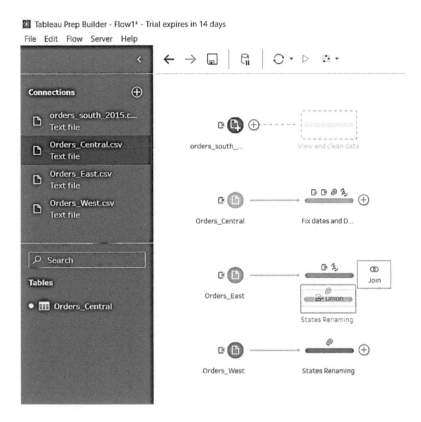

FIGURE 3.58   Output.

Step 22. Similarly, move and drop the next cleaning step to add it to the union created above (Figure 3.59).

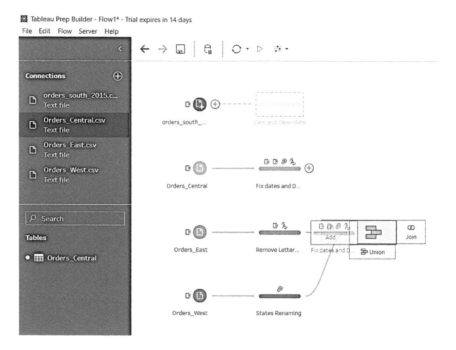

FIGURE 3.59   Output.

Step 23. Drag the remaining steps also to the existing Union flow to combine all files into a single table (Figure 3.60).

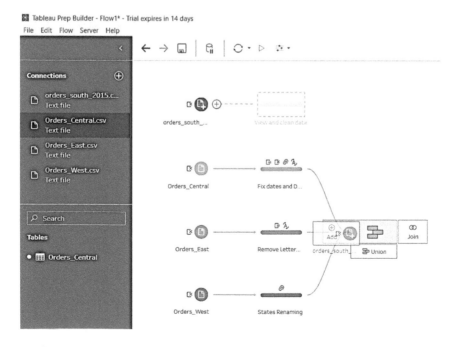

FIGURE 3.60   Output.

Step 24. In the summary pane, we see a list of mismatched fields resulting from naming differences. Click on the Show only mismatched fields
check box.

Step 25. Merge the mismatched fields to their respective counterparts. For
instance, drag and drop the Product field to merge with the Product Name
field, Discounts field with the Discount field, etc. (Figure 3.61).

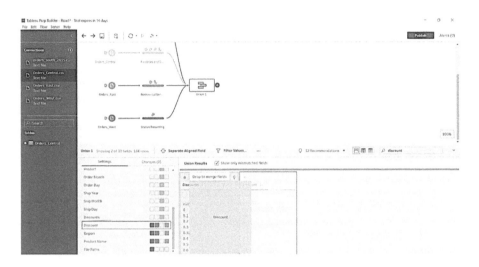

FIGURE 3.61   Output.

KEY NOTES

- Tableau may be used to connect to all frequently used and accessible data
  sources such as Text files, Excel files, PDF files, JSON files, and many more.
- Data Extracts, which are preserved subsets of data, can be used to improve
  performance and make use of Tableau features that were previously unavailable or not supported in the original data source.
- A relational database, or more specifically, a Relational Database
  Management System (RDBMS), is the most widely used type of database. It
  has several tables, each with a different primary key.
- It might be necessary to merge data from different tables, either from dif-
  ferent sources or from a single source. Tableau can link tables via the Data
  pane, which is available from the Data menu.
- Data blending is a function of Tableau that is quite helpful. It is used to look
  at data from several interconnected data sources from one viewpoint.
- After connecting the data to Tableau, you may sort the data using the Sort
  Fields option.
- Tableau Prep is a data preparation tool made for analysts and business users
  who may encounter difficulties preparing data on their own if they lack the
  necessary ETL skills.

TEST YOUR SKILLS

1. Enlist diverse categories of data sources that can be connected in Tableau Desktop.
2. Compare the similarities and differences between data joining and data blending in Tableau.
3. Install Tableau Prep in your system and observe the different components in its interface.
4. Elaborate Primary and Secondary data sources with reference to data blending.
5. Create a free account on public data repositories such as Kaggle, GitHub, and UCI. Download some sample datasets to do the necessary data pre-processing steps such as removing nulls and data cleaning from the dataset. Perform all the data pre-processing steps in Tableau Prep. Finally, import the cleaned dataset in Tableau Desktop or Tableau Public.

REFERENCES

[1] Meier, Marleen. *Mastering Tableau 2023: Implement Advanced Business Intelligence Techniques, Analytics, and Machine Learning Models with Tableau*. United Kingdom, Packt Publishing, 2023.

[2] Sleeper, Ryan. *Innovative Tableau: 100 More Tips, Tutorials, and Strategies*. United States, O'Reilly Media, 2020.

[3] Milligan, Joshua N. *Learning Tableau 2019: Tools for Business Intelligence, Data Prep, and Visual Analytics*, 3rd Edition. India, Packt Publishing, 2019.

[4] Loth, Alexander. *Visual Analytics with Tableau*. United States, Wiley, 2019.

[5] Costello, Tim, and Blackshear, Lori. *Prepare Your Data for Tableau: A Practical Guide to the Tableau Data Prep Tool*. Germany, Apress, 2019.

[6] Sleeper, Ryan. *Practical Tableau: 100 Tips, Tutorials, and Strategies from a Tableau Zen Master*. United States, O'Reilly Media, 2018.

[7] Khan, Arshad. *Jumpstart Tableau: A Step-By-Step Guide to Better Data Visualization*. United States, Apress, 2016.

[8] Acharya, Seema, and Chellappan, Subhashini. *Pro Tableau: A Step-by-Step Guide*. United States, Apress, 2016.

4 Table Calculations and Level of Detail

4.1 INTRODUCTION TO CALCULATIONS

We can do calculations on your data and generate new data from data that is already present in the data source with the help of calculations. This allows us to add fields to the data source instantaneously and conduct complex analyses on our own [1]. Learning how to use Tableau presents several challenges, the first of which is determining when we need to do a calculation. Numerous objectives can be achieved with the use of calculations. Some instances include:

- Data segmentation
- Modifying a field's data type
- Filtering the outcomes
- Calculating ratios
- Data aggregation
    In Tableau, the calculation requires the following four elements:
    1. **Tableau Functions:** The members or values of a field can be modified using function statements. For example, SUM (expression), LEN (string), etc. are some of the Tableau functions.
    2. **Fields:** A field represents any dimension or measure in the data source. Brackets [] are frequently used to denote a field in a computation, such as [Sales] and [Quantity].
    3. **Literal Expression:** Literal expressions depict the values of constants.
    4. **Operators:** An operation between the operands is represented by an operator, which is a symbol. These include +, -, *, /, %, ==, =, >, \, >=, \=, ! =, <>, ^, AND, OR, NOT, (), and other operators that you can use in Tableau computations.
        Let us discuss each of these components in detail.

DOI: 10.1201/9781003429593-4

4.2 TABLEAU FUNCTIONS

Numerous calculations are required in data analysis. To the fields being studied in Tableau, calculations have been made using the calculation editor. The numerous built-in functions in Tableau make it easier to create expressions for challenging calculations [2]. A list of Tableau functions is provided, and it is divided into the following five categories:

1. **Number Functions:** The number function is a means of computation used in mathematical calculations. All they accept as inputs are numbers. Here are some instances of Tableau's numerical functions (Table 4.1).
2. **String Functions:** To work with the string, one uses string functions as listed below (Table 4.2).
3. **Date Functions:** There are numerous date functions in Tableau, and each one makes use of the date_part string, which indicates the day, month, or year of the date. Let us examine a few crucial instances of date functions (Table 4.3).

TABLE 4.1

Number Functions Supported in Tableau

Function	Description
ABS (number)	Yields the absolute value of the number provided.
COS (number)	Yields the cosine of the number (angle); the angle should be in radians.
DEGREES (Num)	Returns radian to degree conversion of the given number.
LOG (Num [, base])	Yields the logarithm of a number. By default, the base of the logarithm is 10.
MAX (Num1, Num2)	Yields the maximum of the two same types of values. Result Null if either argument is Null.
MIN (Num1, Num2)	Yields the minimum of the two same types of values. If either argument is Null, the result is Null.
PI ()	Yields the value of numeric constant pi = 3.14159.
POWER (Num, pow)	Calculate the number to the specified power.
RADIANS (Num)	Transforms argument from degrees to radians.
ROUND (Num, [precision])	Numbers are rounded to a certain number of digits given by precision. If no decimals are given, then the number is rounded to the nearest integer.
SIGN (Num)	Yields the sign of argument. If the number is less than 0, the output is −1; if the number is equal to 0, the output is 0; if the number is greater than 0, the output is +1.
SIN (Num)	Yields the sine of an angle given in radians.
SQRT (Num)	Yields the square root of a quantity.
SQUARE (Num)	Yields the square of the argument.
TAN (Num)	Yields the tangent of a number (angle); the angle should be in radians.

TABLE 4.2
String Functions Supported in Tableau

Function	Definition
ASCII (str)	Yields the ASCII code for the first character of the string.
CHAR (Num)	Yields character corresponding to ASCII code.
CONTAINS (str, substr)	Outcome is True if a string contains the specified substring.
ENDSWITH (str, substr)	Yields True if the given string ends with the specified substring. It ignores any trailing white spaces while doing so.
FIND (str, substr)	Yields the substring's index position in the string or 0 if the substring is not found in the string.
LEN (str)	Yields the length of the string.
LOWER (str)	Produces modified string in lowercase.
LTRIM (str)	Removes any left-side spaces in a string.
MAX (p, q)	Yields the maximum of a and b strings.
MIN (p, q)	Returns the minimum of p and q strings.
REPLACE (str, substr, newstr)	Substitutes a string with a new one after searching the string for a substring. The string remains unchanged if the substring cannot be located.
RTRIM (str)	Yields string with any trailing spaces removed.
SPLIT (str, delimiter)	Yields a substring by splitting a string into a sequence of subparts using a delimiter character.
STARTSWITH (str, substr)	Yields True if the string begins with a specified substring. It ignores any of the leading whitespaces present.
TRIM (str)	Removes the leading and trailing whitespaces and yields the string.
UPPER (str)	Yields string, with all characters, uppercased.

TABLE 4.3
Date Functions Supported in Tableau

Function	Definition
DATEADD (date_part, increase, date_value)	Yields an increase that is added to the "date_value" argument.
DATENAME (date_part, date_value, [start_of_week])	Yields "date_part" of "date_value" as a string. The argument "start_of_week" is non-compulsory.
DAY (date_value)	Yields the given date's day as an integer value.
NOW ()	Yields the present date and time.

4. **Logical Functions:** A Boolean output is generated by these functions after evaluating specified expressions. Several crucial illustrations of logical operation are listed in Table 4.4.

5. **Aggregate Functions:** We can restructure or alter the level of detail in your data using aggregate functions. Let us examine a few crucial aggregate function instances (Table 4.5).

TABLE 4.4
Logical Functions Supported in Tableau

Function	Description
<First expr> IN <Sec expr>	Yields TRUE if any value in first and second expression matches.
IF < First expr > AND < Sec expr > THEN <then> END	Executes a logical AND on two expressions. If both are True, then the outcome is True, else False.
IF < First expr > OR < Sec expr > THEN <then> END	Executes a logical OR on two expressions. If one is True, then the outcome is True, else False.
CASE <Test Expression> WHEN <Val1> THEN <outcome1> WHEN <Val2> THEN <outcome2>... ELSE <default outcome> END	Achieves logical assessments and returns suitable values.
IF <TestExpr> THEN <then> ELSE <else> END	Examines an expression and executes <outcome> value for first true <expr>.
IF < TestExpr1> THEN <outcome1> ELSEIF < TestExpr2> THEN <outcome2> ... ELSE <default outcome > END	Examines a sequence of expressions and executes <outcome> value for first true <expr>.
ISDATE (parameter)	Yields true if a given parameter is valid date.
ISNULL (expression)	Yields true if expression evaluates to NULL.

TABLE 4.5
Aggregate Functions Supported in Tableau

Function	Definition
AVG (Test Expression)	Yields the mean of all the values in the expression with numeric fields only.
CORR (First Expr1, Sec Expr2)	Yields the Pearson correlation between two expressions.
COUNT (Test Expression)	Yields the count of items returned from the expression; null values are not counted.
COVAR (First Expr1, Sec Expr2)	Yields the sample covariance between the two expressions.
MAX (Test Expression)	Yields the maximum of a given sequence or expression.
MEDIAN (Test Expression)	Yields the expression's median value over all records.
MIN (Test Expression)	Yields the minimum of all values in the expression.
STDEV (Test Expression)	Yields the standard deviation of sample data.
SUM (Test Expression)	Yields the expression's sum. SUM is only applicable to numeric fields.
VAR (Test Expression)	Yields the variance of sample data; variance is just the square of the standard deviation.

4.3   TABLEAU OPERATORS

To perform specific logical and mathematical processes, the compiler uses symbols called operators [3]. Tableau has a multitude of operators that can be used to construct formulas and computed fields. The types of operators and the order in which they should be used are as follows:

1. Operators in general
2. Operators in mathematics
3. Operators for relations (relational)
4. Logical or assertive operators

4.3.1   GENERAL OPERATORS

This group includes the operators that we typically employ in general quantitative computation, such as addition and subtraction (Table 4.6).

4.3.2   ARITHMETIC OPERATORS

Mathematical operators are those that assist in carrying out arithmetic computations on various fields of given source data (Table 4.7).

TABLE 4.6
General Operators in Tableau

Operator	Description
+ (For Addition)	Applied while adding days to dates, concatenating strings, and adding numerals.
– (For Subtraction)	Applied in a variety of actions, such as taking days off dates and subtracting figures.

TABLE 4.7
Arithmetic Operators in Tableau

Operator	Description
* (Multiplication)	Arithmetic multiplication on numerals
/ (Division)	Arithmetic division on numerals
% (Modulus sign)	Arithmetic remainder on numerals
^ (Power)	Calculate raised to the power on numerals

TABLE 4.8
Relational Operators in Tableau

Operator	Description
Num1 > Num2	Examine for greater than between Num1 and Num2 numerals
Num1 >= Num2	Examine for greater than or equal in Num1 and Num2 numerals
Num1 < Num2	Examine for less than between Num1 and Num2 numerals
Num1 <= Num2	Examine for less than or equal to in Num1 and Num2 numerals
Num1 == Num2	Examine for equality between Num1 and Num2 numerals
Num1 ! = Num2	Examine for inequality between Num1 and Num2 numerals

4.3.3 RELATIONAL OPERATORS

A binary operator that receives two operands as input, compares their values, and outputs the result is known as a relational operator or comparison operator. A comparison operator is typically used in loops and conditional expressions to determine whether to proceed with execution based on the comparison result (Table 4.8).

4.3.4 LOGICAL OPERATORS

There are three fundamental directives in the logical operator:

- The operator denoted as "AND" or logical conjunction
- Operator for logical disjunction or "OR"
- The operator for logical negation or "NOT"
  1. **"AND" or Logical Conjunction:** If both conditions are met, the operator will return True. It will return false if one of the conditions is false (Figure 4.1).

AND	TRUE	FALSE
TRUE	TRUE	FALSE
FALSE	FALSE	FALSE

FIGURE 4.1   Logical AND operator in Tableau.

  2. **Logical Disjunction or "OR":** If one or both criteria are true, the logical disjunction or "OR" operator will return True; otherwise, it will produce False (Figure 4.2).

OR	TRUE	FALSE
TRUE	TRUE	TRUE
FALSE	TRUE	FALSE

FIGURE 4.2   Logical OR operator in Tableau.

3. **Logical Negation or "NOT":** If the condition is False, the operator will produce a True, whereas for a True condition, NOT will yield False (Figure 4.3).

NOT	TRUE	FALSE
NOT	FALSE	TRUE

FIGURE 4.3 Logical NOT operator in Tableau.

4.3.5 PRECEDENCE OF OPERATOR

The operator's order of priority known as "Precedence" is described in the table below. The table with the highest priority is in the top row. Certain operators share the same precedence when they are in the same row. Two operators are analyzed in the formula from left to right if their precedence is equal (Figure 4.4).

Rank of Precedence	Operators
I.	~ (Negation)
II.	^ (Raise to power)
III.	*, /, %
IV.	+, -
V.	==, >, <, >=, <=, !=
VI.	NOT
VII.	AND
VIII.	OR

FIGURE 4.4 Operator precedence order in Tableau.

4.4 TABLEAU CALCULATIONS

Tableau's calculations, also known as computations, enable users to create new data from existing data sources [4,5]. This allows users to add new fields dynamically and perform sophisticated analyses. However, determining when to use these calculations can be challenging. Tableau calculates fields based on preexisting data, generates new fields or columns with regulated values, and saves them to the data source [6]. The original data is kept intact to prevent modification. To construct calculated fields in Tableau, you can use one of three main calculation types:

- Simple expressions
- Calculations in tables
- Expressions of level of detail (LOD).

4.4.1 SIMPLE EXPRESSIONS

Tableau allows for row-level and display-level modifications using simple expressions. Numeric, string, and date calculations are performed using built-in functions in the formula editor. Applying calculations to fields is simple, such as subtracting values or using aggregate functions. To create a calculation field and use numeric functions, follow these steps:

Step 1. Get the Sample-Superstore dataset connected (Figure 4.5).

FIGURE 4.5   Output.

> **Step 2.** Create a calculated field by opening a new worksheet, selecting Analysis from the menu and following the instructions in Figure 4.6.

FIGURE 4.6   Output.

Step 3. It launches a calculation editor that displays a list of all of Tableau's functions. To view the list of all possible functions, rename the calculation as "DemoCalculation" and click the arrow on the far-right side of the screen (Figure 4.7).

FIGURE 4.7 Output.

Step 4. We develop a formula that deducts the discount from the profit and rounds off the result to see the rounded-off difference between the goods' profit and discount. Drag and drop the required dimensions into the calculation box (Figure 4.8).

FIGURE 4.8 Output.

Step 5. To demonstrate the profit and discount margin in products, drag and drop the "DemoCalculation" field in the column header and the sub-category "Dimension" under the rows header (Figure 4.9).

FIGURE 4.9   Output.

Step 6. To compute the average sales numbers for various products and develop a new formula for the same, we can utilize the aggregate function AVG() (Figure 4.10).

FIGURE 4.10   Output.

Step 7. At this point, the average sales for the various product subcategories are visible (Figure 4.11).

FIGURE 4.11 Output.

4.4.2 TABLE CALCULATIONS

To apply a transformation or calculation to values displayed on a visualization, a table calculation is used. The calculated field is only applied to the local data of Tableau. These calculations rely on the selected visualization and disregard any other dimensions or measures that are removed from the visualization [7,8]. Table calculations apply to the whole table. Table calculations have various applications, such as transforming values to rankings, showing running totals, and displaying the percentage of the total. The types of table calculations are as follows:

- Difference from calculation
- Percent difference from calculation
- Moving calculation
- Percent of total calculation
- Percentile calculation
- Rank calculation
- Running total calculation

Tableau's "Quick Table calculations" feature allows users to quickly apply common table calculations to visualizations, such as calculating an average on an entire column. This feature is used to create calculations using the most common settings for that calculation type. The following are the steps applied in quick table calculations:

Step 1. As in the example above, connect to the Sample-Superstore dataset and launch a new worksheet. Choose "Create Calculated Field" from the "Analysis" panel.

Step 2. We want to view different table calculations. For this, drag YEAR(Order_Date) in the Columns header and QUARTER(Order_Date) and MONTH(Order_Date) in the Rows header (Figure 4.12).

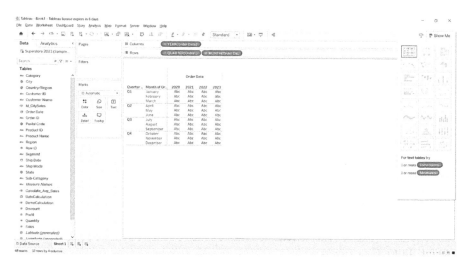

FIGURE 4.12   Output.

Step 3. To view sales values in the table, drag the Sales field and drop it in the *Text* Marks area (Figure 4.13).

FIGURE 4.13   Output.

Step 4. The table is displayed as shown in Figure 4.14.

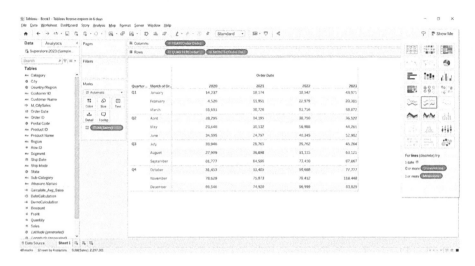

FIGURE 4.14   Output.

Step 5. Choose the "Add Table Calculation" option after right-clicking SUM(Sales) on the Marks shelf (Figure 4.15).

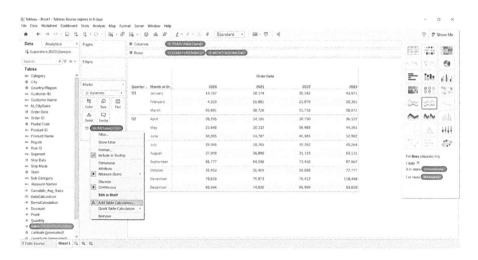

FIGURE 4.15   Output.

Step 6. Choose "Difference From" under Calculation Type and Table (across) under the Compute Using in the Table Calculation dialog box that appears. Once complete, click the "X" button from the upper corner to close the Table Calculation dialog box (Figure 4.16).

FIGURE 4.16 Output.

Step 7. The data values in the visualization are subjected to the computation (Figure 4.17).

Quarter..	Month of Or..	2020	2021	2022	2023
Q1	January		3,937	360	25,429
	February		7,432	11,027	-2,678
	March		-16,965	12,990	7,156
Q2	April		5,900	4,555	-2,229
	May		6,483	26,856	-12,727
	June		-9,798	15,547	12,637
Q3	July		-5,181	10,497	6,002
	August		8,989	-5,783	32,006
	September		-17,181	8,814	14,457
Q4	October		-48	28,283	18,089
	November		-2,656	3,439	39,036
	December		5,374	22,080	-13,170

FIGURE 4.17 Output.

Note: To modify a table calculation, we can right-click on the measure that is being transformed using a table calculation and click on "Alter Table Calculation."

4.5 LEVEL OF DETAIL (LOD) EXPRESSIONS

Level of detail expressions, or LOD expressions for short, allow us to compute values at both the data source and visualization levels [9, 10]. But we may decide how fine a granularity we wish to compute with LOD expressions. There are three different levels at which they can be carried out: fully independent (FIXED), less granular (EXCLUDE), and more granular (INCLUDE) level [11]. The format of the level of detail statement is as described below (Figure 4.18).

{[FIXED | INCLUDE | EXCLUDE] <dimension declaration>: <aggregate expression>}

FIGURE 4.18   Syntax of writing LOD expression.

According to the syntax, the LOD expressions need to be completely enclosed within curly braces.

4.5.1 Types of LOD Expressions

LOD expressions come in three primary categories.

1. **FIXED LOD:**
    The FIXED level of detail expressions utilizes the provided dimensions to calculate values ignoring the view level of detail, i.e., regardless of the other dimensions in the view. The FIXED level of detail expressions ignores all other filters in the view, except the context, data source, and extract filters. To compute the total sales for each region, use the following FIXED level of detail expression (Figure 4.19).

{FIXED [Region]: Average Sales (SUM)}

FIGURE 4.19   Syntax of writing FIXED LOD expression.

To display total sales by region, this level of detail expression—named [Sales by Region]—is subsequently set to Text. Here, [Region] and [State] are the view levels of detail. However, the dimensions indicated in the computation (here, Region) are the only dimensions taken into consideration by FIXED level of detail expressions. Let us create an example for FIXED LOD expression to view sum of sales per shipping mode in Tableau using the below steps:
    Step 1. To aggregate a measure onto the relevant dimension, control-click and drag it onto the Data pane. Here, with Sample-Superstore data

connected in the Tableau worksheet, we press the ctrl key with a mouse click on Sales measure and drag-drop it on Ship Mode dimension (Figure 4.20).

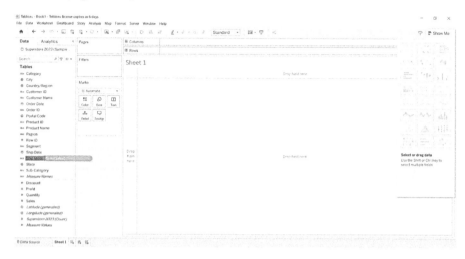

FIGURE 4.20   Output.

Step 2. A new field named Sales (Ship Mode) appears as a FIXED LOD calculation (Figure 4.21).

FIGURE 4.21   Output.

Step 3. The aggregation in the aggregate expression will come from the default aggregation on the measure. This is usually SUM. At this point, right-click on the new field and click on "Edit Calculation" to modify the LOD or change the aggregation (Figure 4.22).

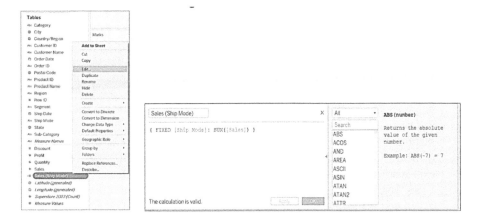

FIGURE 4.22 Output.

Step 4. After that, bring the computed field Sales (Ship Mode) to the Text shelf beneath the Marks card and the Ship Mode and the Sub-Category field to the Rows shelf. Additionally, drag the Ship Mode field to the shelf of color. As a result, the view that follows displays a fixed value for each sub-category (Figure 4.23).

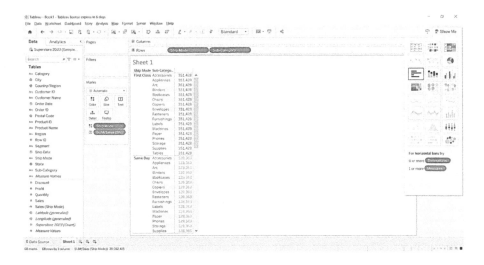

FIGURE 4.23 Output.

Every ship mode exhibits the same sales value. This is because we have fixed the dimension "Ship Mode" for the "Sales" amount computation.

2. **INCLUDE LOD:** The equations for the INCLUDE level of detail calculate values by utilizing the given dimensions along with any other dimensions present in the view. INCLUDE level of detail expressions are particularly helpful when a dimension that is not in the view is included. INCLUDE can be useful when you want to reaggregate data at a higher level of information in your view while still performing calculations at a finer level of detail in the database. Fields reliant on the INCLUDE level of detail expressions change as dimensions are added or deleted from the display. Using INCLUDE LOD, let us examine the sample above. Total sales are calculated per shipping mode using the INCLUDE level of detail expressed below (Figures 4.24 and 4.25).

{INCLUDE [Ship Mode]: SUM([Sales])}

FIGURE 4.24   Syntax of writing INCLUDE LOD expression.

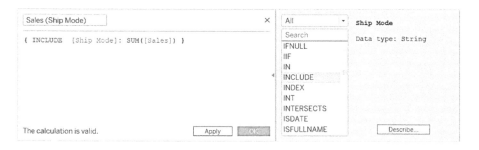

FIGURE 4.25   Output.

For every ship mode in the example above, the sales amounts would have varied if the keyword had been INCLUDE rather than FIXED. In evaluating the expression, INCLUDE considers the dimension in the expression ([Ship Mode]) as well as any supplementary dimensions in the view such as ([Sub-Category]) (Figure 4.26).

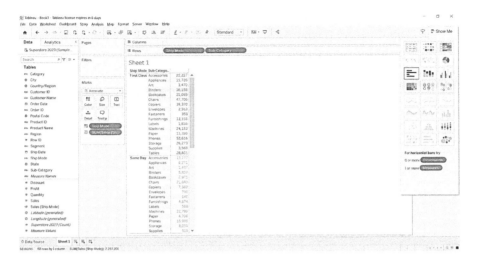

FIGURE 4.26 Output.

Here, we can observe distinct sales values for each ship mode with sub-category:

3. **EXCLUDE LOD:** Level of detail expressions that begin with EXCLUDE designate dimensions to be excluded from the view level of detail. Specifically, expressions for the EXCLUDE level of detail delete dimensions from the view level of detail by expressly removing them from it. When eliminating a dimension from the view, EXCLUDE level of detail expressions are extremely helpful. If there are not any dimensions to omit in row-level expressions, EXCLUDE cannot be utilized. They can alter other LODs or a view-level computation.

We construct a level of detail expression that eliminates [Ship Mode] from the total of [Sales], which we call "Sales (Ship Mode)" (Figure 4.27).

FIGURE 4.27 Output.

Examine the view below, which separates the total sales by Ship Mode and Sub-Category (Figure 4.28).

FIGURE 4.28   Output.

Since the ship mode dimension has been eliminated, we have noticed in the view above that the sales figures are constant for all shipment options.

KEY NOTES

- Users can compute and generate new data from preexisting data sources using Tableau functions.
- The five categories that they fall under are aggregate functions, logical, date, string, and numeric functions.
- There are four sorts of operators: general, arithmetic, relational, and logical.
- Operators are symbols used for mathematical and logical operations.
- Tableau uses four different calculation types—numerical, string, date, and table—for both data source and display calculations.
- Level of detail (LOD) expressions allow for computation at both the display and data source levels.

TEST YOUR SKILLS

1. What is the purpose of a parameter in Tableau?
2. Differentiate between the two types of connections in Tableau, i.e., live connection and an extract.
3. Define the need for a "Calculated Field." Describe how to make a calculated field for a dataset of your choice by performing a simple calculation.
4. Discuss various types of operators and functions supported in Tableau.

5. Define table calculations. Enlist the different types of table calculations allowed in Tableau.
6. Describe different LOD expressions in Tableau with suitable examples.

REFERENCES

1. Sarsfield, Patrick, et al. *Maximizing Tableau Server: A Beginner's Guide to Accessing, Sharing, and Managing Content on Tableau Server*. United Kingdom, Packt Publishing, 2021.
2. Sleeper, Ryan. *Innovative Tableau: 100 More Tips, Tutorials, and Strategies*. United States, O'Reilly Media, 2020.
3. Milligan, Joshua N. *Learning Tableau 2019: Tools for Business Intelligence, Data Prep, and Visual Analytics*, 3rd Edition. India, Packt Publishing, 2019.
4. Loth, Alexander. *Visual Analytics with Tableau*. United States, Wiley, 2019.
5. Costello, Tim, and Blackshear, Lori. *Prepare Your Data for Tableau: A Practical Guide to the Tableau Data Prep Tool*. Germany, Apress, 2019.
6. Sleeper, Ryan. *Practical Tableau: 100 Tips, Tutorials, and Strategies from a Tableau Zen Master*. United States, O'Reilly Media, 2018.
7. Khan, Arshad. *Jumpstart Tableau: A Step-By-Step Guide to Better Data Visualization*. United States, Apress, 2016.
8. Acharya, Seema, and Chellappan, Subhashini. *Pro Tableau: A Step-by-Step Guide*. United States, Apress, 2016.
9. Murray, Daniel G. *Tableau Your Data! Fast and Easy Visual Analysis with Tableau Software*. Germany, Wiley, 2016.
10. Milligan, Joshua N. *Learning Tableau: Leverage the Power of Tableau 9. 0 to Design Rich Data Visualizations and Build Fully Interactive Dashboards*. United Kingdom, Packt Publishing, 2015.
11. Monsey, Molly, and Sochan, Paul. *Tableau for Dummies*. Germany, Wiley, 2015.

5 Sorting and Filters in Tableau

5.1 FILTERS IN TABLEAU

Filtering is removing a group of results containing a specific value or combination of values. The filtering tool in Tableau allows for both the use of field values in simple applications and more intricate calculations or context-based filters [1]. Tableau offers an extensive range of filter choices as compared to other visualization applications. In Tableau, the source dataset is cleaned using filters, eliminating unnecessary records. For data processing, Tableau settings employ a range of filters; some of the filters are extract filter, data source filter, context filter, dimension filter, measure filter, and table calculation filter [2].

5.1.1 TYPES OF FILTERS IN TABLEAU

To increase performance or draw attention to the necessary information, all applications employ filters to shrink the dataset and remove irrelevant data. For greater efficiency, Tableau offers a variety of filters for the given dataset. Each filter has a different purpose, and their execution order on a dataset might have a significant impact on performance [3, 4]. Tableau uses a variety of filters, some of which are outlined below:

1. Dimension filtering
2. Measures filtering
3. Dates filtering
4. Extract filtering
5. Context filtering
6. Condition filtering
7. Quick filtering
8. Table calculation filtering
   Let us discuss each of these filters with their implementation details:

1. Dimension Filter: These are only available for the dimension field in Tableau. The following examples of filtering use groups of numbers or texts with logical expressions that are less than or greater than constraints. Only values in dimension filters can be used for filtering. As an example of a data source for applying dimension filters to an item subdivision, consider Sample-Superstore. We must create an illustration that displays the profit for each product sub-category based on the shipping method, as shown below:
Step 1 Move the sub-categories of the dimension field to the Rows shelf.

DOI: 10.1201/9781003429593-5

Step 2 Continue with the Columns shelf and the measure field profit (Figure 5.1).

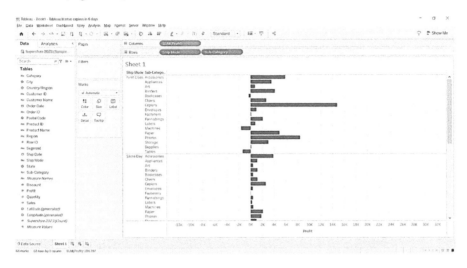

FIGURE 5.1   Output.

Step 3 To open the Filter dialog box, move the Sub-Category to the Filter's shelf (Figure 5.2).

FIGURE 5.2   Output.

Step 4 To deselect every segment, at the bottom of that list, select the None button. Then, in the dialog box's bottom-right corner, click the Exclude button. Lastly, choose Labels and Storage, and then press the OK button (Figure 5.3).

FIGURE 5.3 Output.

Step 5 The screenshot below shows the result, without the two categories listed above (Figure 5.4).

FIGURE 5.4 Output.

2. **Measures Filters:** The measure fields are subjected to these filters, and the filtering is determined by calculations performed on the measured fields. Therefore, while dimension filters only use values to filter, measure filters use calculations based on fields.

Step 1 To use dimension selections on the mean profit value Sample-Superstore data source, follow these steps.

Step 2 In the screenshot below, drag the ship mode and sub-category dimensions in the Rows header and the Average of Profit in the Columns header first (Figure 5.5).

FIGURE 5.5 Output.

Step 3 Now, drag Profit measure in the Filters section and set the filter types as Average and click Next (Figure 5.6).

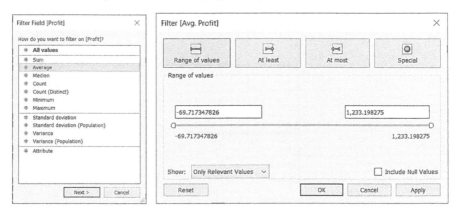

FIGURE 5.6 Output.

Step 4 At this point, a new dialog box appears, where we can configure the value range, the minimum and maximum values, and any special values to be checked. In this case, the range is set to 0–1,233, with all values remaining positive. Press "Apply" and "Ok" (Figure 5.7).

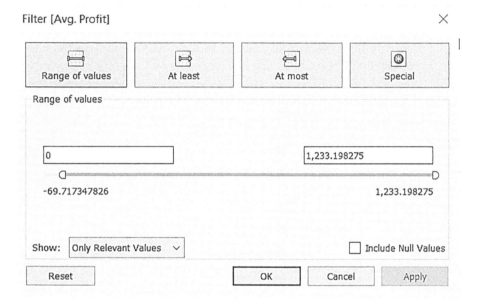

FIGURE 5.7   Output.

Step 5 The output is displayed as the below image (Figure 5.8).

FIGURE 5.8   Output.

Note: Users can try to set at least and at most values themselves.

3. **Dates Filter:** Tableau uniquely handles date fields, letting you filter data by absolute dates, relative dates (as compared to today), or date ranges. When you drag a date field to the filter shelf, these options appear. Let us consider the following example:

Step 1 Move the Order Date to the Column shelf and the Sum (Profit) to rows that are our measure parameter after connecting to the Sample-Superstore data source (Figure 5.9).

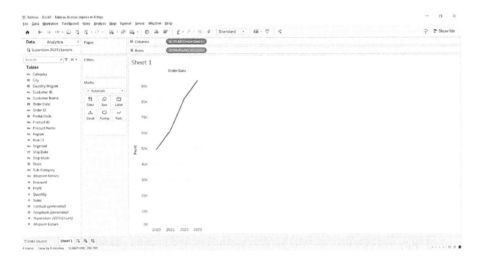

FIGURE 5.9 Output.

Step 2 Next, in the filter dialog box, select the Range of year/date, then move the field Order Date to the Filter shelf, and click Next (Figure 5.10).

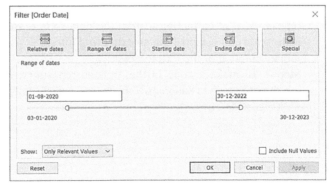

FIGURE 5.10 Output.

Step 3 Below is a display of the profit values for the specified date range (Figure 5.11).

FIGURE 5.11   Output.

Step 4 We can also set relative dates, starting and ending dates for filtering results.

4. **Extract Filter:** The data gathered from the data source is filtered using the extract filter. If the user takes the data out of the data source, this filter is applied. Once the text file has been linked to Tableau, both the Live and Extract buttons can be discovered in the top-right position of the Data Source tab. A live connection links the data source to the data. The extract connection ensures a copy is locally created for the data in the Tableau repository after extracting it from the data source. Below are the detailed instructions for establishing an extracting filter. Let us discuss the practical implementation of the Extract filter.

Step 1 To make a copy in the Tableau repository, connect the Sample-Superstore data source to Tableau and select the "Extract" radio button (Figure 5.12).

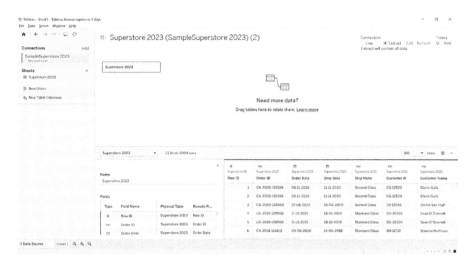

FIGURE 5.12   Output.

Step 2 Next, select the "Add" option located under the Filters heading in the top-right position. The "Edit Data Source Filters" window appears. Select the "Add" option that is displayed in the window.

Step 3 In Figure 5.13, we can observe that the "Add Filter" window appears to let you choose your filter condition. Any field can be selected and added as an extract filter. We have chosen "Ship Mode" as the extract filter in this instance. Press the OK button.

FIGURE 5.13   Output.

Step 4 The filter window seen in the screenshot below opens after you click the OK button. Here, we select the "Same Day" filter value. Click OK (Figure 5.14).

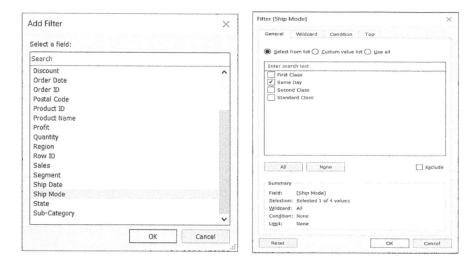

FIGURE 5.14   Output.

Step 5 The new filter is added in the Data Source filters. Click OK (Figure 5.15).

FIGURE 5.15   Output.

Step 6 In the extracted data values, we can observe all the rows filtered for the value "Same Day" in the shipping mode column (Figure 5.16).

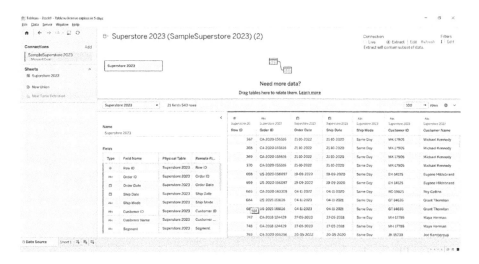

FIGURE 5.16   Output.

5. **Context Filter:** Tableau's normal filters operate independently of one another, which means that each one reads every row in the source data and produces a unique output. But in some cases, we might want the additional filter to handle only the records returned by the initial filter; when this occurs, the additional filter is known as a dependent filter because it only handles data that has passed through the context filter. Context filters serve two main purposes:

- **Enhances Performance:** Queries may run slow on a large data source or when a lot of filters are applied. Single or more context filters can be set to enhance working.
- **Generates a Numerical or Top N Filter that is Dependent:** We may initially define a context filter to include only relevant data, followed by a top N or numbers filter.

Using the Sample-Superstore, we can use a context filter to find the top three profitable sub-categories of products for the category called Office Supplies. We can follow the below steps to achieve the desired output.

Step 1 In Tableau, create a new worksheet and link it to the Sample-Superstore data source.

Step 2 Move the Profit to the Rows and the Sub-Category and Category to the Columns shelves, respectively. Choose bar graph as the type of chart (Figure 5.17).

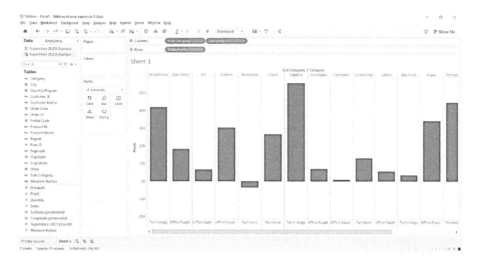

FIGURE 5.17   Output.

> **Step 3** Move the category dimension to the Filters and then choose "Office Supplies" from the drop-down menu. Press "Apply" and "OK" (Figure 5.18).

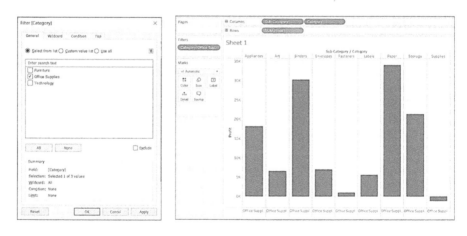

FIGURE 5.18   Output.

> **Step 4** Move the Sub-Category with the required dimensions to the Filter box. Click the Top tab, choose By Field, set the parameter to Top, and enter 3 as the value in the filter window.
>
> **Step 5** The chart in Figure 5.19 above displays the top three profit-making sub-categories under the Office Supplies category of products.

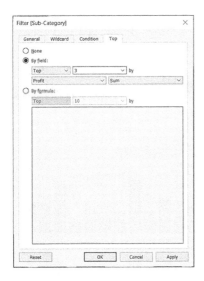
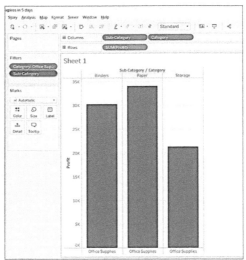

FIGURE 5.19   Output.

6. **Condition Filter:** In Tableau, condition filtering is used to conditionally apply existing filters. These conditions can be as simple as finding just sales that are greater than a certain amount, or as complex as creating a range filter. For example, consider the Sample-Superstore data source and identify the product sub-category that falls under various segments and whose overall sales surpass 50k. The steps to implement a condition filter are as follows:

   Step 1 In Tableau, link it to the Sample-Superstores data source.

   Step 2 Move the dimensions segment as well as Sales onto the Rows shelf.

   Step 3 Now, move the field Sub-Category to the Column shelf. Select the bar graph option to visualize the given scenario (Figure 5.20).

FIGURE 5.20   Output.

Step 4 Move the Sub-Category dimension to the Filters shelf in step four. Click the "Condition" tab in the filter settings dialog box and then choose the "By field" radio button. Pick the field "Sales" and the "Sum" function from the drop-down menu. Use the operator greater than equal to with the value 50,000. Click Apply and OK.

Step 5 The chart in Figure 5.21 displays the sub-category sales whose net sales worth is greater than or equal to 50k.

 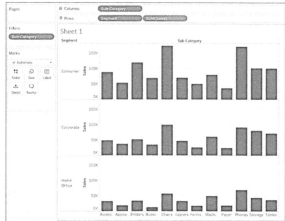

FIGURE 5.21 Output.

7. **Quick Filters:** Using Tableau's right-click menu on measurements and dimensions, a variety of filter types are easily accessible. These filters, also referred to as "Quick filters," are sufficiently functional to address most regular filtering requirements. Tableau's quick filters and their applications are listed in Table 5.1.

Let us apply a quick filter to retrieve the product quantity, product names, and order year of those customers whose names start with "R":

TABLE 5.1
List of Quick Filters in Tableau

Filter	Purpose
Single value (list)	It only chooses one value from the list at a time.
Single value (drop-down)	It allows you to choose just one value from a list of options.
Multiple values (list)	It can choose more than one value from a list.
Different values (drop-down)	This option allows you to choose one or more values from the list.
Multiple values (custom list)	It picks a value or values and looks for them.
Single value (slider)	It chooses a single value by dragging a horizontal slider.
Wildcard match	Values with special characters are selected.

Step 1 Open a new worksheet in Tableau and connect it to data source naming the Superstore. Drag the Year (from the date of order) in the Column and drag Customer Name and Product Name in the Row shelves, respectively. Drag the Sum (Quantity) in Text marks. The following output is displayed (Figure 5.22).

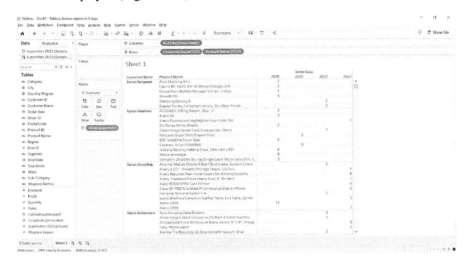

FIGURE 5.22   Output.

Step 2 Choose the Filter option by performing a right-press on the Customer Name column (Figure 5.23).

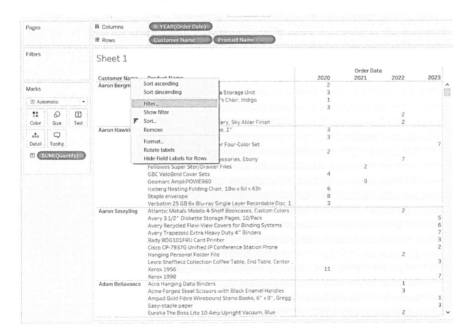

FIGURE 5.23   Output.

Step 3 In the dialog box for filter settings, click on the Wildcard tab, and in Match value, type "R" and select the Starts with radio button. Click Apply and OK (Figure 5.24).

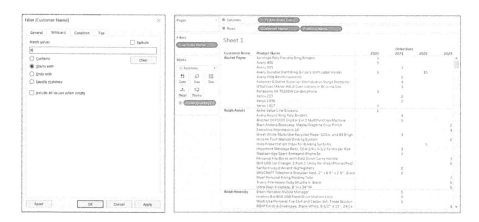

FIGURE 5.24   Output.

Step 4 The result is displayed in the above image where the order details of only those customers whose names start with "R." But this is a static filter for only one condition. We can add quick filters to make the filtration process more dynamic.

Step 5 We can also show filter, edit, or clear the filters as per our requirement. After that, move the Product Name dimension to the shelf of filters. Select the Show Filter option by right-clicking the Customer Name filter. Do the same process for the Product Name filter (Figure 5.25).

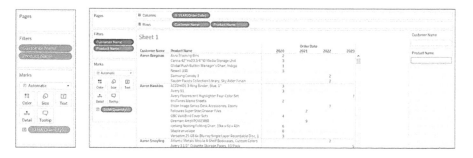

FIGURE 5.25   Output.

Step 6 We can see textboxes for both the filters on the extreme right end of the screen. Select the small drop-down option that is located next to the text field to see the quick filters that are available (Figure 5.26).

FIGURE 5.26   Output.

Step 7 Here, we can observe the list of all available quick filters as discussed in Table 5.1. We can apply each of these filters to view the results. For the Customer Name filter, let us select the first filter named Single Value (list), and for Product Name, select Multiple Values (drop-down) (Figure 5.27).

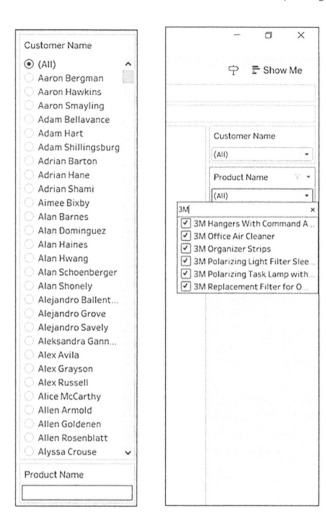

FIGURE 5.27   Output.

Step 8 The output after selecting the above quick filters (Figure 5.28).

FIGURE 5.28   Output.

Step 9 Similarly, users can select other filter options as given in Table 5.1 and observe the different results obtained.

8. **Table Calculation Filter:** Since table calculation filters are applied last in the order of operations, they do not remove underlying data from the data-set. This means that Tableau applies table calculation filters to the current view's results after evaluating any table calculations. A table calculation filter can be made by creating a calculated field and then adding it to the Filters shelf. If a table calculation filter is to be applied to the totals when they are displayed in a view, you can choose Apply to totals from the filter's drop-down menu (located on the Filters shelf). You can select when to apply a table calculation filter to totals using this option. Let us apply table calculation filter to totals.

Step 1 Open a new worksheet in Tableau and connect it to the Sample-Superstore data source. Drag the Order Date to Rows now. On Rows, right-click Order Date and choose Month. Once more, right-click Rows' Order Date and choose Discrete.

Step 2 Next, drag Sales to Text in the Marks shelf.

Step 3 Once again on Rows, right-click Order Date and choose Sort. Choose Descending under Sort Order in the Sort dialog box and then click OK (Figure 5.29).

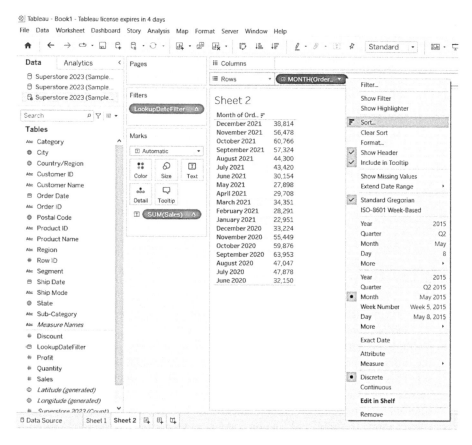

FIGURE 5.29   Output.

Step 4 Select Quick Table Calculation by right-clicking on Sales in Text. Select the Moving Average option as shown in Figure 5.30.

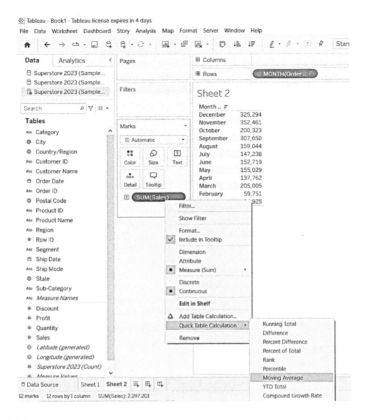

FIGURE 5.30 Output.

Step 5 In the next step, we need to create a Filter for the View. To create a calculated field for this, select the Analysis menu and then click the Create Calculated Field option (Figure 5.31).

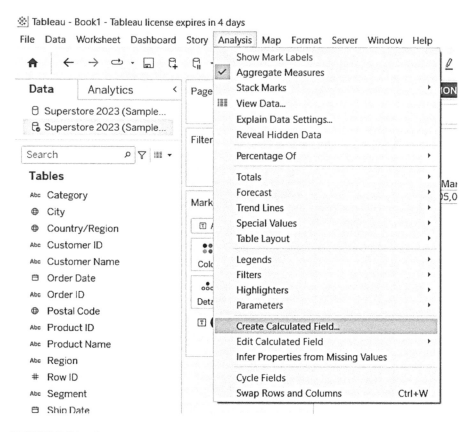

FIGURE 5.31   Output.

> **Step 6** Type the field name, "LookupDateFilter," and construct the formula
> in the dialog box of the calculated field option: lookup(min(([Order
> Date])),0) (Figure 5.32).

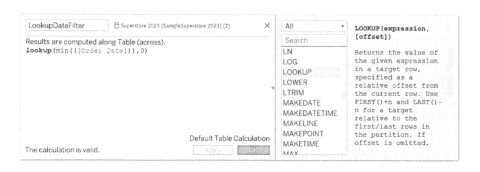

FIGURE 5.32   Output.

Step 7 Right-click LookupDateFilter under Measures and choose Convert to Continuous (Figure 5.33).

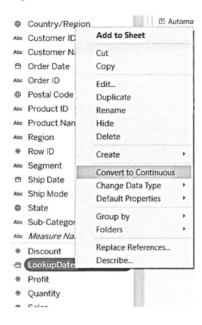

FIGURE 5.33 Output.

Step 8 Drag the Date Lookup Filter to the Filters tab from Measures.
Step 9 Choose the desired dates from the Filter box that appears, and then select OK (Figure 5.34).

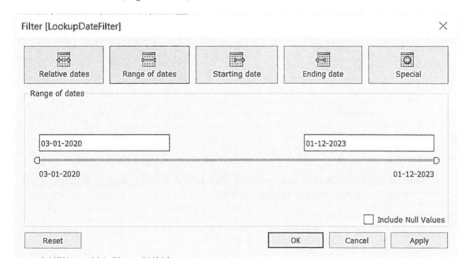

FIGURE 5.34 Output.

Step 10 Using a visualization to display grand totals in the Analytics pane: Drag and drop Totals above the Grand Totals by Row or Column option in the Add Totals dialog box located under Summarize in the Analytics pane (Figure 5.35).

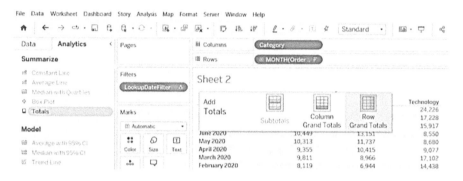

FIGURE 5.35   Output.

Step 11 The output is displayed as follows (Figure 5.36).

Month of Ord.. F	Furniture	Category Office Supplies	Technology	Grand Total
August 2021	15,979	13,238	15,082	44,300
July 2021	16,529	11,920	14,971	43,420
June 2021	10,342	9,034	10,777	30,154
May 2021	10,255	8,160	9,483	27,898
April 2021	9,188	10,773	9,746	29,708
March 2021	10,783	12,518	11,049	34,351
February 2021	8,703	11,270	8,318	28,291
January 2021	9,125	7,686	6,139	22,951
December 2020	15,173	8,394	9,656	33,224
November 2020	21,317	15,559	18,573	55,449
October 2020	21,505	17,360	21,011	59,876
September 2020	19,229	20,499	24,226	63,953
August 2020	14,480	15,338	17,047	47,047
July 2020	13,986	17,975	15,917	47,878
June 2020	10,449	13,151	8,550	32,150
May 2020	10,313	11,737	8,680	30,730

Pages
Filters
LookupDateFilter
Marks
Automatic
Color   Size   Text
Detail   Tooltip
SUM(Sales)

iii Columns   Category
Rows   MONTH(Order..

Sheet 2

FIGURE 5.36   Output.

Step 12 Right-click on LookupDateFilter in the Filters shelf and select the Apply to totals option (Figure 5.37).

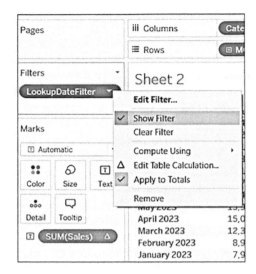

FIGURE 5.37   Output.

> **Step 13** Again right-click on LookupDateFilter and select the Show Filter
> option (Figure 5.38).

FIGURE 5.38   Output.

> **Step 14** Now, we select dates in the filter, say May 2021 to May 2023, and
> we can see the filtered grand total (Figure 5.39).

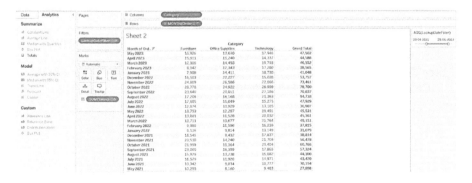

FIGURE 5.39   Output.

5.2 SORTING IN TABLEAU

We discussed the basics of sorting in Tableau in the previous chapter. In this chapter, we will discuss some advanced concepts related to sorting using multiple fields in Tableau. Sorting allows us to have control over various dimensions that are loaded from data source and visible in the worksheet. By altering a visualization's sort order, we can bring attention to the message we are attempting to get through. We can arrange our visuals in whatever way we desire, whether we are using text (like state names) or numeric data (such as sales or profit figures). When designing a visualization, it is essential to sort the measures because it makes it simpler for us to comprehend the facts being displayed [5,6]. The need for layered sorting arises when the view has several dimensions. Tableau offers a variety of sorting options, some of which are more popularly used than others based on ease of use. Sorting options include manual sorting, sorting by a field, alphabetical sorting, and nested sorting [7]. The table can be sorted using a field on the view, the default sort setting, and occasionally a sort icon that appears in the worksheet. The various techniques of sorting are listed below:

- Toolbar sorting
- Axis sorting
- Manual sorting
- Nested sorting
  - Using the Sort dialog box
  - Using the Combine field
  - Using the Rank method
- Custom sorting using parameter

Let us discuss each of these techniques in detail.

5.2.1 TOOLBAR SORTING

Sorting using the toolbar is easy. Two options for sorting it into ascending or descending instantly are located just above the columns area where you may add your fields, as implemented in the example below:

Step 1 Open a new worksheet and establish a connection to the data source for Sample-Superstore.

Step 2 Move the Category dimension to the Rows shelf and measure it in the Columns shelf in step 2 (Figure 5.40).

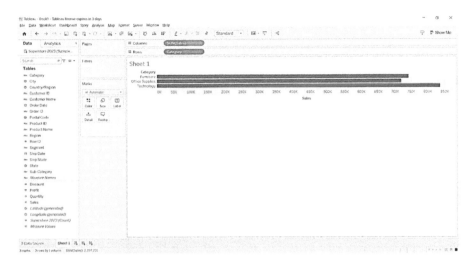

FIGURE 5.40   Output.

Step 3 In the toolbar above, we can observe three icons that are meant for swapping and visualizing.

Step 4 The first icon is used for swapping data visible in rows and columns. The effect of using the swapping operation gives the following output (Figure 5.41).

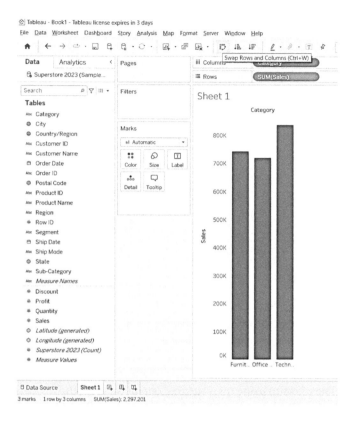

FIGURE 5.41   Output.

Step 5 On using the second icon 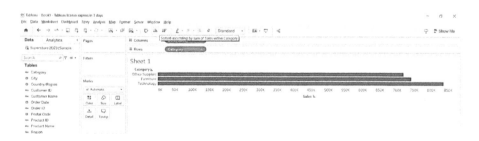, we can sort the data in ascending order. The data used for sorting is given under the measures field used within the dimension field used (Figure 5.42).

FIGURE 5.42   Output.

Step 6 Similarly, the third icon ⬇️ sorts the data in descending order (Figure 5.43).

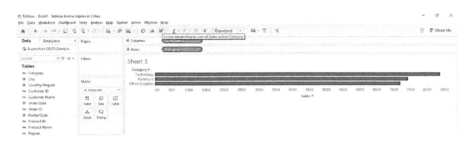

FIGURE 5.43   Output.

5.2.2   AXIS SORTING

For axis sorting, you can click the sorting symbol next to the continuous field axis; in this case, it is sales. It will sort it into descending first, ascending second, and then back to default. Let us consider the following example of using axis sorting in Sales and Category (Figures 5.44 and 5.45).

FIGURE 5.44   Output.

FIGURE 5.45   Output.

5.2.3 MANUAL SORTING

To manually sort your data, i.e., decide the order of data by manually changing the order up or down. Essentially, we can sort or order our field members in the exact order we want. We can implement this using right-click on categories or your specific dimension field and select sorting and then choose the Manual option (Figure 5.46).

FIGURE 5.46   Output.

In the filter dialog box manually, we can arrange the order of values as per our choice (Figure 5.47).

Sort [Category]   ×

Sort By
Manual   ▼

Furniture
Technology
Office Supplies

↺ Clear

FIGURE 5.47   Output.

The output is visible as follows (Figure 5.48).

FIGURE 5.48 Output.

5.2.4 NESTED SORTING

In Tableau, when you have data spread across multiple sections, you can sort it in two ways: nested sorting and non-nested sorting. Non-nested sorting looks at the values across all sections and keeps the same order of values in each section. This might make the sorting appear incorrect within a single section, but it consistently reflects how the values compare when aggregated across all sections. In contrast, nested sorting assesses values separately within each section, rather than considering them together across all sections. Consequently, nested sorts look correct within the context of each section but don't provide an overview of how the values compare across all sections. When you use nested sorting, the sorting order remains consistent as you navigate through dimensions, and you can choose the field that determines the column order.

5.2.4.1 Nested Sorting Using the Sort Box

Let us consider an example of implementing nested sort for arranging sales across sub-categories under various product categories:

Step 1 Open a new worksheet and establish a connection to the data source for Sample-Superstore.

Step 2 Move the measure Sales in Columns and Category dimension in the Rows shelves, respectively.

Step 3 Also, move the Sub-Category and drop in the Row shelf. As the below image displays it, how the view looks like is shown in Figure 5.49.

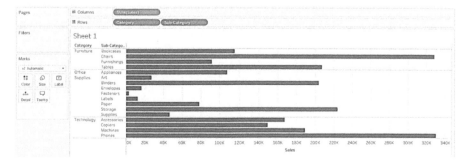

FIGURE 5.49 Output.

Step 4 Here, we observe the sub-categories within the categories in the view. The sub-categories are embedded into categories, so we refer to it as "nested" in categories.

Step 5 Since it is sub-categories that are to be sorted, right-click sub-categories and click on the Sort option (Figure 5.50).

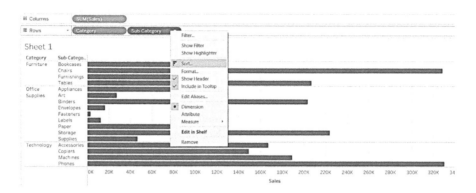

FIGURE 5.50 Output.

Step 6 Inside the Sort dialog box, select the Nested option. You can sort it either ascending or descending order (Figure 5.51).

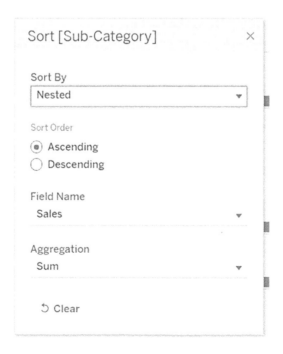

FIGURE 5.51 Output.

Step 7 After sorting, the result is displayed as follows (Figure 5.52).

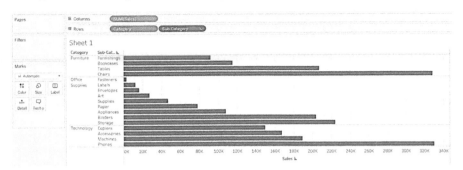

FIGURE 5.52 Output.

5.2.4.2 Nested Sorting Using the Combined Field

The Combined field can be created by selecting different dimensions and combining them together to form a new field. It can be regarded as a cross-product of dimensions selected from the data source. Let us consider the region and sub-categories dimensions which follow a hierarchy and the issue faced is that data is not sorted based on the values but based on the sub-categories. Now suppose we want to display the sales of regions for sub-categories in decreasing or increasing order. For solving this problem, we can use the Combined field for sorting:

Step 1 Launch a new worksheet and establish a connection to the data source for Sample-Superstore.

Step 2 Move the sales to the Columns and the region and sub-category dimensions to the Rows shelves, respectively.

Step 3 Let us create a combined field with region and sub-category. For this, click Region dimension, press the ctrl key, and right-press on the Sub-Category dimension. Next, click the Create option and choose the Combined field (Figure 5.53).

FIGURE 5.53 Output.

Step 4 The newly added Combined field is visible in dimensions (Figure 5.54).

Abc Region

Abc Region & Sub-Category (Combined)

\# Row ID

Abc Segment

☐ Ship Date

Abc Ship Mode

⊕ State

Abc Sub-Category

FIGURE 5.54   Output.

Step 5 Drag this Combined field before the Category on the Row shelf (Figure 5.55).

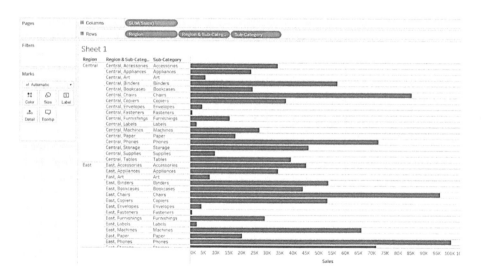

FIGURE 5.55   Output.

Step 6 At the Sum aggregation level, right-click on the Combined field, choose Sort by Field, and then sort Descending by Sales (Figure 5.56).

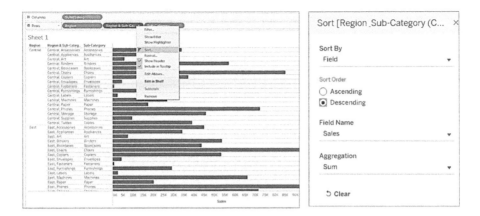

FIGURE 5.56 Output.

Step 7 Choose the Combined field (Region & Sub-Category (Combined)) by right-clicking on it and uncheck the Show Header (Figure 5.57).

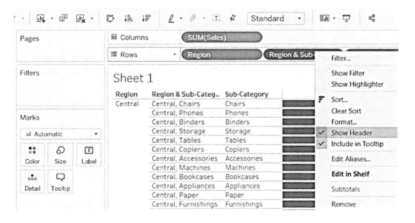

FIGURE 5.57 Output.

Step 8 The final sorted output for sales of sub-categories for regions is displayed as follows (Figure 5.58).

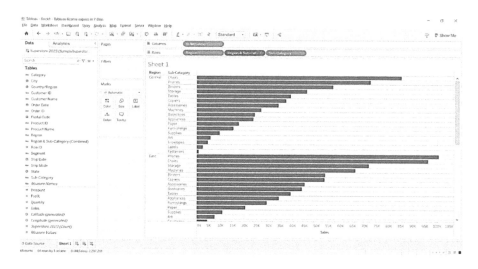

FIGURE 5.58   Output.

5.2.4.3   Nested Sorting Using Rank function

As its name implies, the rank function is used to assign a rank to any measure (number-related) that exists in the dataset. This rank can also be used to sort nested columns. Let us consider the following steps for implementing nested sorting:

Step 1 On the mark card, move the sales, region, and sub-category to rows, and the sales to columns (Figure 5.59).

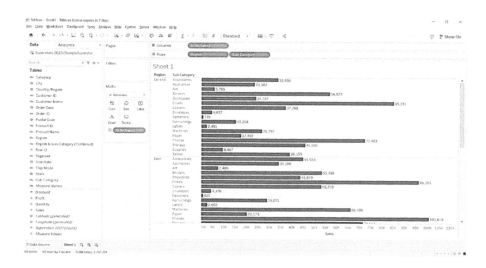

FIGURE 5.59   Output.

Step 2 To select the Quick Table Calculation option, select Rank by clicking right on the Sum (Sales) on the mark card (Figure 5.60).

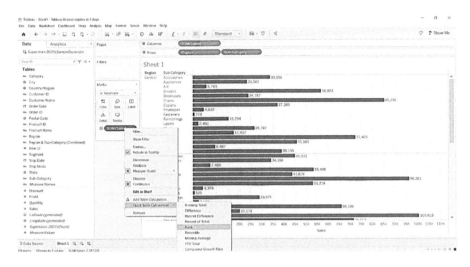

FIGURE 5.60   Output.

Step 3 Perform a second right-clicking on Sum (Sales) and choose compute using Pane Down (Figure 5.61).

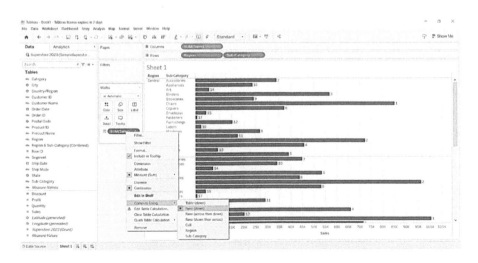

FIGURE 5.61   Output.

Step 4 Drag Sales to the Row shelf and then select Discrete with a right-click (Figure 5.62).

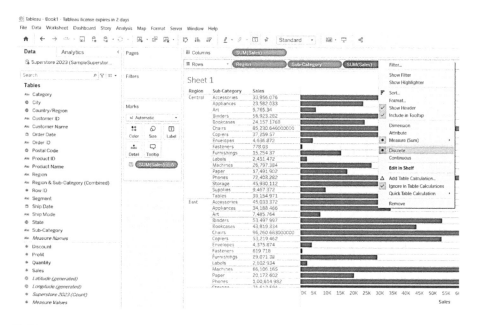

FIGURE 5.62   Output.

Step 5 Place Sales before the Sub-Category and then by right-clicking right on Sales, uncheck Show Header (Figure 5.63).

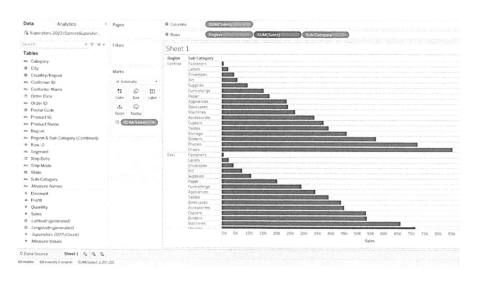

FIGURE 5.63   Output.

Step 6 In this example, data is sorted by region and sub-category. Now, you have a bar chart that is sorted by two dimensions. This allows some nice interactivity.

5.2.5 CUSTOM SORTING

Over the years, Tableau has made significant advancements to its sorting capabilities, including the addition of nested sorting in version 2018.2. This has made it easier for users to sort without getting confused, although occasionally the user interface and default selections are insufficient. For instance, Tableau inserts the axes header at the bottom of the window while many measurements are being displayed on the columns shelf. When hovering, the sort symbol is visible at the top, although this is not always the best option for novice users, and if we create custom headers, we may require different options. In a calculation, filter, or reference line, a workbook variable called a parameter are strings, numbers, or other type of value that can be used in place of a constant. Using the Sample-Superstore dataset, we will create a parameter to enable custom sorting.

Step 1 Open a new worksheet and establish a connection to the data source for Sample-Superstore.

Step 2 Drag the State dimension from the Rows shelf to the Columns shelf after dragging the sales, profit, quantity, and discount measurements from the Rows shelf.

Step 3 Select Bars for each measure in the Mark card from the Mark type (Figure 5.64).

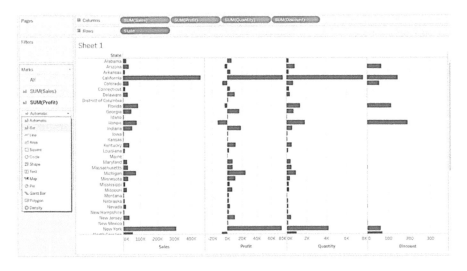

FIGURE 5.64 Output.

Step 4 Select Create Parameter by clicking the drop-down arrow in the Data pane's upper right corner. Enter the name "Sorting Parameter" to create a new parameter. Enter the names of the measures as the values, and choose string as the data type, i.e., sales, profit, quantity, and discount. Click OK (Figure 5.65).

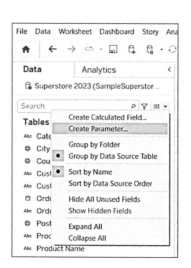

FIGURE 5.65 Output.

Step 5 Next, we make a calculated field that references the parameter selection naming "Select Parameter." To choose the field to sort by dynamically, we can use a case statement and the Sort By parameter. To compute the total, the fields for sum, profit, quantity, and discount must be combined (Figure 5.66).

FIGURE 5.66 Output.

Step 6 The final step completes the picture by instructing our sheet to use the Sort By field in the State field. Sort can be chosen by right-clicking on the State pill in the columns shelf (Figure 5.67).

FIGURE 5.67 Output.

Step 7 After that, choose Field in the Sort Choose the calculated field "Selection Parameter" that we recently created as the Field Name by selecting Descending from the drop-down menu for the Sort Order (Figure 5.68).

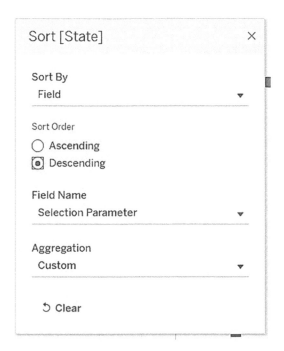

FIGURE 5.68 Output.

Step 8 Now right-click the parameter named "Sorting Parameter" that we created and select the Show Parameter option to display the parameter for choice (Figure 5.69).

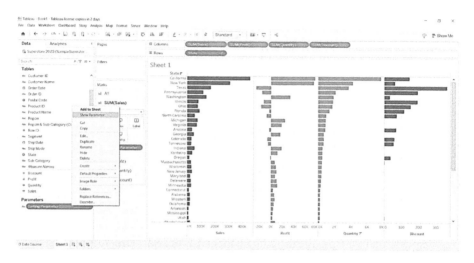

FIGURE 5.69   Output.

Step 9 The final display is given in Figure 5.70.

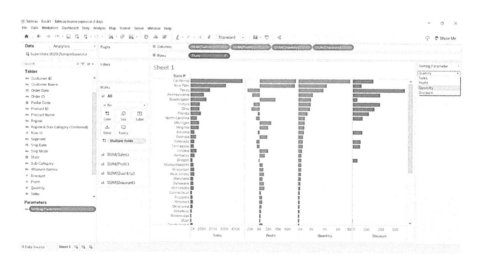

FIGURE 5.70   Output.

Step 10 If we choose Sales in "Sorting Parameter," we get the following output (Figure 5.71).

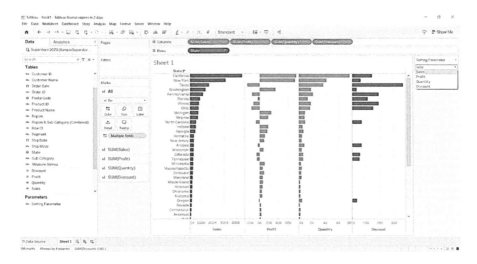

FIGURE 5.71 Output.

Step 11 For better color display, we can drag the parameter "Sorting Parameter" to the colors option in the Marks card (Figure 5.72).

FIGURE 5.72 Output.

Step 12 The result will now change color with changing parameters (Figure 5.73).

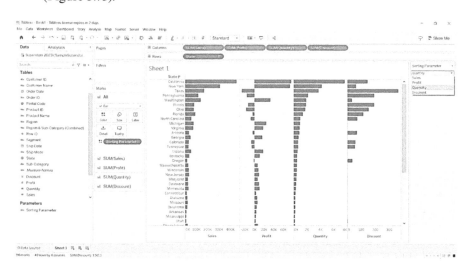

FIGURE 5.73　Output.

5.3　GROUP, HIERARCHY, AND SET IN TABLEAU

Sometimes, a dimension may have several values, and driving visual analytics over that many dimension values is a tedious task. This might not provide any insightful information as well. However, by combining multiple dimension values based on their similarities, we can form groups that we can then analyze easily. This can be implemented in Tableau by creating group, hierarchy, or set as per their requirements.

5.3.1　CREATING AND MANAGING GROUP

These groups may convey insights in a much effective manner as compared to the insights conveyed by individual dimension values. Therefore, "*Group*" feature is quite useful in Tableau projects. The Group feature in Tableau allows us to integrate various dimension values into specific groups or categories. Consider the data source Sample-Superstore as an example. The group can be used to acquire the values of Office Supplies and Technology as an aggregate. Once the group is created, the graphics can display the total worth of the furniture and office supply categories. Below are the detailed steps for creating a group:

Step 1 As shown in Figure 5.74, perform a right-clicking on the Category field and select "Create" and then choose the "Group" option.

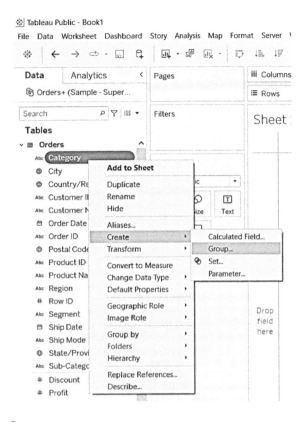

FIGURE 5.74   Output.

Step 2 The "Create Group" window is displayed. Next, write the group's name. Choose the individuals you wish to be grouped with. Then, click on the "Group" option (Figure 5.75).

FIGURE 5.75   Output.

Step 3 Create a group called Furniture and Office Supplies in the "Edit Group" window. Next, to create the group, click the OK button.

Step 4 The dimension list is updated with the field name Category (Group). This helps visualize the group of people that are present in a field.

Step 5 To view Sum (Sales) for various categories, drag Sales in columns and the Category (Group) dimension in the Rows header (Figure 5.76).

FIGURE 5.76   Output.

5.3.2 Creating Hierarchy Structure

A hierarchical structure, resembling a tree, is used to represent the level-wise configuration. Relationship-based data can be used in Tableau to create hierarchies. To perform additional actions, similar and related data are grouped into hierarchical structures.

Take Sample-Superstore as an example of a data source, along with its dimensions and measures, and proceed as follows:

Step 1 Go to the worksheet and establish a connection with the data source for Sample-Superstore. In order to establish a hierarchy, choose a dimension and then right-click on it. Select the "Hierarchy" menu. Click the "Create Hierarchy" option that is displayed in the screenshot below (Figure 5.77).

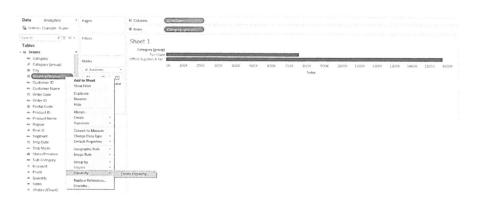

FIGURE 5.77   Output.

Step 2 After this, a "Create Hierarchy" window opens. Entering the hierarchy's name here, we press the OK button. It establishes a hierarchy as seen in Figure 5.78.

FIGURE 5.78 Output.

Step 3 In order to add another field, we can drag and drop a field, like the State field, straight on top of another field in the hierarchy. This adds the State field to the hierarchy of the Country/Region (Figure 5.79).

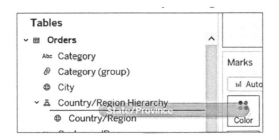

FIGURE 5.79 Output.

Step 4 By performing a right-click on the hierarchy and choosing "Remove Hierarchy," we can remove the hierarchy that was created (Figure 5.80).

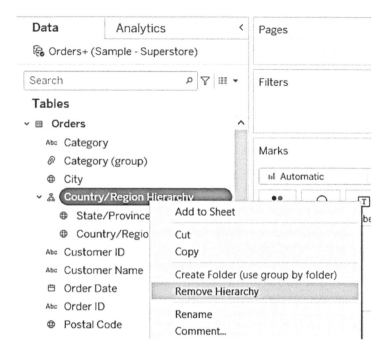

FIGURE 5.80 Output.

5.3.3 COMBINING DIMENSIONS INTO SETS

With Tableau *Sets*, you can provide your audience immediate access to a visualization or dashboard so they can manage some components of their examination. Set actions have the ability to modify a set's values when you select marks in the view. It thus becomes an essential part of Tableau. Sets are custom fields in Tableau 002C that are used to store the subset of data corresponding to a specific condition. By choosing members from a list or a visualization, you can instantly construct a set. By creating your own conditions or choosing the top/bottom few records in a measure, you can get the same result. Dynamic sets are sets that automatically adapt to changes in the underlying data. They are limited to one dimensional models.

Making a dynamic set involves the following steps:

Step 1 Let's build the Sets by taking into account the data source for Sample-Superstore. Open the worksheet. Now, right-click on a dimension Sub-Category.

Step 2 Next step is to click the "Create" option and then select the "Set" option (Figure 5.81).

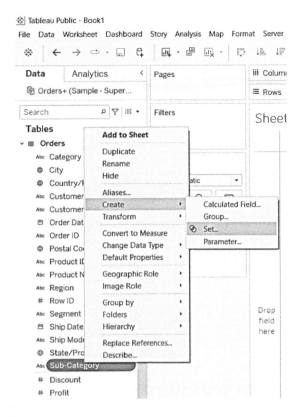

FIGURE 5.81   Output.

Step 3 This opens the Create Set dialog box in which we can configure the set. The following tabs can be used to configure your set:

a. General: To choose one or more values that will be considered while calculating the set, use the General tab.

b. Alternatively, you can always take into account all members, irrespective of the addition or removal of new members, by using the "All" option (Figure 5.82).

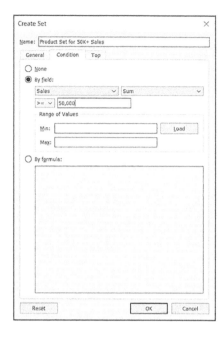

FIGURE 5.82 Output.

    c. Create rules that specify which members should be included in the set by using the Condition tab. For example, as the image above shows, you could develop a criterion based on total sales that only takes into account goods that sell for more than $50,000.

    d. To impose limitations on which members belong in the set, use the "Top" tab. For example, you could establish a cap on overall sales that only applies to the top ten best-selling items.

    e. Click OK when finished. The Data window's dimensions include the new set. The field is marked as a set by the set icon, which looks like two intersecting bubbles as displayed in Figure 5.83.

FIGURE 5.83 Output.

    f. Drag the newly created set into the column's header and right-click to select the option "Show Members in Set" (Figure 5.84).

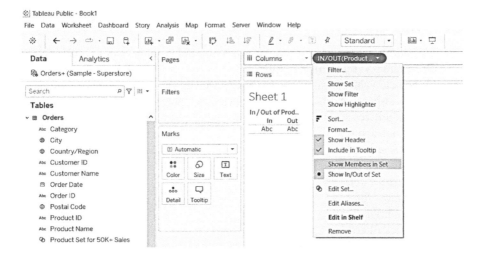

FIGURE 5.84 Output.

    g. Drag the Sales measure in the rows header to visualize the sales of the top ten sub-categories whose net sales worth is above 50k (Figure 5.85).

    h. We can also edit and make changes in the set by selecting the set → right-click the set → select the "Edit Set" option to make desired changes in it. Users can try editing the above created set as a practice task.

FIGURE 5.85   Output.

KEY NOTES

- The elimination of specific numbers or a range of numbers from a collection of outcomes is referred to as filtering.
- Using field values in simple scenarios as well as more complex calculations or context-based filters are both supported by Tableau's filtering tool.
- Tableau utilizes a variety of filter types, which are listed below:
  - Dimension filter
  - Measure filter
  - Dates filter
  - Extract filter
  - Context filter
  - Condition filter
  - Quick filters
  - Table calculation filter
- Sorting allows us to have control over various dimensions that are loaded from data source and visible in the worksheet.
- The various techniques of sorting are listed below:
  - Toolbar sorting
  - Axis sorting
  - Manual sorting
  - Nested sorting
  - Using the Sort dialog box

- • Using the Combine field
- • Using the Rank method
- Custom sorting using parameter

TEST YOUR SKILLS

1. Discuss the use of filters in Tableau.
2. Compare the different types of filters in a tabular format with use-case/ examples.
3. What is a context filter and what are the steps to create the Context Filter Tableau?
4. Discuss the shortcomings of context filters in Tableau?
5. Differentiate between parameters and filters in Tableau.
6. Is it possible to create cascading filters without using context filters?
7. Discuss different types of sorting methods supported in Tableau with examples for each.

REFERENCES

1. Sleeper, Ryan. *Innovative Tableau: 100 More Tips, Tutorials, and Strategies*. United States, O'Reilly Media, 2020.
2. Meier, Marleen. *Mastering Tableau 2023: Implement Advanced Business Intelligence Techniques, Analytics, and Machine Learning Models with Tableau*. United Kingdom, Packt Publishing, 2023.
3. Munroe, Kirk. *Data Modeling with Tableau: A Practical Guide to Building Data Models Using Tableau Prep and Tableau Desktop*. United Kingdom, Packt Publishing, 2022.
4. Sarsfield, Patrick, et al. *Maximizing Tableau Server: A Beginner's Guide to Accessing, Sharing, and Managing Content on Tableau Server*. United Kingdom, Packt Publishing, 2021.
5. Milligan, Joshua N. *Learning Tableau 2019: Tools for Business Intelligence, Data Prep, and Visual Analytics*, 3rd Edition. India, Packt Publishing, 2019.
6. Loth, Alexander. *Visual Analytics with Tableau*. United States, Wiley, 2019.
7. Costello, Tim, and Blackshear, Lori. *Prepare Your Data for Tableau: A Practical Guide to the Tableau Data Prep Tool*. Germany, Apress, 2019.

6 Charts in Tableau

6.1 INTRODUCING CHARTS IN TABLEAU

Data visualization is essential for presenting trends and influencing opinions. Charts, commonly used in Tableau, offer various analytical techniques in a visual manner, including comparison, relationship, distribution, and composition [1]. Each chart has its own meaning, so choose based on the information you want to provide and the conclusions you want your audience to derive [2]. Tableau provides various chart types for data visualization.

6.1.1 TYPES OF CHARTS IN TABLEAU

Tableau is a Business Intelligence software that helps to visualize data by allowing users to create various charts and graphs using the "Show Me" tab. With 24 different charts available, users can choose from various visualizations like text tables, heat maps, symbols, and more [3]. Each chart has a minimal set of dimensions, measurements, and bins (Figure 6.1).

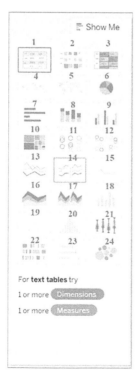

1. Text Table
2. Heat Map
3. Highlighted Table
4. Symbol Map
5. Filled Map
6. Pie Chart
7. Horizontal Bar Chart
8. Stacked Bar Chart
9. Side-by-Side Bar Chart
10. Tree Map
11. Circle View
12. Side-by-side Circle View
13. Line Chart (Continuous)
14. Line Chart Discrete
15. Dual Line Chart
16. Area Chart (Continuous)
17. Area Chart (Discrete)
18. Dual Combination
19. Scatter Plot
20. Histogram
21. Box and Whisker Plot
22. Gantt Chart
23. Bullet Graph
24. Packed Bubble

FIGURE 6.1 Different types of charts in "Show Me" of Tableau.

DOI: 10.1201/9781003429593-6

1. **Text Table:** Tableau text table or Tableau Crosstab is a data visualization tool that displays individual values in columns and rows but requires careful processing to identify patterns or insights (Figure 6.2).

Minimum Requirements for Text Table:

❖ 1 or more Dimensions
❖ 1 or more Measures

FIGURE 6.2   Text table.

2. **Heat Map:** A heat map shows the correlation between two data variables as well as the ratings of these variables. Typically, several factors are used to display this rating information, such as different shades of the same color and varying sizes (Figure 6.3).

Minimum Requirements for Heat Map:

❖ 1 or more dimensions
❖ 1 or 2 measures

FIGURE 6.3   Heat map.

3. **Highlight Table:** Highlight tables can be used to highlight the data in a text table. They use color intensity to accelerate the process of selecting the most significant values from a span of different values. In addition, different dimensions are indicated by rows and columns. Highlight tables are easy to read and understand as compared to Crosstab (Figure 6.4).

Highlight Table for Region-wise sales of each Shipping Mode

Region	First Class	Same Day	Second Class	Standard Class
Central	58,914	20,415	103,550	320,291
East	113,742	44,236	118,822	415,029
South	49,333	21,017	93,759	227,614
West	129,762	43,604	150,541	415,907

Minimum Requirements for Highlight Table:

❖ 1 or more dimensions
❖ Exactly 1 measure

FIGURE 6.4   Highlight table.

4. **Symbol Map:** A symbol map lets users interpret data by mapping quantitative values onto geographic locations using icons or symbols. These symbols are frequently represented by a round shape, but icons can take any shape. The symbols in the map represent certain values in a data set and can differ in size, shape, or color to represent the variation of the data (Figure 6.5).

Minimum Requirements for Symbol Map:

❖ 1 Geographic Dimension
❖ 0 or more Dimensions
❖ 0 to 2 Measures

FIGURE 6.5   Symbol map.

5. **Filled Map:** Tableau includes a wide range of mapping features and numerous options for displaying data spatially across multiple geographical regions. A filled map is a sort of chart where multiple geographic regions can be shown on the map with areas colored based on a measure or dimension (Figure 6.6).

Minimum Requirements for Filled Map:

❖ 1 Geographic Dimension
❖ 0 or more Dimensions
❖ 0 to 2 Measures

FIGURE 6.6   Filled map.

6. **Pie Chart:** A pie chart is a circular diagram divided into portions, used in business intelligence tools like Tableau, to display performance data by category, area, and segment, allowing for examination of sales, profitability, and statistical characteristics (Figure 6.7).

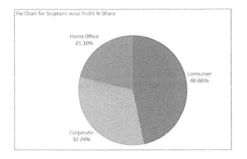

Minimum Requirements for Pie Chart:

❖ 1 or more Dimensions
❖ 1 or 2 Measure

FIGURE 6.7 Pie chart.

7. **Horizontal Bar Chart:** A bar chart divides data into rectangular bars for easy comparison. Ideal for comparing two or more data values with minimal data groups, bar charts display discrete data and are not suitable for continuous data. Tableau's "Show Me" option can create bar charts (Figure 6.8).

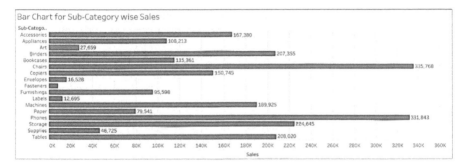

Minimum Requirements for Horizontal Bar Chart:

❖ 0 or more Dimensions
❖ 1 or more Measures

FIGURE 6.8 Horizontal bar chart.

8. **Stacked Bar Chart:** In Tableau, stacked bars are a specific kind of bar chart that uses segmented bars to show values. To provide more information on the field and regions, each bar in this illustration is broken into many segments or sections. With this, you can compare both the major data variables and the distribution of minor variables in each bar (Figure 6.9).

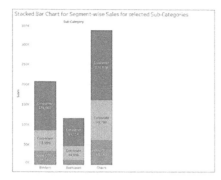

Minimum Requirements for Stacked Bar Chart:

❖ 1 or more Dimensions
❖ 1 or more Measures

FIGURE 6.9   Stacked bar chart.

9. **Side-by-Side Bar Chart:** Tableau offers unique comparison charts, such as the shared axis or side-by-side bar chart. These charts allow users to view multiple measures compared to a single dimension or dimensions compared to a single measure. To create these charts, three fields are required, and the bars are divided into colored segments. In the bar graph, the segments inside a category bar are stacked and positioned next to every other field (Figure 6.10).

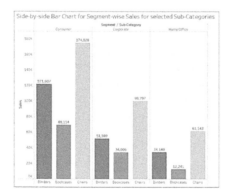

Minimum Requirements for Side-by-side Bar Chart:

❖ 1 or more Dimensions
❖ 1 or more Measures

FIGURE 6.10   Side-by-side bar chart.

10. **Tree Map:** A Treemap is a visual representation of data elements, dividing them into smaller rectangles based on their relation to the total data. It provides a comprehensive view of the data set, while each individual rectangle illustrates the relationship between the subsets (Figure 6.11).

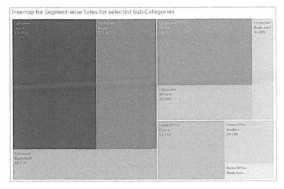

Minimum Requirements for Treemap:

❖ 1 or more Dimensions
❖ 1 or 2 Measures

FIGURE 6.11   Tree map.

11. **Circle View:** The Circle View is a chart type that is ideal for comparative analysis, allowing users to customize its features. The default shape is a circle, which can be changed to suit their preferences. The keys for the data sets determine the mark's color and size, with higher profits resulting in larger circles. This persuasive chart type allows for simultaneous comparison of multiple categories (Figure 6.12).

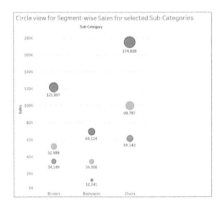

Minimum Requirements for Circle View chart:

❖ 1 or more Dimensions
❖ 1 or more Measures

FIGURE 6.12   Circle view.

12. **Circle View, Side by Side:** Tableau's Side-by-Side Circle View is an expanded version of the circle view, allowing for side-by-side comparison of multiple measures. It allows for quick identification of trends and variances across multiple dimensions or measures by displaying multiple circle views side by side (Figure 6.13).

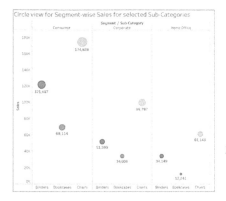

Minimum Requirements for Side-by-Side Circle View:

❖ 1 or more Dimensions
❖ 1 or more Measures (at least 3 fields)

FIGURE 6.13   Side-by-side circle view.

13. **Line Chart:** A date field is an essential component of line charts, which are excellent for showing trends and changes over time. Line charts come in three varieties: continuous, discrete, and dual. Please consider the following notes while creating a Line Plot.

- While discrete fields have a fixed set of values, continuous fields can have an infinite number of values [4]. Tableau indicates whether a field is continuous or discrete by showing discrete fields as blue and continuous fields as green.
- A date dimension is necessary for Tableau to generate a line chart. Only our dates will determine if we are drawing a discrete or continuous line.
- If our dates are discrete, then we are going to get the discrete line chart; however, if our dates are continuous, we will obtain a continuous line graph.
- A dual-line chart, also known as a dual-axis chart, allows for the representation of more than one measure using two different axis ranges (Figure 6.14).

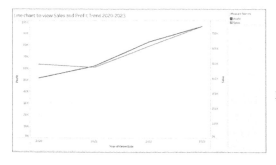

Minimum Requirements for Line Chart:

❖ 1 Date dimension
❖ 0 or more other Dimensions
❖ 1 or more Measures

FIGURE 6.14   Line chart.

14. **Area Chart:** Area charts in Tableau show relationships between different dimensions in a dataset by displaying the proportion of totals or percentages of specific values of the data. Dimensions and values can be analyzed by observing the area under each line and its variation over time (Figure 6.15).

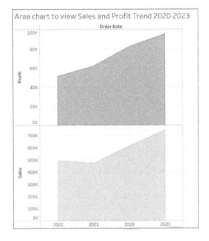

Minimum Requirements for Area Chart:

❖ 1 Date Dimension
❖ 0 or more other Dimensions
❖ 1 or more Measures

FIGURE 6.15   Area chart.

15. **Combination Chart:** Combination graphs display various data types on the same chart, including columns, lines, and areas. Dual-axis combination charts, also known as combo charts, combine multiple chart types and save real state by combining views. There is a common shared axis, similar to an X-axis for a date, and two different axes, like a Y-axis on extreme left and right ends, respectively, for two different measures (Figure 6.16).

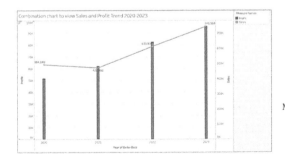

Minimum Requirements for Combination chart:

❖ 1 Date dimension
❖ 0 or more Dimensions
❖ 2 Measures

FIGURE 6.16   Combination chart.

16. **Scatter Plot:** Scatter plots demonstrate two measure values or comparable value fields as an individual dot on a chart, with two on the x-axis and one on the y-axis. To view and evaluate hidden trends, trend lines can be added to Tableau alongside the scatter plot's dotted points (Figure 6.17).

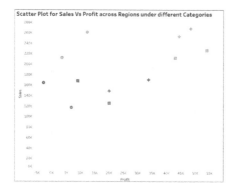

Minimum Requirements for Scatter Plot:

❖ 0 or more Dimensions
❖ 2 to 4 Measures

FIGURE 6.17   Scatter plot.

17. **Histogram:** Histograms are graphs that display value distribution along an axis, providing statistical information about the probability distribution of values occurring in equal-sized intervals, enabling insightful and informative analysis (Figure 6.18).

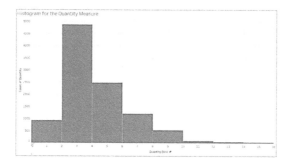

Minimum Requirements for Histogram:

❖ 1 measure (bin field)

FIGURE 6.18   Histogram.

18. **Box and Whisker Plots:** Box and whisker plots are useful charts for displaying data and the distribution of a measure. They show ranges within variables, such as outliers, the median, the mode, and a majority of data points in the "box." These visuals aid in comparing the distribution of multiple variables against each other (Figure 6.19).

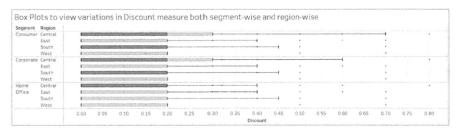

Minimum Requirements for Box and Whisker Plot:

❖ 0 or more Dimensions
❖ 1 or more Measures

FIGURE 6.19   Box and whisker plot.

19. **Gantt Chart:** The horizontal bar chart that shows the duration of an event for multiple values is Gantt Chart, providing detailed representations of data values in various formats like yearly, quarterly, monthly, weekly, or daily. Its ability to assign different colors for each year or month makes it easier to track data trends over time, making it a valuable tool (Figure 6.20).

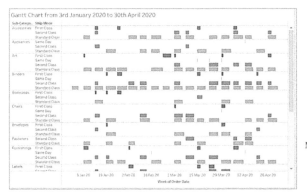

Minimum Requirements for Gantt Chart:

❖ 1 Date Dimension
❖ 1 or more Dimensions
❖ 0-2 Measures

FIGURE 6.20   Gantt chart.

20. **Bullet Graph:** A bullet chart is an advanced bar chart that allows the comparison of two measures on one single bar. The primary measure is represented by a dark bar, and the secondary measure is represented as a reference line beneath it. The reference line can be divided into segments such as 60%, 80%, and 100%, making bullet charts highly informative and accommodating more detail and data (Figure 6.21).

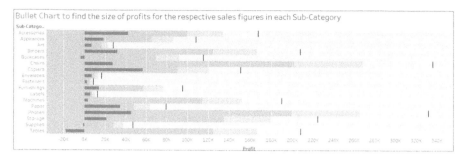

Minimum Requirements for Bullet Chart:

❖ 0 or more Dimensions
❖ 2 Measures

FIGURE 6.21   Bullet graph.

21. **Packed Bubble:** A bubble chart is a graphical representation that shows data in the form of bubbles or circles of various sizes and colors. It can represent various variables, with dimension field values represented as separate bubbles and measure field values defining the size and color of the bubble. This allows for the analysis of a plot with at least three variables, making it a simple yet insightful visual graph (Figure 6.22).

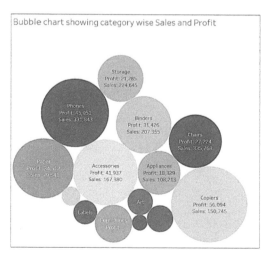

Minimum Requirements for Bubble Chart:

❖ 1 or more Dimensions
❖ 1 or 2 Measures

FIGURE 6.22   Packed bubble chart.

6.1.2   WHEN TO CHOOSE WHICH CHART?

Tableau offers 24 different graphs and charts, each with its unique usability and representation of data. The visualization used depends on the user's questions, data features (dimensions and measures), and their requirement to present insights [5,6]. For example, displaying sales growth year over year requires a different visualization than demonstrating profit earned and product discounts. Understanding user needs helps choose the appropriate visualization method. A comprehensive list of nine types of information can be displayed with visualization, based on the most used types of applications. This helps users choose the right chart for different visualization requirements. Let us consider each of these criteria listed in Table 6.1.

TABLE 6.1
Criteria for Choosing Different Charts

S. No.	Information	Description	What Sort of Query Does This Graph Address?	Suitable Chart Types
1.	Variation over time	One of the core types of visualizations is demonstrating how a metric has evolved over time.	• How has this measurement evolved over the past 12 months? • When was maximum fluctuation observed? • How recently did this measure change?	• Line plots • Slope graphs • Highlight tables.
2.	Correlation between data	Sometimes, we're dealing with two variables and are trying to figure out how they are related.	• Are these two actions connected? How firmly? • What metrics are more closely related than others? • How closely are these measurements related?	• Scatter plots • Highlight table
3.	Magnitude or scale of variables	Magnitude illustrates the difference in size or worth between two or more distinct objects. For instance, we would like to compare and show the magnitude of sales for various states.	• Which member of this dimension has the highest measure? • Do there exist any unique dimensions? • How much of a difference exists between these dimensions' lowest and highest measurements?	• Bar graph • Packed bubble graph • Line graph

(Continued)

TABLE 6.1 (*Continued*)
Criteria for Choosing Different Charts

S. No.	Information	Description	What Sort of Query Does This Graph Address?	Suitable Chart Types
4.	Deviation of data from baseline	Deviation graphs display the variance between a number and a reference point, such as the average or median. A deviation chart can be used by the user to identify which products have exceptionally high or low profit margins.	• How far off the mean does this measurement deviate? • What significance do the variations in this measure have? • Are the variances following a pattern?	• Bullet graphs • Bar charts • Combination charts
5.	Distribution of data to find the frequency	We examine the distribution to determine the frequency of events within a population. A distribution chart may be the best solution for displaying the age distribution of survey respondents or the volume of incoming calls by day.	• Are incidents grouped around a particular probability? • Which segment of the population makes the most purchases? • When are the busiest hours of our workday?	• Box plots • Pareto graphs • Population pyramids • Histograms
6.	Ranking values in order of importance	We may want to present not only the size of a value but also the corresponding significance of each member of our dimension. Using a ranking chart, you can highlight the top ten salespeople or underperforming regions.	• What percentage of staff in the organization perform below par? • How much capital do our top ten clients bring in? • What are the values of our ten assets with the lowest revenue?	• Rank computations fit into bar charts. • The top n sets or important progress markers.

(*Continued*)

TABLE 6.1 (*Continued*)
Criteria for Choosing Different Charts

S. No.	Information	Description	What Sort of Query Does This Graph Address?	Suitable Chart Types
7.	Composition or part-to-whole	Part-to-whole charts are used to illustrate the contribution of each component to a whole, such as a region's contribution to overall sales or the cost of each shipping option for a specific product.	• What percentage of the total does this value make up? • How does the expense distribution alter annually? • Do various products make up varying percentages of regional sales?	• Tree maps; • Pie graph; • Area graph; • Stacked bar graph
8.	Spatial distribution	Spatial charts can be used to visualize the distinct geographic trends, areas, and locations in our data. Two examples of spatial maps are a map of the busiest airport terminals and a map of all sales throughout the country.	• Which metropolitan area has the biggest sales? • How far away are our clients from the distribution centers? • Which airport entrance receives the most visitors?	• Symbol map • Filled map • Point distribution map • Density map
9.	Flow path	Maps that depict movement over time, like Sankey diagrams, can be viewed as flow charts. To visualize movement, Flow maps depict the path through time as well as the path between origin and destination.	• Which shipping route is the longest or most time-intensive? • How long will people stand outside the gates? • What are chokepoints in the traffic of the city?	• Flow plots like maps

6.2   COLOR SCHEMES AND PALETTES IN TABLEAU

Color is crucial in creating effective charts and graphs. A good color scheme enhances the story the data tells, while a poor one may detract from it [7,8]. This section outlines various color palettes used in data visualization and provides best practices for using color in Tableau. There are two main categories of color schemes: black and white, and red and green:

1. Qualitative color palettes
2. Quantitative color palettes

The color scheme used in visualization is determined by the characteristics of the data being color-mapped. Let us discuss each of these in detail.

6.2.1   QUALITATIVE OR CATEGORICAL COLOR PALETTE

Tableau is perfect for fields with values that do not naturally follow a precise sequence since it uses a categorical palette to give various colors to discrete values in a field, often a dimension when dropped on the Color mark on the Marks card. The following are the instructions for opening the Edit Colors dialog box and altering a field's color value:

Step 1. Select in the upper-right corner of the color legend to change the colors for values in a field, like the Sub-Category field within the sample superstore data source (Figure 6.23).

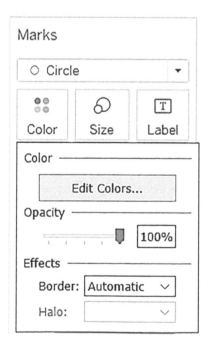

FIGURE 6.23   Output.

Step 2. In Tableau Desktop, Colors can be edited from the context menu tab, while in Tableau's Server or Cloud version, the box to Edit Colors is the default option (Figure 6.24).

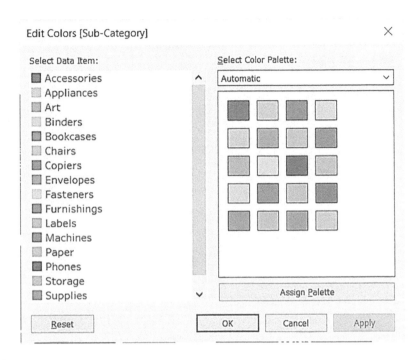

FIGURE 6.24   Output.

Step 3. Double-click the item to the left under "Select Data Item" to change its color. Right now, select a new color from the palette there (Figure 6.25).

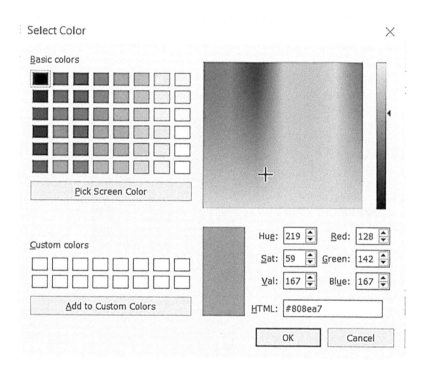

FIGURE 6.25   Output.

Step 4. Select the desired color. Then, click Apply and OK.

Step 5. In the Edit Color dialog box, users can select a different color palette. Categorical palettes, like Tableau 10, are suitable for discrete fields without inherent order, while ordinal palettes, like Blue, Orange, and Green, are suitable for fields with associated order, like dates or numbers (Figure 6.26).

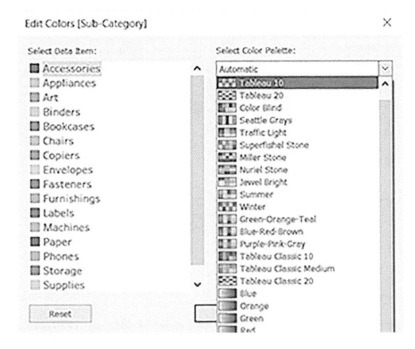

FIGURE 6.26 Output.

Step 6. Select a color palette, click Assign Palette, and then to use the new palette, select Reset in the Edit Colors dialog box. This way we can assign colors to the field members (Figure 6.27).

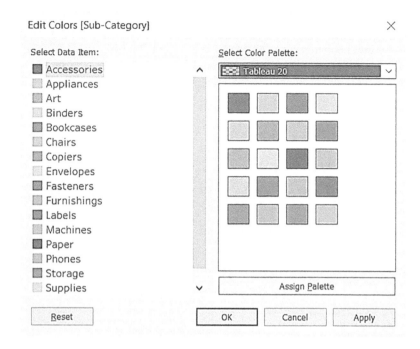

FIGURE 6.27 Output.

6.2.2 QUANTITATIVE COLOR PALETTE

Tableau will show a quantitative legend with a range of different continuous colors if you set a field with continuous values on the mark card. You can alter the colors distribution and other features of the color legend. Click on the color legend's upper-right corner to change the colors for a measurement like sales or profit. Tableau Server and Tableau Cloud by default display the Edit Colors dialog box. There are two categories of quantitative color palettes:

1. Diverging Palette

In a field with both negative and positive values, the default color ranges are two, and a diverge color palette appears in the Edit Colors window. To group values into uniform steps or bins, select Stepped Color. For example, in the given color, five steps display five colors in the diverging palette (Figure 6.28).

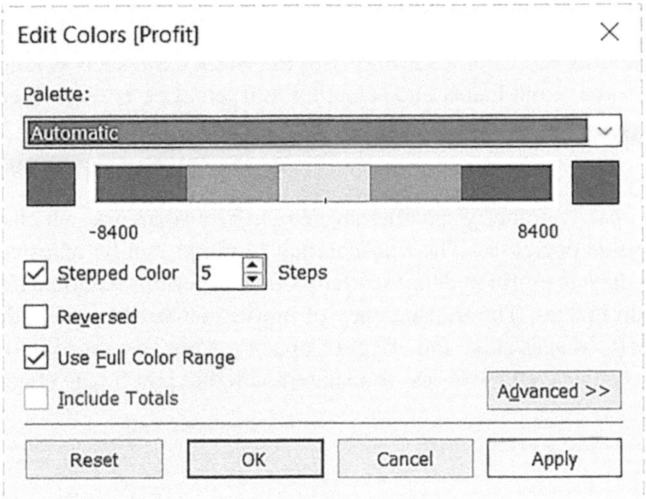

FIGURE 6.28   Output.

2. Sequential Palette

In a field with all values being positive or negative, the default range uses a single-color range, having a squared colored box on the right corner. The Edit Colors dialog box has a *Sequential Palette*. The Stepped Color option can divide the values in to uniform steps or bins, each with its own color. For example, 5 steps display 5 colors in a diverging palette (Figure 6.29).

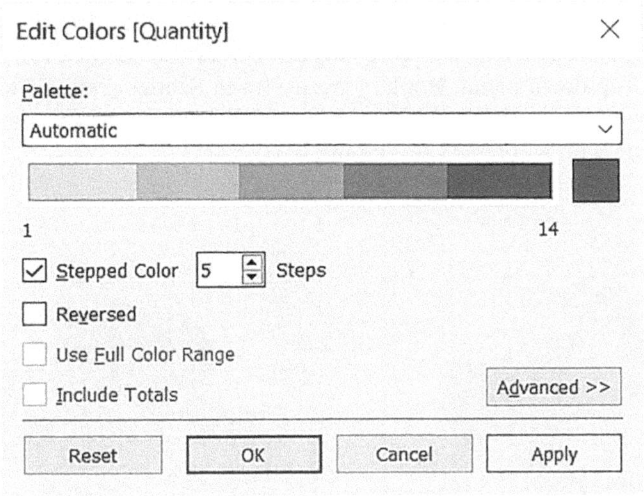

FIGURE 6.29   Output.

6.2.3 Configuring Color Effects

Users can configure more color settings with the Mark card, such as adjusting opacity, marking borders and halos, and selecting markers. Let us discuss each of these briefly:

1. **Opacity**

   The opacity property specifies an element's transparency, which increases as the value decreases. The transparency of marks can be adjusted using a slider, which is useful in dense scatter plots or superimposed data on maps or backdrop images. The transparency of marks increases as the slider moves to the left. Images show the effect of opacity, with 27% more transparency in the left image and 93% less transparency in the right image (Figure 6.30).

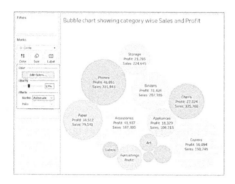

FIGURE 6.30 Opacity difference in bubble charts.

2. **Mark Border**

   Tableau defaults to no borders around markers, but all mark types can have their borders enabled. To configure borders, choose a color from the Color drop-down menu. Borders are useful in Scatter plots, Circle views, and Bubble charts for visually separating closely spaced marks, as shown in the figure with no borders set (Figure 6.31).

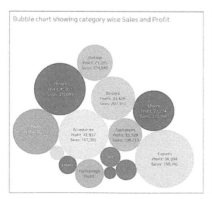

FIGURE 6.31 Mark borders in chart.

3. Mark Halos

Marks in visualizations can be surrounded by a contrasting color or hue, known as a halo, to enhance their visibility against a background image or map. This feature is available when the visualization contains a background image or map. To apply a halo, choose a mark halo color from the Color menu control. The illustration shows that the second image clearly shows the marked halos property in black, while the first image does not show the halos effect (Figures 6.32 and 6.33).

FIGURE 6.32   Mark halos in map.

FIGURE 6.33   Mark halos with borders in map.

4. Select Markers

Tableau Desktop allows users to reveal or hide points along a line and use the marker effect. The Line mark type allows users to display all points, just a few, or none. To configure markers, users can select a marker from the Effects section using the Color drop-down menu (Figure 6.34).

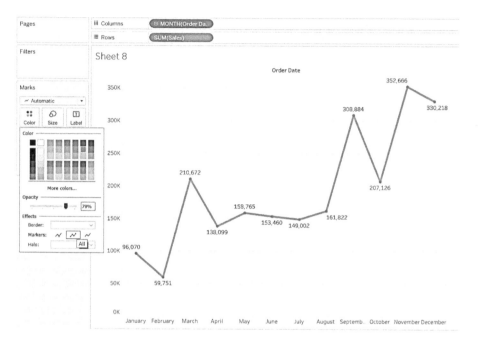

FIGURE 6.34   Markers in line chart.

6.3   COLOR CHOOSING BEST PRACTICES

Tableau offers various types of charts and graphs for effective data visualization. However, it is crucial to choose colors wisely to create a mature and professional look and feel for the visualization, as this may not serve the intended purpose [8]. Let us observe the below-given points closely:

I. **Make Use of Color to Create Associations:** For instance, you may use orange to symbolize a company's success in terms of safety, deep green to symbolize profits, or light green to symbolize environmental sustainability.

II. **Use a Single Color to Show Continuous Data:** To display continuous data, use a single color: For observing changes in a single statistic over time, such as the unemployment rate or an infection rate.

III. **Use Contrasting Colors to Differentiate:** To highlight variations in sales, use contrasting colors like Red and Green to compare eastern and western regions.

IV. **Use Color to Highlight Essential Information:** Colors can highlight important information, such as red or orange, while lighter shades like gray can highlight less important variables.

V. **Avoid Using Colors that are Difficult to Distinguish:** Avoid excessive use of colors in visualizations to avoid confusion and use easily distinguishable colors to represent different information.

KEY NOTES

- Charts and graphs are the largest family of visual representations, presenting various analytical techniques in a visual manner.
- Tableau is a tool for data visualization that allows the creation of various charts and graphs using the "Show Me" tab. There are 24 different charts available in Tableau, depending on the number of dimensions, measures, and bins.
- Effective charts are often created using color, as a good color scheme enhances the story you want the data to tell.
- There are two main categories of color scheme for data visualization: qualitative color palettes and quantitative color palettes.
- Effective charts are often created using color, as a poor color scheme can conceal or detract from the visualization's goal.

TEST YOUR SKILLS

1. Define dual-axis and blended-axis charts.
2. Define the Gantt chart.
3. Define a histogram chart.
4. Differentiate between a stacked bar chart and a stacked column chart.
5. Discuss various color schemes supported in Tableau.
6. Elaborate color choosing best practices in Tableau.

REFERENCES

[1] Munroe, Kirk. *Data Modeling with Tableau: A Practical Guide to Building Data Models Using Tableau Prep and Tableau Desktop.* United Kingdom, Packt Publishing, 2022.
[2] Sarsfield, Patrick, et al. *Maximizing Tableau Server: A Beginner's Guide to Accessing, Sharing, and Managing Content on Tableau Server.* United Kingdom, Packt Publishing, 2021.
[3] Sleeper, Ryan. *Innovative Tableau: 100 More Tips, Tutorials, and Strategies.* United States, O'Reilly Media, 2020.
[4] Milligan, Joshua N. *Learning Tableau 2019: Tools for Business Intelligence, Data Prep, and Visual Analytics*, 3rd Edition. India, Packt Publishing, 2019.
[5] Acharya, Seema, and Chellappan, Subhashini. *Pro Tableau: A Step-by-Step Guide.* United States, Apress, 2016.
[6] Murray, Daniel G. *Tableau Your Data! Fast and Easy Visual Analysis with Tableau Software.* Germany, Wiley, 2016.
[7] Milligan, Joshua N. *Learning Tableau: Leverage the Power of Tableau 9. 0 to Design Rich Data Visualizations and Build Fully Interactive Dashboards.* United Kingdom, Packt Publishing, 2015.
[8] Monsey, Molly, and Sochan, Paul. *Tableau for Dummies.* Germany, Wiley, 2015.

7 Comparison Charts in Tableau

7.1 INTRODUCTION TO COMPARISON CHARTS

Comparison is a crucial step in data analysis, allowing for in-depth insights into trends and patterns. By comparing key data points, we can uncover hidden insights and uncover hidden patterns [1]. Comparison charts can be used to compare the performance of two or more critical metrics, such as sales revenue, profit earned, and discounts. In business, comparison charts can be used to compare popularity and customer loyalty for different products and services [1,2]. They can also help compare team performance on a weekly, month-to-month, or year-to-year basis [3]. In digital marketing, comparison charts can help establish the primary source of traffic. The major types of comparison charts that we will discuss in this chapter are as follows:

- Text table
- Bar chart
- Column chart
- Lollipop chart
- Line chart
- Time series and trendlines

Let us discuss each of these briefly.

7.1.1 TEXT TABLE

In Tableau, text tables—also called pivot tables or cross-tabs—are often created by arranging two dimensions: one on the Rows level and the other on the Columns level. Text tables employ the type of text mark. You can create a text table with sales totals broken down by year as well as category using the guidelines provided below:

Step 1. Let us first establish a connection to the Superstore dataset. Subsequently, move the field of the order date to Columns. It is evident that Tableau generates column headings by aggregating the date by year.

Step 2. After that, drag the dimension of the "Sub-Category" and place it to Rows. The result is shown in Figure 7.1.

Pages	iii Columns	⊞ YEAR(Order Date)		
	≡ Rows	Sub-Category		

Text Table that shows Sales Totals by Year and Category

		Order Date		
Sub-Catego..	2020	2021	2022	2023
Accessories	Abc	Abc	Abc	Abc
Appliances	Abc	Abc	Abc	Abc
Art	Abc	Abc	Abc	Abc
Binders	Abc	Abc	Abc	Abc
Bookcases	Abc	Abc	Abc	Abc
Chairs	Abc	Abc	Abc	Abc
Copiers	Abc	Abc	Abc	Abc
Envelopes	Abc	Abc	Abc	Abc
Fasteners	Abc	Abc	Abc	Abc
Furnishings	Abc	Abc	Abc	Abc
Labels	Abc	Abc	Abc	Abc
Machines	Abc	Abc	Abc	Abc
Paper	Abc	Abc	Abc	Abc
Phones	Abc	Abc	Abc	Abc
Storage	Abc	Abc	Abc	Abc
Supplies	Abc	Abc	Abc	Abc
Tables	Abc	Abc	Abc	Abc

Marks: Automatic — Color, Size, Text, Detail, Tooltip — Filters

FIGURE 7.1   Output.

Step 3. Under the Marks card, move the "Sales" measure to Text. We realize that the metric by default is aggregated by Tableau as a sum (Figure 7.2).

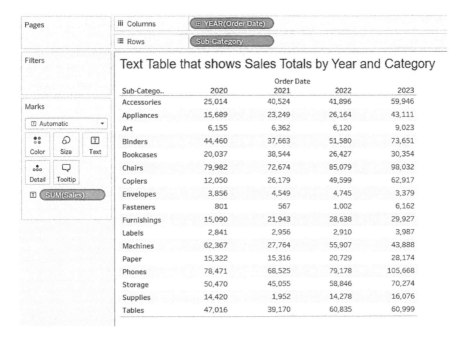

Pages	iii Columns	⊞ YEAR(Order Date)		
	≡ Rows	Sub-Category		

Text Table that shows Sales Totals by Year and Category

		Order Date		
Sub-Catego..	2020	2021	2022	2023
Accessories	25,014	40,524	41,896	59,946
Appliances	15,689	23,249	26,164	43,111
Art	6,155	6,362	6,120	9,023
Binders	44,460	37,663	51,580	73,651
Bookcases	20,037	38,544	26,427	30,354
Chairs	79,982	72,674	85,079	98,032
Copiers	12,050	26,179	49,599	62,917
Envelopes	3,856	4,549	4,745	3,379
Fasteners	801	567	1,002	6,162
Furnishings	15,090	21,943	28,638	29,927
Labels	2,841	2,956	2,910	3,987
Machines	62,367	27,764	55,907	43,888
Paper	15,322	15,316	20,729	28,174
Phones	78,471	68,525	79,178	105,668
Storage	50,470	45,055	58,846	70,274
Supplies	14,420	1,952	14,278	16,076
Tables	47,016	39,170	60,835	60,999

Marks: Automatic — Color, Size, Text, Detail, Tooltip — SUM(Sales) — Filters

FIGURE 7.2   Output.

Step 4. Text is the default mark type used for tables by Tableau. Total sales for a specific year and sub-category are shown in each cell of the table. It is evident that the sub-categories of phones and chairs consistently had the highest sales each year.

Step 5. Slide the Region dimension to the left of the adjacent pill for the "Sub-Category" field by dragging it to Rows (Figure 7.3).

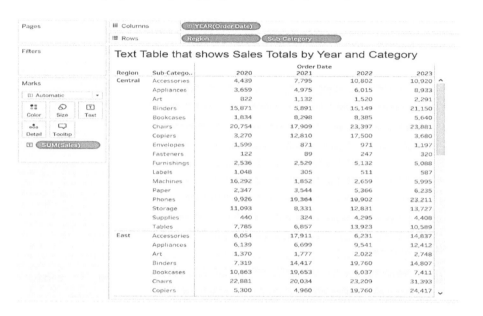

FIGURE 7.3 Output.

Step 6. The quantity (or numeric) values in the table are hard to interpret and do not provide any relevant details. For deeper insights, we can use a table computation to reveal percentages of the total rather than just raw numerical data.

Step 7. To create a table calculation that shows percentages, step 7 involves right-clicking the SUM(Sales) element on the Marks panel and selecting "Add Table Calculation" (Figure 7.4).

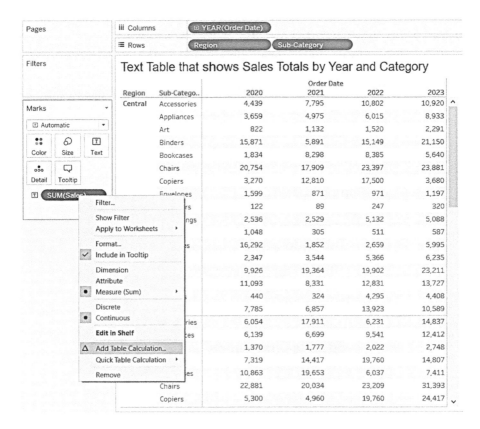

Pages	iii Columns	🗓 YEAR(Order Date)			
	≡ Rows	Region	Sub-Category		

Text Table that shows Sales Totals by Year and Category

			Order Date		
Region	Sub-Catego..	2020	2021	2022	2023
Central	Accessories	4,439	7,795	10,802	10,920
	Appliances	3,659	4,975	6,015	8,933
	Art	822	1,132	1,520	2,291
	Binders	15,871	5,891	15,149	21,150
	Bookcases	1,834	8,298	8,385	5,640
	Chairs	20,754	17,909	23,397	23,881
	Copiers	3,270	12,810	17,500	3,680
	Envelopes	1,599	871	971	1,197
	rs	122	89	247	320
	ngs	2,536	2,529	5,132	5,088
		1,048	305	511	587
	es	16,292	1,852	2,659	5,995
		2,347	3,544	5,366	6,235
		9,926	19,364	19,902	23,211
		11,093	8,331	12,831	13,727
		440	324	4,295	4,408
		7,785	6,857	13,923	10,589
	ries	6,054	17,911	6,231	14,837
	es	6,139	6,699	9,541	12,412
		1,370	1,777	2,022	2,748
		7,319	14,417	19,760	14,807
	es	10,863	19,653	6,037	7,411
	Chairs	22,881	20,034	23,209	31,393
	Copiers	5,300	4,960	19,760	24,417

Marks: Automatic

Color | Size | Text
Detail | Tooltip
SUM(Sale)

Context menu (popup):
- Filter...
- Show Filter
- Apply to Worksheets ▸
- Format...
- ✓ Include in Tooltip
- Dimension
- Attribute
- • Measure (Sum) ▸
- Discrete
- • Continuous
- **Edit in Shelf**
- △ Add Table Calculation...
- Quick Table Calculation ▸
- Remove

FIGURE 7.4   Output.

Step 8. Pick "Pane (Down)" under "Compute Using" and change the Calculation Type to "Percent of Total" in the Table Calculation popup box (Figure 7.5).

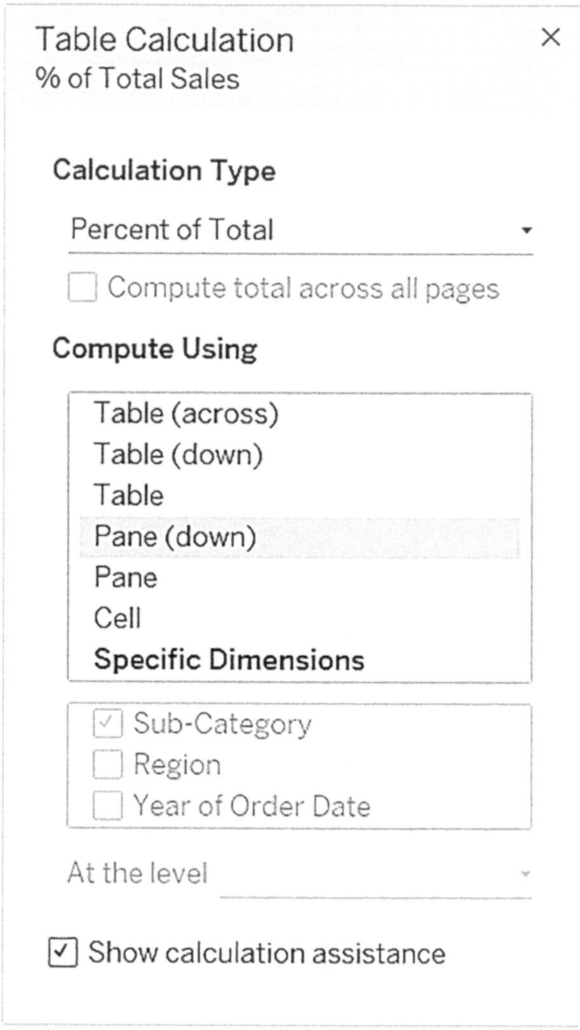

Table Calculation   ×
% of Total Sales

Calculation Type

Percent of Total   ▾

☐ Compute total across all pages

Compute Using

Table (across)
Table (down)
Table
Pane (down)
Pane
Cell
Specific Dimensions

☑ Sub-Category
☐ Region
☐ Year of Order Date

At the level   ▾

☑ Show calculation assistance

FIGURE 7.5   Output.

Step 9. Take note that this time, Pane (Down) is the right option since it indicates that the computation must be carried out within each of the table's panes from top to bottom (Figure 7.6).

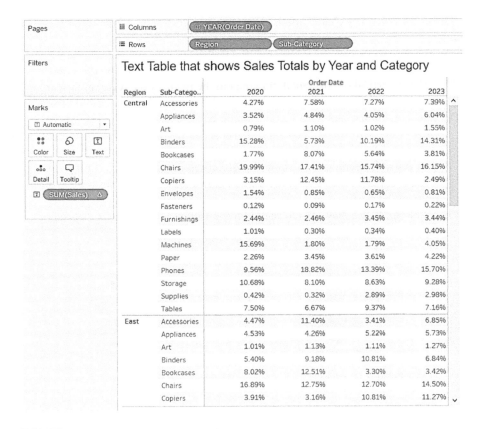

Pages						
	Columns	YEAR(Order Date)				
	Rows	Region	Sub-Category			

Text Table that shows Sales Totals by Year and Category

Region	Sub-Catego..	Order Date 2020	2021	2022	2023
Central	Accessories	4.27%	7.58%	7.27%	7.39%
	Appliances	3.52%	4.84%	4.05%	6.04%
	Art	0.79%	1.10%	1.02%	1.55%
	Binders	15.28%	5.73%	10.19%	14.31%
	Bookcases	1.77%	8.07%	5.64%	3.81%
	Chairs	19.99%	17.41%	15.74%	16.15%
	Copiers	3.15%	12.45%	11.78%	2.49%
	Envelopes	1.54%	0.85%	0.65%	0.81%
	Fasteners	0.12%	0.09%	0.17%	0.22%
	Furnishings	2.44%	2.46%	3.45%	3.44%
	Labels	1.01%	0.30%	0.34%	0.40%
	Machines	15.69%	1.80%	1.79%	4.05%
	Paper	2.26%	3.45%	3.61%	4.22%
	Phones	9.56%	18.82%	13.39%	15.70%
	Storage	10.68%	8.10%	8.63%	9.28%
	Supplies	0.42%	0.32%	2.89%	2.98%
	Tables	7.50%	6.67%	9.37%	7.16%
East	Accessories	4.47%	11.40%	3.41%	6.85%
	Appliances	4.53%	4.26%	5.22%	5.73%
	Art	1.01%	1.13%	1.11%	1.27%
	Binders	5.40%	9.18%	10.81%	6.84%
	Bookcases	8.02%	12.51%	3.30%	3.42%
	Chairs	16.89%	12.75%	12.70%	14.50%
	Copiers	3.91%	3.16%	10.81%	11.27%

Marks
- Automatic
- Color / Size / Text
- Detail / Tooltip
- SUM(Sales)

FIGURE 7.6   Output.

7.1.2 BAR GRAPH FOR COMPARISON

The categorical data of a dataset are displayed in a bar chart or graph. Each category's value is represented by a bar whose length varies according to it [4,5]. As a result, the data can be visualized right away (Figure 7.7).

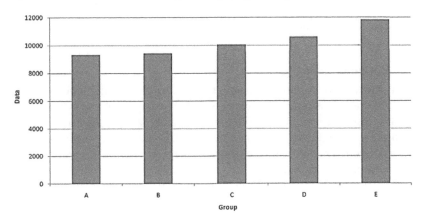

FIGURE 7.7   A sample bar chart.

Below are some key characteristics that set a bar graph apart from other types of graphs:

I. The width and spacing between each rectangular bar should be the same.
II. Either a vertical or horizontal drawing can be made of the rectangular bars.
III. The rectangular bars' height is equal to the data they are supposed to depict.
IV. The rectangular bars must be on a single base, with the starting point typically being zero (0). If necessary, a graph can be set with a starting point different than 0.
V. One possible technique to show the quantitative measures is through bar charts, which plot them in either a vertical fashion on the y-axis or horizontally on the x-axis.
VI. Additionally, we may set a measure on the Columns block and a dimension on the Rows block to construct a bar chart (Figure 7.8).

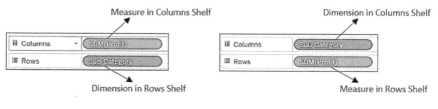

A. Horizontal Bar Chart　　　　　　　B. Vertical Bar Chart

FIGURE 7.8　Setting for creating bar chart.

Tableau offers several variations of bar charts. A few popular ones are:

1. Horizontal bar chart
2. Vertical bar (column) chart
3. Stacked bar charts
4. Grouped or side-by-side bar chart

Let us discuss the implementation of each of these charts in details in the following sections.

7.1.2.1　Horizontal Bar Chart

The most general and easy to understand type of bar chart is the typical horizontal bar chart. To create this type of bar chart, we place the quantitative measure such as profit, sales, discount, etc. in the Columns shelf and place a categorical dimension field such as region and category in the Rows shelf. Following are the instructions for creating a horizontal bar chart to demonstrate category-by-category profit analysis in the Sample-Superstore data source:

Step 1. First, establish a connection to the Sample-Superstore data source. Orders, Returns, and People tables can all be connected by dragging them together (Figure 7.9).

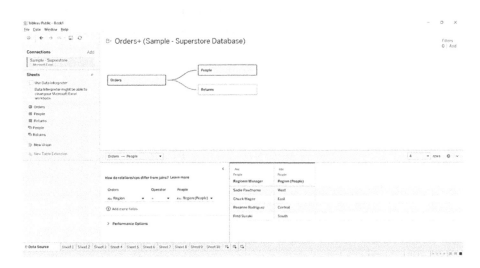

FIGURE 7.9 Output.

Step 2. Start a fresh worksheet. Move to place the "Profit" metric to the Columns block and the "Category" field to the Rows block (Figure 7.10).

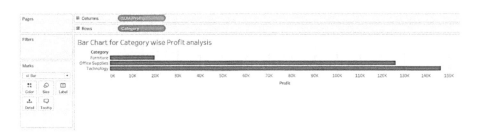

FIGURE 7.10 Output.

At this point, we see that row headers are visible and the data is compiled by category. Horizontal bars are produced in accordance with profit values when the profit measure is combined as a sum.

Step 3. Automatically, we observe that bar marks are selected under the Marks card (Figure 7.11).

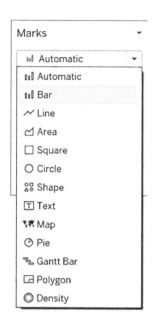

FIGURE 7.11   Output.

Step 4. In this instance, the marks are bars, and they are horizontal. For every
mark, the total profit for that year is represented by its length. Under the
Marks card, drag the profit measurements to the labels (Figure 7.12).

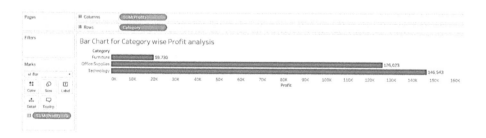

FIGURE 7.12   Output.

7.1.2.2   Vertical Bar (Column) Chart

The orientation of horizontal bar charts can be changed to vertical bars. Such type of
bar charts is also called Column charts. The only difference lies in the orientation of
the axis. To create this type of bar chart, we place the quantitative measures such as
profit, sales and discount in the Rows shelf and place a categorical dimension field such
as region and category in the Columns shelf. Observe the suggested steps to produce a
vertical bar chart that shows total sales over the course of a four-year timeframe:

Step 1. First, establish a connection to the Sample-Superstore data source. Move the "Sales" measure to the Rows and the "Order-Date" dimension to the Columns. Since we used the Date dimension, Tableau applies Line as the default mark type (Figure 7.13).

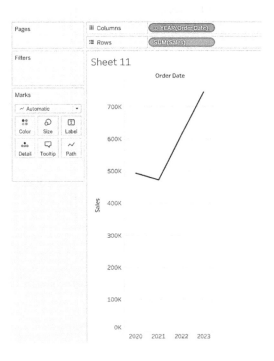

FIGURE 7.13   Output.

Step 2. Pick "Bar marks" from the Marks card's drop-down menu (Figure 7.14).

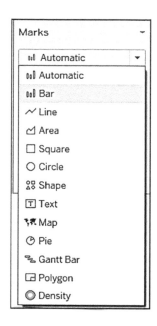

FIGURE 7.14 Output.

Step 3. As soon as we select the bar marks, the view changes to bar chart with vertical column like bars (Figure 7.15).

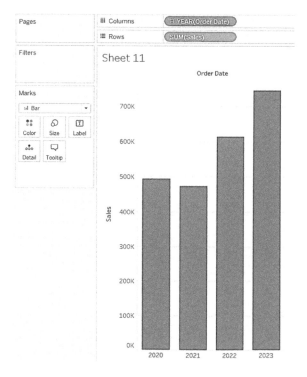

FIGURE 7.15 Output.

Step 4. Every vertical bar that is made has a length that corresponds to the overall sales for that particular year. Here, we may also add the Region information to expand the data presented in the Bar Chart. Drag Region to the Columns or Rows shelf to accomplish this. A sequence of region-specific annual sales will result from this (Figure 7.16).

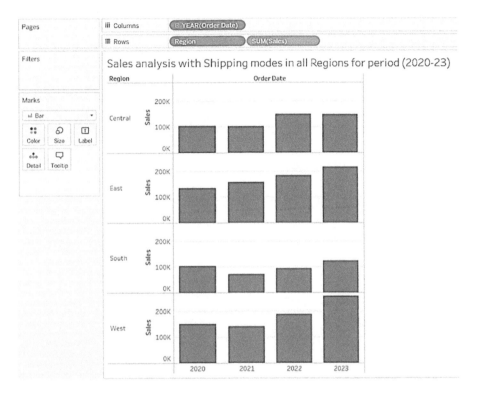

FIGURE 7.16   Output.

Step 5. To create labels and color variation in the generated bar graphs, we drag Sales measure to Color and Labels in the Marks card.

Step 6. Here, we can see a series of colored and labeled bar charts in Figure 7.17. Users can modify the color scheme of bar chart as per the requirement.

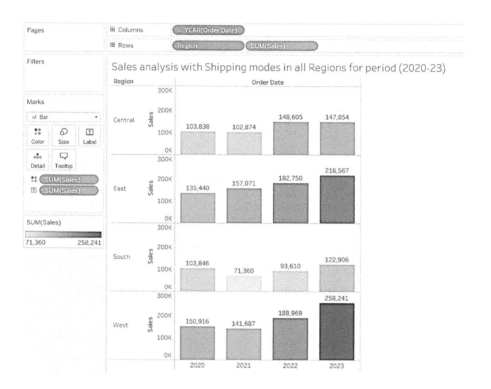

FIGURE 7.17   Output.

7.1.2.3   Stacked Bar Chart

Tableau supports a stacked bar chart, which displays values in the form of segmented bars. These bars are divided into sections, providing specific details about the field used. Dimensions like categories, regions, product type, and profit can be segmented. For example, a segmented bar chart can display sales for each product in multiple geographic locations, providing additional data for thorough study and better decision-making. This type of bar chart is ideal for analyzing data in various fields. The steps required for creating a stacked bar chart are given below:

Step 1. Let us consider the previous example where we created a series of vertical bar charts to display region-wise sales per year (2020–2023) as shown in Figure 7.18.

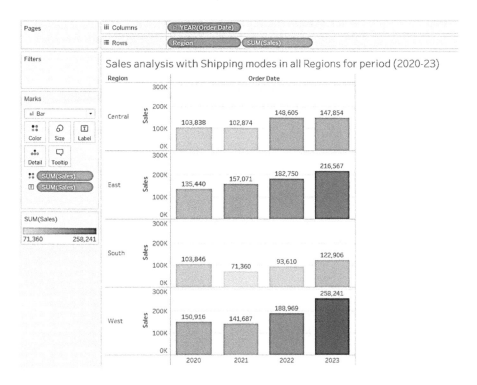

FIGURE 7.18 Output.

Step 2. To view the contribution of each shipping mode in region-wise yearly sales, bring the "Ship Mode" field to the Colors in Marks panel, generating a stacked bar graph with segments for different shipping modes (Figure 7.19).

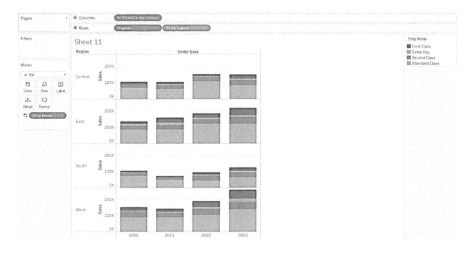

FIGURE 7.19 Output.

Step 7. Let us try to apply filters for regions to view sales for a particular region at a time. For this, drag Regions to Filters card. Select all values from list and click OK (Figure 7.20).

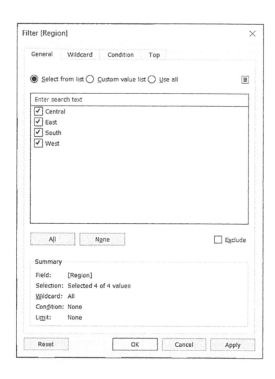

FIGURE 7.20   Output.

Step 8. To show the filter, apply right-click on the "Regions" filter and pick the option for "Show Filter" (Figure 7.21).

FIGURE 7.21   Output.

Step 9. The filter is visible on the extreme right pane of the worksheet, and by default, all regions are checked. Users can select and deselect regions according to their needs, such as showing Sales for Central and East regions (Figure 7.22).

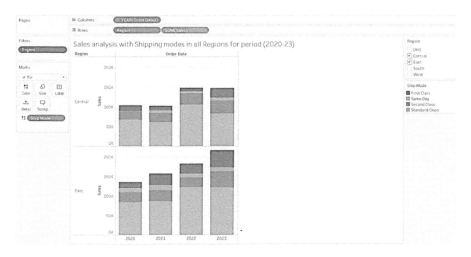

FIGURE 7.22   Output.

Step 10. We can also add totals to Stacked Bars, i.e., a combined total for each bar instead of each segment. For this browse through the "Analytics pane" bring the "Reference Line" into the view and release it on the option for "Cell " (Figure 7.23).

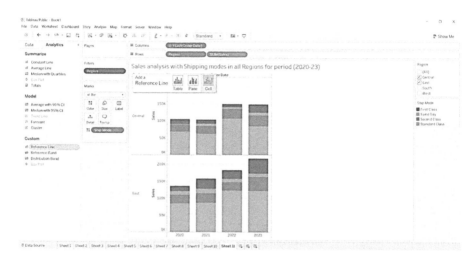

FIGURE 7.23   Output.

Step 11. As appears in the illustration below, in the Edit Line box, update the "Label" to Value, and the aggregate value for SUM(Sales) to Sum. Set the "Line" under Formatting to "None" (Figure 7.24).

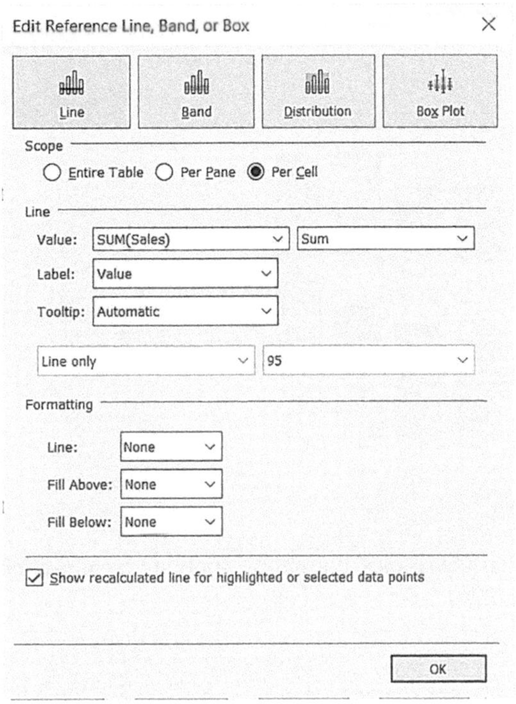

FIGURE 7.24   Output.

Step 12. Subsequently, select OK to dismiss the reference line, band, or box edit dialog box. It now shows the sales totals at the top of each bar in the bar graph mode (Figure 7.25).

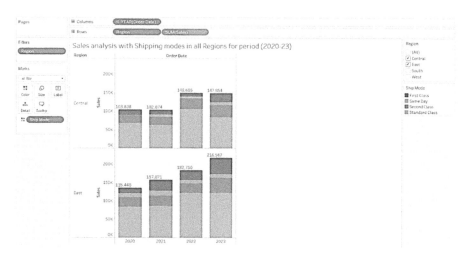

FIGURE 7.25   Output.

Step 13. In the bar chart, pick Format by applying a right-click on any of the totals (Figure 7.26).

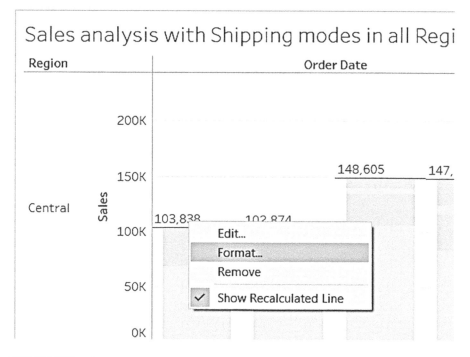

FIGURE 7.26   Output.

Step 14. Access the "Alignment" setting in the Format window's Reference Line Label section, and then select the "Center" option to align horizontally (Figure 7.27).

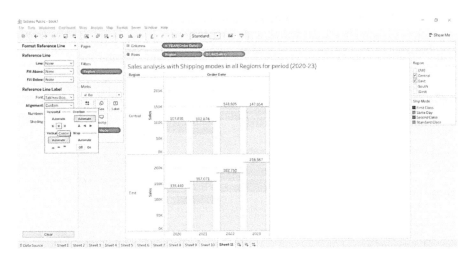

FIGURE 7.27 Output.

Step 15. The output is now flawlessly modeled to show annual sales totals on each bar that is segmented (Figure 7.28).

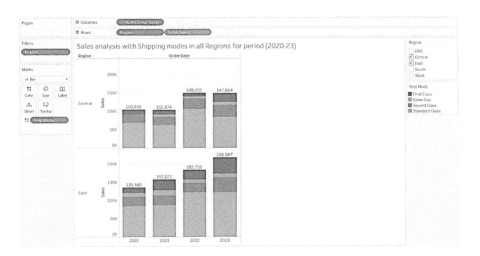

FIGURE 7.28 Output.

7.1.2.4 Grouped or Side-by-Side Bar Chart

Tableau supports the Grouped Bar Chart, also acknowledged as side-by-side, clustered, or shared-axis bar charts. This type of bar chart is useful for comparing and displaying data side by side, with two or more measures placed next to each other. The rectangular bars are grouped by position for one categorical variable, with the same colors displaying the measures within each group. It can be created in vertical or horizontal orientation. The stages to create a side-by-side bar plot to compare segment-wise profit, sales, and discount measures.

Step 1. Launch a new worksheet and establish connection to the Superstore dataset. Place the fields for the "Category" in addition to "Sub-Category" on the Columns block (Figure 7.29).

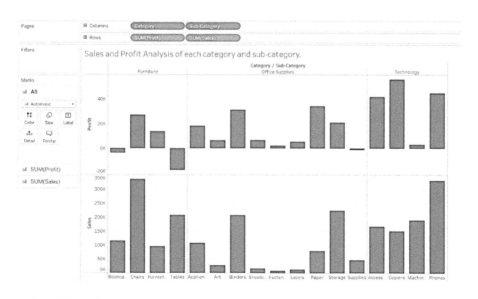

FIGURE 7.29 Output.

Step 2. Drag measures Sales and Profit to Rows shelf. Also add a suitable title (Figure 7.30).

FIGURE 7.30 Output.

Step 3. Click on "Show Me" tab to select the side-by-side parallel bar plot (Figure 7.31).

FIGURE 7.31 Output.

Step 4. Once selected, the side-by-side corresponding bars are created comparing sales and profit with data grouped by category and further sub-categories (Figure 7.32).

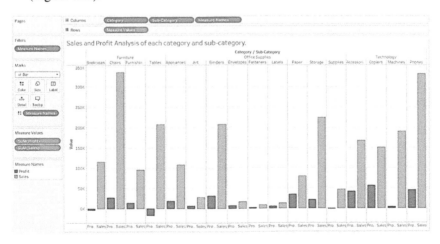

FIGURE 7.32 Output.

Step 5. We can modify the colors representing each bar, add borders to bar and make necessary changes as required. To add data labels to each bar we select Label under Marks card and check the Show Mark Labels checkbox (Figure 7.33).

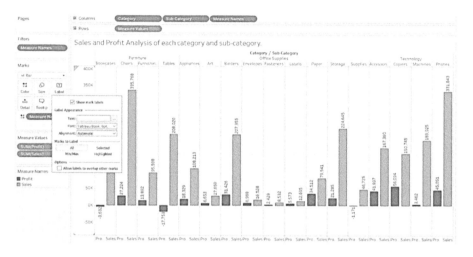

FIGURE 7.33   Output.

This will add respective labels to each label.

Step 6. We can also combine the Stacked chart with the created Grouped bar graph to display the share of each segment in Sales and Profit values. For this, drag the Segment field to Color under Marks Card. The modified graph is visible as below (Figure 7.34).

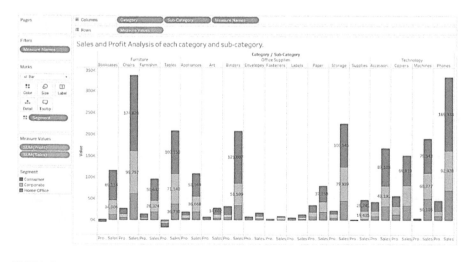

FIGURE 7.34   Output.

Step 7. For better display, we change the alignment and label value direction to "Up" in Label under Marks card. The output is displayed below (Figure 7.35).

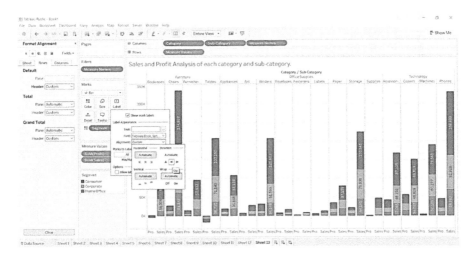

FIGURE 7.35   Output.

Such a chart is known as a Grouped Stacked Bar Chart.

7.1.3   Lollipop Chart for Presentation

A composite dual-axis chart with bars and circles is called a lollipop chart. Dual-axis charts, commonly referred to as combination (combo) charts, are a style of visualization that combines two distinct chart types in one graph. Two sets of data can be displayed simultaneously because the two chart types have different y-axis but the same x-axis. Lollipop charts, like bar charts, are used to compare categorical data. It is a bar chart variation that has a circle chart at the end to emphasize the importance of the data. The major properties of a lollipop chart are as follows:

    I. The magnitude is determined by the length of the bar.
   II. Additionally, color can be used to indicate a category or magnitude.
  III. To emphasize the importance, size can also be utilized.
  IV. Additionally, icons of categories can be used in place of circles to convey information about those categories in a more logical way (Figure 7.36).

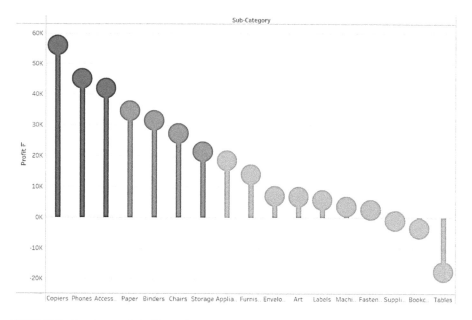

FIGURE 7.36   A sample lollipop chart.

However, the value represented by the bar is exaggerated due to circle at the end. The lollipop chart not only stretches the bar length but blurs the border as well. Particularly when the circle size is large or not comparable, it makes precise comparison challenging for viewers.

The phases to generate a lollipop chart as follows:

Step 1. To create a new worksheet, connect to the Sample-Superstore data source, place the "sub-category" in the Rows block, and the "profit" measure in the Columns block (Figure 7.37).

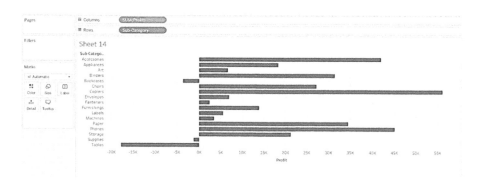

FIGURE 7.37   Output.

Step 2. Drag Profit once again to create a dual-axis graph (Figure 7.38).

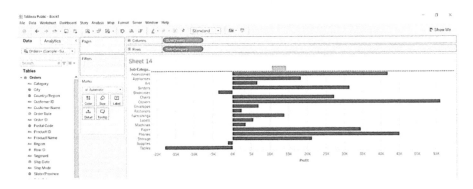

FIGURE 7.38   Output.

Step 3. The dual-axis graph so created is shown in Figure 7.39.

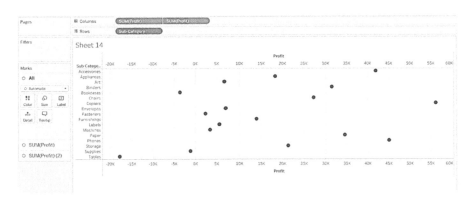

FIGURE 7.39   Output.

Step 4. Process Right-click the Profit axis above and choose Synchronize Axis while deselecting "Show Header" (Figure 7.40).

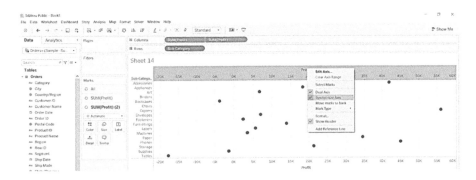

FIGURE 7.40   Output.

Step 5. Now in the Marks card select Bar marks instead of Automatic for first axis Sum (Profit) and select Circle for second axis Sum (Profit) 2. This will generate a Bar chart ending with a circle chart (Figure 7.41).

FIGURE 7.41   Output.

Step 6. To make the shape of bars to resemble Lollipop, we need to open the size marks of first axis and reduce the size of bars. Next, open the size marks of second axis and increase the size of circles (Figure 7.42).

FIGURE 7.42   Output.

Step 7. We can swap the axis and view the exact Lollipop shape graph (Figure 7.43).

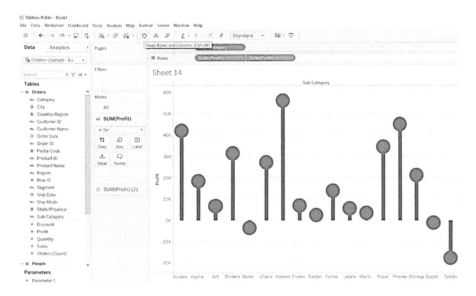

FIGURE 7.43 Output.

Step 8. Drag Profit measure to color marks of both the axis and arrange bars in descending order to create a visually appealing Lollipop chart. Also, drag the Profit measure to Label marks of second axis only (Figure 7.44).

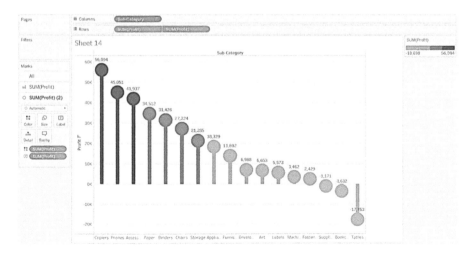

FIGURE 7.44 Output.

Here in the output, we can visualize a lollipop chart showing product sub-category-wise profit in decreasing order. The Blue-Orange diverging color scheme well enhances the chart display with the darkest blue representing the bar for the highest earned profit sub-category with value and deep orange colored bar signifies the loss-making sub-categories.

7.1.4 Line Chart in Tableau

A line chart, also known as a line graph or line plot, links data points using a line to identify trends and forecast future values. It typically has a vertical y-axis representing quantitative values and a horizontal x-axis indicating a time dimension. Line charts can display one or several lines depending on the analysis type. A single-line chart allows users to identify changes and trends within the data, while a line chart with multiple lines uses different colors for comparison. A line chart with fewer lines is easier to interpret, while plotting too many lines can increase confusion and make it difficult to understand.

Create a line chart by following the instructions below to display total sales and profit for all years (2020–2023) and illustrate a trend.

Step 1. Open a new worksheet by connecting to the given Superstore data collection.

Step 2. Place the "Order-Date" field to the Columns block. As we can see, Tableau constructs column headings and aggregates the date by year. Additionally, drag the Sales aggregated by the Sum function measure into Rows. This will instantly generate a single-line line graph connecting the two axes (Figure 7.45).

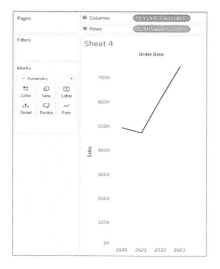
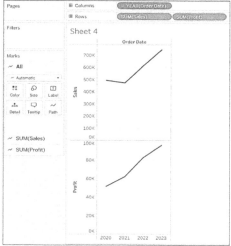

FIGURE 7.45 Output.

Step 3. The Profit measure should be shifted to Rows and placed to the right of the Sales metric. It is evident that distinct parts are created for Sales and Profit, each utilizing a distinct Y-axis value scale.

Step 4. A blended-axis chart that is easier for viewers to interpret and compare numbers can be made by aligning or combining axes when displaying various measures in a single-line chart. To accomplish this, drag the SUM(Profit) field from Rows to the Sales axis to create a blended axis. When the mouse button released, the profit and sales metrics will employ a blended axis, as indicated by the two weak green parallel bars in the upcoming figure. The graph that will be produced on the blended axes is as follows (Figure 7.46):

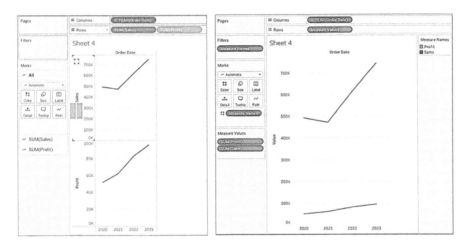

FIGURE 7.46 Output.

Step 5. Click the drop-down arrow in the Year (Order-Date) column of the Columns shelf and select Month from the bottom area of the context menu to examine a continuous range of values over the years. This will allow you to get deeper into the generated lines (Figure 7.47).

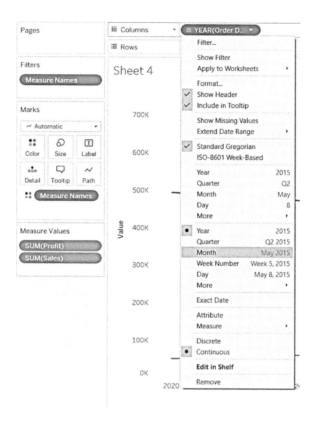

FIGURE 7.47   Output.

Step 6. Now add a suitable title and the output can be seen below (Figure 7.48).

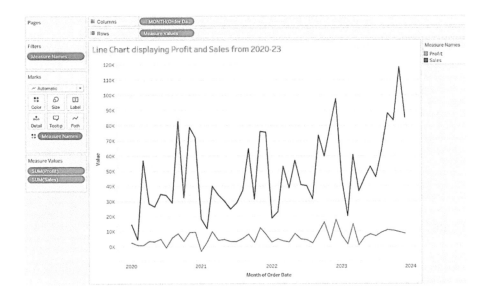

FIGURE 7.48   Output.

In the output shown above, we can see that right before each year's conclusion, the figures seem to suddenly increase significantly. *Seasonality* is the term for such a pattern. In the parts that follow, we will talk more about seasonality.

7.2   STUDYING CHANGES ACROSS TIME: TRENDS AND FORECASTING

Time is a crucial factor in data recording, and time series analysis is a method of examining a set of time series data points over a period [7]. This method identifies uniform patterns in data, forms trends, cyclic or seasonal variances, and can be used for time series forecasting to predict future events. Time is not only a data quantity but also a primary axis on which the data relies (Figure 7.49).

FIGURE 7.49 An example of a line chart.

Time series analysis is a crucial tool in various industries, particularly in non-stationary data, population trend analysis, retail, finance, and economics. It helps predict changes in factors like currency and sales and is used in shares and stock market analysis [8]. It is also useful for forecasting weather changes and helping meteorologists predict future climate change. In the medical field, time series analysis aids in heart rate monitoring, brain monitoring, and predicting heart attack possibilities. Overall, time series analysis plays a vital role in various industries and businesses.

7.2.1 COMPONENTS OF TIME SERIES

A *Time Series* is composed up of all the different factors or causes that continually alter the values of an observation.

Time series components can be categorized into three groups (Figure 7.50).

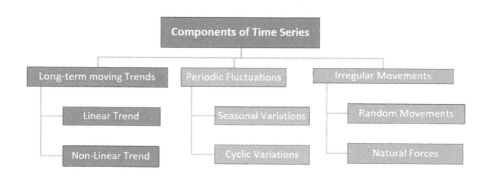

FIGURE 7.50 Components of time series.

7.2.1.1 Trend

A trend is a long-term, smooth, and average trend of data that indicates an increase, decrease, or constant over time [7,8]. It can be observed in scenarios such as population, crop production, sale, demand, birth, and death rates, and can be upwards, downwards, or constant. The overall trend must be upwards, downwards, or constant (Figure 7.51).

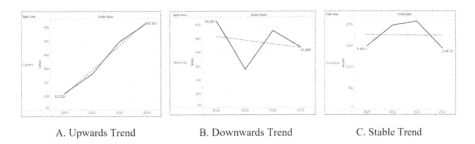

| A. Upwards Trend | B. Downwards Trend | C. Stable Trend |

FIGURE 7.51 Types of trends in Tableau.

The graphs show solid lines for data points and dotted lines for the trend line. If the time series values are plotted, the data clustering pattern indicates the type of trend. *Linear* trends are those where data points are grouped around a straight line, while non-linear or *Curvilinear* trends are not (Figure 7.52).

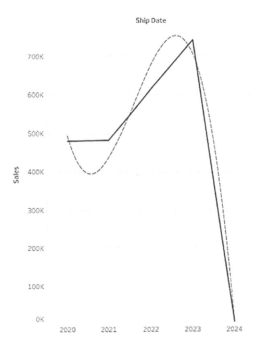

FIGURE 7.52 A non-linear trend example.

7.2.1.2   Periodic Fluctuations

Periodic Fluctuations are components in a time series that recur at specific intervals over a specific period, acting in a regular yet occasional manner due to their periodic recurrence nature. These can be further categorized into two categories described as follows:

A. **Seasonal Variations:** A repeated pattern in data over a predetermined time period—daily, weekly, monthly, or annual—caused by events such as weather, holidays, special occasions, and human behavior is referred to as "Seasonality" in data. Sales of fans, woolens, and crops during the Rabi and Kharif seasons are a few examples (Figure 7.53).

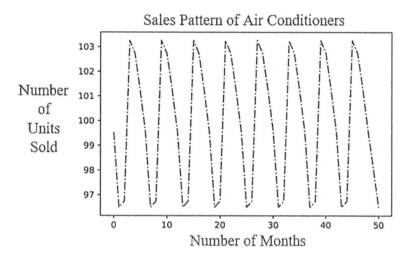

FIGURE 7.53   An example of seasonal variations.

B. **Cyclic Variations:** Cyclicity refers to the repeated patterns or variations in data over an unspecified time interval, often caused by factors like economic cycles and trends. It is not limited to a fixed time and can be of different frequencies, making it difficult to identify and model. In business scenarios, cyclic motions like the "Business Cycle" can have four stages: prosperity, recession, depression, and recovery, influenced by internal and external economic forces (Figure 7.54).

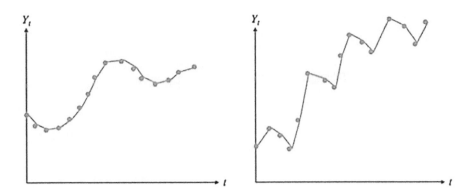

FIGURE 7.54 Examples of cyclic variations without and with seasonality.

7.2.1.3 Irregular Movements – Noise and Outliers

Irregular patterns are sudden, random fluctuations in nature, often uncontrollable and caused by natural calamities like earthquakes, floods, war, famines, or changes in government policies. They can be observed in graphs like the one showing a sudden spike in sales, highlighting the importance of understanding, and managing these patterns (Figures 7.55 and 7.56).

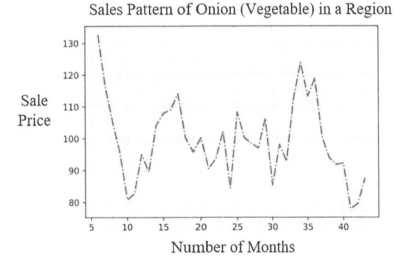

FIGURE 7.55 Example for irregular movements.

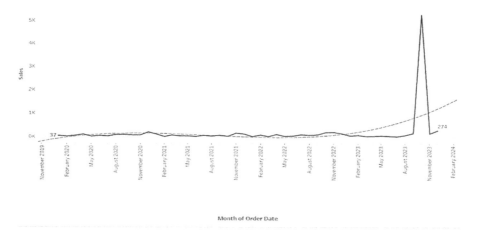

FIGURE 7.56 Example for outlier.

7.2.1.4 Noise

Noise in time series data refers to random fluctuations in data that are not based on an underlying pattern or trend. These fluctuations can be caused by measurement errors, process fluctuations, or data recording or processing errors. The presence of noise makes it difficult to identify the underlying trend or pattern, making it crucial to remove or reduce the noise before further analysis.

7.2.1.5 Outliers

Outliers are data points in time series data that are significantly different from the rest, often due to errors in measurement, sudden extreme events, or variations in data-generating processes. These outliers can significantly impact the outcomes of time series analysis by skewing the statistical properties of the data.

7.2.2 DECOMPOSITION MODELS FOR TIME SERIES ANALYSIS

In order to split a time series into its four constituent pieces, we usually use the following two models:

1. Additive model for Time Series Decomposition
2. Multiplicative model for Time Series Decomposition (Figure 7.57)

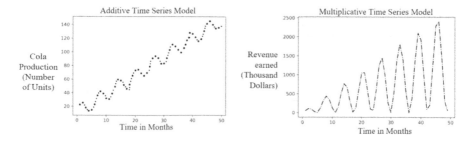

FIGURE 7.57 Time series models.

I. Additive Model

For seasonal variance that is largely stable or consistent throughout time, the additive approach works well. The contributions made by each model component are put together to create an additive model. Hence, the sum of all four elements is provided for a certain observation in a time series.

Observation = Trend + Seasonal Variations + Cyclical Variations + Irregular Variations

II. Multiplicative Model

Multiplicative models can greatly enhance the quality of forecasts for data when the level (magnitude) of the data influences the trend or seasonality. Here, as time goes on, the seasonal fluctuation gets bigger. The relationship between the four-time series components in this model is multiplicative. Therefore, a certain observation is characterized as the product of these four components:

Observation = Trend * Seasonal Variations * Cyclical Variations * Irregular Variations

7.2.2.1 Which Model to Choose and When?

For seasonal modeling, we have two options: the multiplicative model and the additive model.

- The multiplicative model is suitable when the seasonality's strength depends on the data's magnitude.
- In contrast, the additive model is suitable when the seasonality's strength remains the same, regardless of the data's magnitude.
- If you are unsure which model to choose, try both and compare their accuracy measures. Go with the one that yields the smaller accuracy measures.

7.2.3 TIME DISTRIBUTION CHARTS IN TABLEAU

Visualizing change over time is a fundamental visualization technique. Charts like slope, highlight table, line, bar chart, and combination chart are used to study and analyze changes across time distribution. These charts require understanding the expected change in the measure and the functionality of the Date fields in Tableau.

Further discussion on time distribution charts will follow.

7.2.3.1 Slope Chart: From Beginning to End

The straight-line equation $y = mx + b$ represents a line on a pair of coordinate axes [x, y]. The letter "m" represents the slope of the line, which measures its steepness. The slope can be positive (upwards), negative (downwards), or zero (horizontally level). Slope charts are a modern version of a simple line chart, displaying only the variation between a start and end point, without including distracting details in between. These angled lines allow quick answers to user queries and may even prompt new questions. Slope charts are useful for comparing two instances, such as two time periods, countries, or regions.

7.2.3.2 Case Study

Simple patterns over time for company components like rate of change in sales, discount, revenue, profit, etc. are also helpfully illustrated using slope charts. Look at the Tableau dataset Sample-Superstore. Assume that we wish to examine, in a single chart, the profit margins for several product sub-categories over a given period, such as the years 2020 and 2023. With the use of a slope chart, we can solve this situation effectively. The actions are listed below:

Step 1. Launch a new worksheet while working with the Superstore dataset.

Step 2. Bring the "Order-Date" field to Columns. Default data aggregation is at the Year level. Set the values to Discrete. Also, drag Profit measure to Rows as seen in second figure. We can observe a simple line chart is visible now (Figure 7.58).

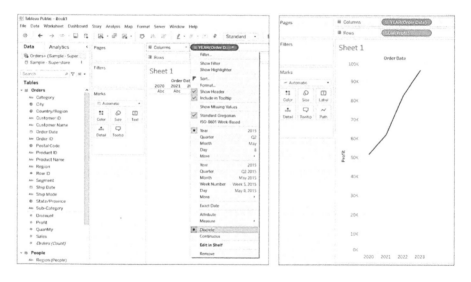

FIGURE 7.58   Output.

Step 3. Drag Order-Date to filters and set Years as filtering criteria. Select two years to compare i.e., 2020 and 2023. Click OK (Figure 7.59).

FIGURE 7.59   Output.

Step 4. Under Marks Card, set "Sub-Category" to Detail and Color. This will create multiple colored sloped-lines for displaying yearly profit of each sub-category (Figure 7.60).

FIGURE 7.60   Output.

> **Step 5.** Let us create a dual-axis slope chart by dragging Profit to create another
> axis as shown in output below (Figure 7.61).

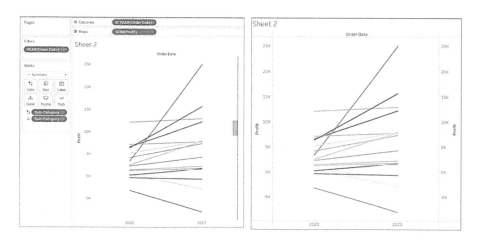

FIGURE 7.61   Output.

Step 6. Now bring "Sub-category" to the Filters panel and select the option of "Show Filter" after right-clicking. Now we can check to select the desired sub-categories and compare their performance in the slope chart (Figure 7.62).

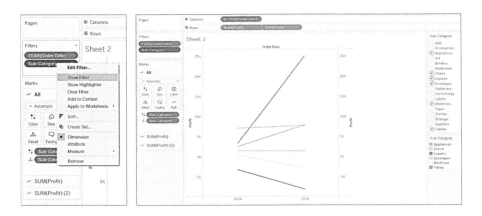

FIGURE 7.62 Output.

Step 7. Drag sub-category dimension to Label under Marks card. The slop chart is ready for view (Figure 7.63).

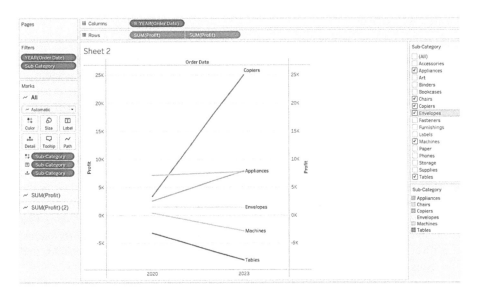

FIGURE 7.63 Output.

Step 8. In order to compare the profit slopes of two or more different product sub-categories we can use shaded slope graph also. For this, we need to change the marks value from "Automatic" to "Area" in the Marks card in both the axis, i.e., Sum (Profit) and Sum (Profit) 2. It will create shaded slope area instead of lines (Figure 7.64).

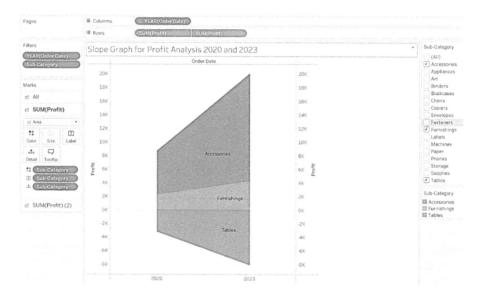

FIGURE 7.64   Output.

The output shows a sharp positive slope for "Accessories" indicating high profit earning from 2020 to 2023, while for "Furnishings", we see a low positive slope indicating slowly increasing profit value. On the other hand, for sub-category "Tables," we observe a sharp negative slope indicating more loss incurred since 2020–2023.

7.2.3.3   Highlight Tables: Identifying Patterns with Color

A highlight table in Tableau is a tool used to segment or split data and highlight important data over a specific time interval. It uses contrasting colors to identify the most and least important values. This can be done using conditional formatting or different color schemes. However, it is important to use comparable measures that significantly differ from each other, avoid using identical colors for similar measures, use a divergent color scheme only when data exceeds a significant threshold, and avoid using multiple colors to avoid confusion.

7.2.3.4   Case Study

Let us create a highlight table to study profit distribution for different sub-categories in a selected time in Superstore dataset. This case study is the same to the one we performed with slope chart. However, this time we analyze profit values using a highlight table instead. The steps are given below:

Step 1. To begin, establish a connection to the Superstore dataset and launch a new spreadsheet.

Step 2. Furthermore, pick the "Sub-Category" field in the Rows block and the "Order-Date" dimension aggregated in Years in the Columns block. Moreover, drag the Profit metric under Marks card's Label and Color fields. A colored highlight table that is shown below is the result (Figure 7.65).

Sub-Category	2020	2021	2022	2023
Accessories	6,403	10,197	9,664	15,672
Appliances	2,565	2,515	5,334	7,915
Art	1,434	1,486	1,463	2,271
Binders	5,203	7,633	10,649	7,941
Bookcases	-346	-2,755	128	-658
Chairs	7,145	6,342	5,948	7,788
Copiers	3,381	9,930	17,743	25,040
Envelopes	1,495	1,977	2,074	1,442
Fasteners	233	182	314	1,699
Furnishings	2,296	3,194	4,091	4,312
Labels	1,286	1,323	1,161	1,803
Machines	408	2,977	2,907	-2,831
Paper	6,589	6,580	9,089	12,254
Phones	12,119	10,458	9,521	12,952
Storage	4,187	3,507	6,227	7,363
Supplies	497	-25	-699	-944
Tables	-3,210	-3,500	-2,950	-8,092

FIGURE 7.65   Output.

Step 3. To enhance the highlight table's appeal, select the desired color scheme from the Marks card and click on the Red-Blue diverging scheme, with shades of Red indicating low profit and Blue indicating high profit values (Figure 7.66).

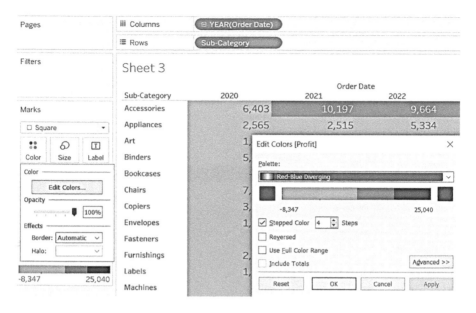

FIGURE 7.66   Output.

Step 4. Choose the Color markings Card and modify the "Border" effect from "Automatic" to a desired color to put a border for each table cell (Figure 7.67).

Sub-Category	2020	2021	2022	2023
Accessories	6,403	10,197	9,664	15,672
Appliances	2,565	2,515	5,334	7,915
Art	1,434	1,486	1,463	2,271
Binders	5,203	7,633	10,649	7,941
Bookcases	-346	-2,755	128	-658
Chairs	7,145	6,342	5,948	7,788
Copiers	3,381	9,930	17,743	25,040
Envelopes	1,495	1,977	2,074	1,442
Fasteners	233	182	314	1,699
	2,296	3,194	4,091	4,312
	1,286	1,323	1,161	1,803
	408	2,977	2,907	-2,831
	6,589	6,580	9,089	12,254
	12,119	10,458	9,521	12,952
	4,187	3,507	6,227	7,363
Supplies	497	-25	-699	-944
Tables	-3,210	-3,500	-2,950	-8,092

FIGURE 7.67   Output.

Step 5. To visualize and compare records of one or more year or specific sub-categories, we can add Order-Date and/or Sub-Category dimensions in Filter and select the desired criteria. Suppose here we apply filters and select the years 2020 and 2023 only for analysis. Similarly, we filter and select a few desired categories only to observe (Figure 7.68).

FIGURE 7.68 Output.

In the output we observe how the profit values for selected sub-categories change over the years from 2020 to 2023.

7.3 TREND LINES AND FORECASTING

Trends are the overall direction of a pattern's development over time, while *forecasts* are projections or predictions of future changes based on historical data [6]. They are often displayed using line graphs with a horizontal axis representing time. Trend lines, or lines of best fit, can be used in visualizations to highlight patterns or trends in user data. They not only predict the persistence of a trend but also recognize correlations between variables. For instance, trend lines can be used to study sales data trends and forecast future scenarios, aiding decision-makers in strategy development.

7.3.1 TYPES OF TREND LINES

To forecast whether a given trend in a variable will continue, trend lines are employed. By simultaneously observing the trends in both variables, it is also helpful to determine the correlation between them. For establishing trend lines, there exist numerous mathematical models. Four alternatives are offered in Tableau namely: linear, logarithmic, exponential, and polynomial (Figure 7.69).

Linear   Logarithmic   Exponential   Polynomial   Power

FIGURE 7.69   Types of trend lines in Tableau.

These trend lines are described as follows:

I. Linear Trend Line

A linear trendline corresponds to the straight line that fits basic linear datasets the best. Data is considered linear if the pattern among the data points resembles a line. In general, something is increasing or diminishing steadily when a linear trendline is present.

Case Study

Let us consider the Sample-Superstore data source. Here, we want to analyze the rate of change in discount measure with respect to Order-Date dimension. Also, we want to visualize the best fit trendline between the two. We will observe the significance of the trend model generated with the help of a trendline equation, p-value parameter along with R-squared statistic value. These values are discussed in detail in later sections:

Step 1. Establish a connection with the Sample-Superstore data source and link the tables for orders, people, and returns (Figure 7.70).

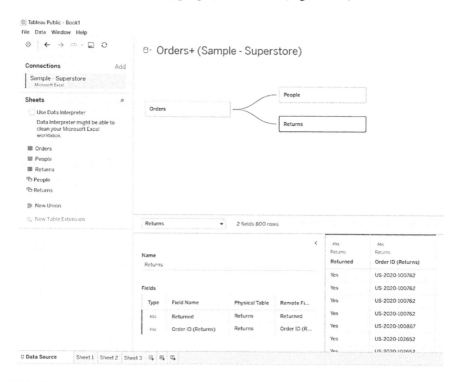

FIGURE 7.70   Output.

Step 2. To build the needed Line chart, open a new worksheet.

Step 3. Place the dimensions of the "Order-Date" in the column shelf and the "Discount" measure on the row shelf. Switch the "Order-Date" detail from Year to Month (Figure 7.71).

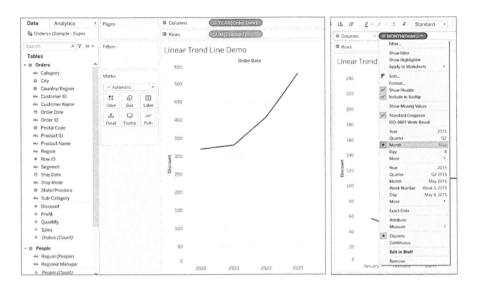

FIGURE 7.71   Output.

Step 4. Choose "Trend line" from the Analytics pane and bring it over the generated line chart. Choose the "Linear" option for the trend line right then (Figure 7.72).

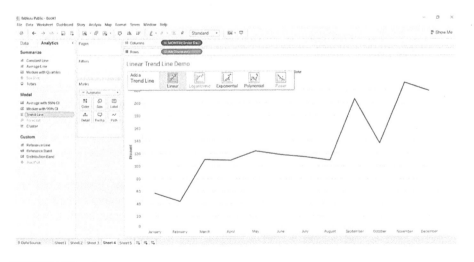

FIGURE 7.72   Output.

Step 5. The best-fitting dotted straight trend line for the line graph will be plotted after the linear trend line has been chosen. To view the characteristics of the plotted line, move the cursor over the trend line (Figure 7.73).

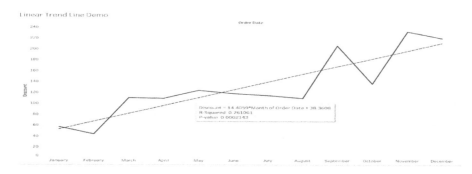

FIGURE 7.73   Output.

Conclusion
- In the explanation of the trend line, we can observe the significant p-value 0.00021 and R-squared statistic is 0.76, i.e., close to 1. This suggests that the trendline model is appropriate.
- The trendline equation describes a linearly increasing pattern of growth between Discount (explanatory variable) and Month Order-Date (response variable).

II. Logarithmic Trend Line

A logarithmic trendline is the most appropriate option when the data's rate of change abruptly increases or decreases before leveling out match a curving line. For example, we can use a logarithmic trendline if our chart shows a quick growth in profits by product category over time, followed by a plateau. We can use positive or negative numbers in a logarithmic trendline.

Example

In this illustration, we use the Superstore dataset and generate a logarithmic trend line to study the relationship of dimensions: Order-Date and Region; with measures: Sales and Quantity. We will analyze the significance of the trend model created by observing the values of parameters namely, p-value (≤0.05) and R-squared statistic (in the range of 0–1). We will discuss the meaning of each parameter in the coming sections. The steps are given below:

Step 1. Place dimension "Order-Date" and "Sales" measure in Columns shelf, along with Discount measure in Rows shelf. This will generate multiple Scatter Plots (2020–2023) to display the yearly Sales and Quantity distribution (Figure 7.74).

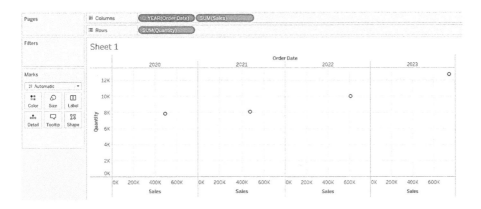

FIGURE 7.74 Output.

Step 2. Now, move the "Region" dimension to Color card under the Marks shelf to examine the annual Sales and Quantity distribution in various regions. Below is the generated scatter plot (Figure 7.75).

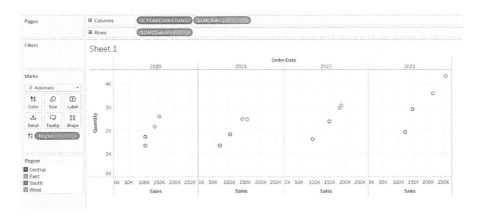

FIGURE 7.75 Output.

Step 3. Pick the option "Trend line" in the Analytics pane and drag it over the generated scatter plots. Choose the Logarithmic trend line at this point (Figure 7.76).

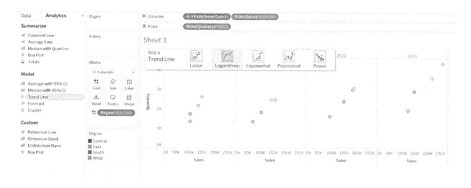

FIGURE 7.76   Output.

Step 4. What follows is the creation of the logarithmic trend lines. We may employ the logarithmic trend curve to show changes in the rate of change between variables (Figure 7.77).

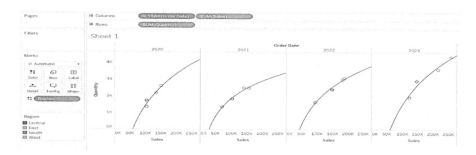

FIGURE 7.77   Output.

Step 5. Give a suitable title to the visualization and hover the mouse cursor over the trend line to observe the logarithmic equation and parameters generated (Figure 7.78).

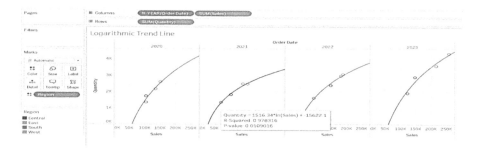

FIGURE 7.78   Output.

Conclusion
- In the above figure, the logarithmic trendlines suggest that for each year the overall rate of change of Quantity with Sales initially increases rapidly across all regions and later levels out slowly.
- Over the years 2020–2023, we observe a comparatively increasing trend in rate of change of Quantity with Sales for West region.
- In the year 2023 graph, the trendline displays a highly increasing rate of change compared to past years and the plateau level for this graph is not reached yet.
- For each trendline, a well-defined logarithmic equation is visible along with significant p-value 0.010 and R-squared statistic 0.97 approx.

Step 6. We can determine the model's overall relevance. Select the Describe Trend model option by right-clicking on a trend line. The developed trendline model's relevance is indicated by multiple parameters that we may observe here (Figure 7.79).

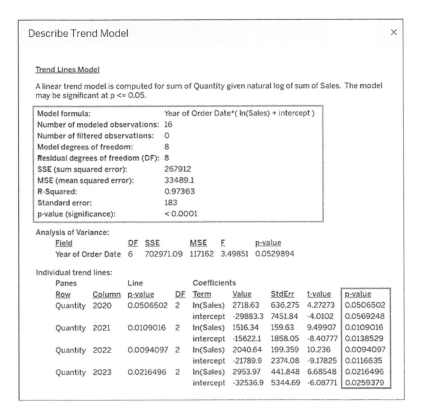

Describe Trend Model   ✕

Trend Lines Model

A linear trend model is computed for sum of Quantity given natural log of sum of Sales. The model may be significant at p <= 0.05.

Model formula:	Year of Order Date*(ln(Sales) + intercept)
Number of modeled observations:	16
Number of filtered observations:	0
Model degrees of freedom:	8
Residual degrees of freedom (DF):	8
SSE (sum squared error):	267912
MSE (mean squared error):	33489.1
R-Squared:	0.97363
Standard error:	183
p-value (significance):	< 0.0001

Analysis of Variance:

Field	DF	SSE	MSE	F	p-value
Year of Order Date	6	702971.09	117162	3.49851	0.0529894

Individual trend lines:

Panes		Line		Coefficients				
Row	Column	p-value	DF	Term	Value	StdErr	t-value	p-value
Quantity	2020	0.0506502	2	ln(Sales)	2718.63	636.275	4.27273	0.0506502
				intercept	-29883.3	7451.84	-4.0102	0.0569248
Quantity	2021	0.0109016	2	ln(Sales)	1516.34	159.63	9.49907	0.0109016
				intercept	-15622.1	1858.05	-8.40777	0.0138529
Quantity	2022	0.0094097	2	ln(Sales)	2040.64	199.359	10.236	0.0094097
				intercept	-21789.9	2374.08	-9.17825	0.0116635
Quantity	2023	0.0216496	2	ln(Sales)	2953.97	441.848	6.68548	0.0216496
				intercept	-32536.9	5344.69	-6.08771	0.0259379

FIGURE 7.79   Output.

Step 7. Here R-squared statistic of model is 0.97 (i.e., close to 1) and p-value (significance) ≤ 0.05. Therefore, the model created is appropriate. Also, the values are in range for each trend line.

III. Exponential Trend Line

When data values upsurge or fall at comparatively faster pace, an exponential trendline—a non-linear or curved line—becomes very useful. An example of an exponential trendline might be a chart showing an exponential increase in profit over time by product category or the increasing rate of cell proliferation in biology. The data cannot, however, be utilized with an exponential trendline if it contains zero (0) or negative values.

Case Study

In this illustration, we use the default Sample-Superstore dataset. Suppose we want to study the yearly rate of change of profit values with sales across each product category and plot trend lines for the same. The steps are given below:

Step 1. Move dimension "Order-Date" and "Sales" measure to Columns shelf, along with "Profit" measure in Rows shelf as displayed in Figure 7.80.

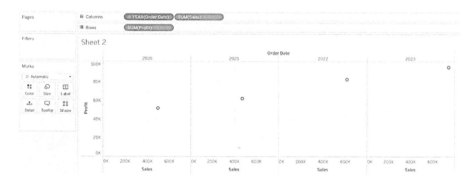

FIGURE 7.80   Output.

Step 2. Plotting the total sales and profit for each year results in a minimal scatter chart, as seen in the above figure. Select the "Sales" measure from the Columns shelf, and then select "Dimension" to get a comprehensive scatter chart with all values shown in it. Bring the "Profit" measure in Rows shelf and convert to Dimension (Figure 7.81).

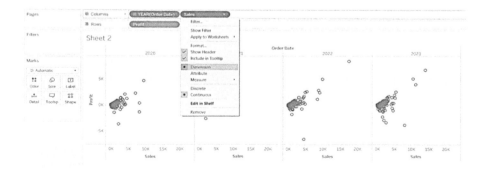

FIGURE 7.81   Output.

Step 3. All product categories are included in the scatter plot that is thus produced, with no distinction made. However, we wish to examine how quickly profit changes in relation to sales for every product category. Place the "Category" field to Color under the Marks panel to do this (Figure 7.82).

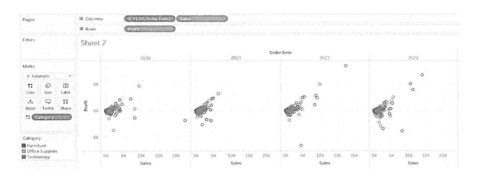

FIGURE 7.82 Output.

Step 4. Proceed to the Analytics tab now and choose "Trend Line" in model section. Drag the trend line over the chart, and then choose the Exponential trend line option (Figure 7.83).

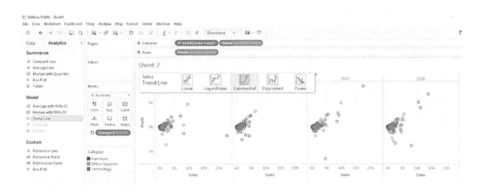

FIGURE 7.83 Output.

Step 5. The output displays exponential trend line for each category (Figure 7.84).

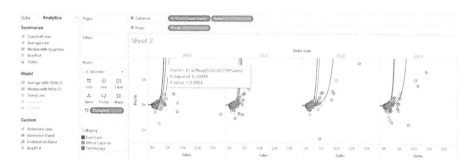

FIGURE 7.84   Output.

Conclusion
- We observe an upwards moving trend with progressing years in the rate of change of profit with sales for each product category.
- On closely analyzing trend lines for all three categories in each year, we can see a relatively higher rate of change in profit with sales for category Technology as compared to furniture and office sales. This can be visualized from the broader path followed by Technology trendline, while the other two trendlines are close to each other and follow almost similar path.
- As we hover cursor over a trendline, we analyze the description of the plotted line. It displays exponential line equation along with significant p-value <0.0001 and R-squared values 0.52.

Step 6. We can also apply filter to Category to select and analyze the desired categories (Figure 7.85).

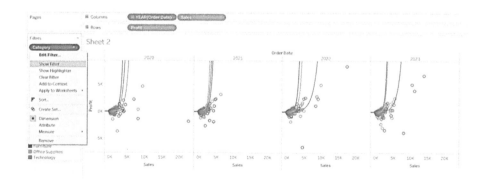

FIGURE 7.85   Output.

Step 7. In the displayed Category filter, we check to select Furniture and Office Supplies categories only to analyze the rate of change of profit with sales for these categories only (Figure 7.86).

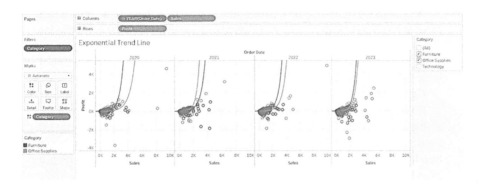

FIGURE 7.86 Output.

Step 8. Subsequently click right on a trend line and choose "Describe Trend Line Model, " all the information about plotted exponential trend lines will appear (Figure 7.87).

Describe Trend Model ×

Trend Lines Model

A linear trend model is computed for natural log of Profit given Sales. The model may be significant at p <= 0.05. The factor Category may be significant at p <= 0.05. The factor Year of Order Date may be significant at p <= 0.05.

Model formula: Category*Year of Order Date*(Sales + intercept)
Number of modeled observations: 5822
Number of filtered observations: 1630
Model degrees of freedom: 16
Residual degrees of freedom (DF): 5806
SSE (sum squared error): 8425.59
MSE (mean squared error): 1.45119
R-Squared: 0.345896
Standard error: 1.20465
p-value (significance): < 0.0001

Analysis of Variance:

Field	DF	SSE	MSE	F	p-value
Category	8	221.50794	27.6885	19.0799	< 0.0001
Year of Order Date	12	128.98816	10.749	7.40705	< 0.0001

Individual trend lines:

Panes		Color	Line		Coefficients				
Row	Column	Category	p-value	DF	Term	Value	StdErr	t-value	p-value
Profit	2020	Office Supplies	< 0.0001	931	Sales	0.0012967	8.339e-05	15.5491	< 0.0001
					intercept	2.11818	0.0439685	48.175	< 0.0001
Profit	2020	Furniture	< 0.0001	278	Sales	0.0018228	0.0001049	17.3712	< 0.0001
					intercept	2.45359	0.0683624	35.8909	< 0.0001
Profit	2021	Office Supplies	< 0.0001	909	Sales	0.0022922	0.0001216	18.8463	< 0.0001
					intercept	2.06192	0.044304	46.5402	< 0.0001
Profit	2021	Furniture	< 0.0001	292	Sales	0.0016373	0.0001027	15.9422	< 0.0001
					intercept	2.61111	0.070196	37.1973	< 0.0001
Profit	2022	Office Supplies	< 0.0001	1179	Sales	0.0016144	8.522e-05	18.9443	< 0.0001
					intercept	2.15124	0.0383998	56.0221	< 0.0001
Profit	2022	Furniture	< 0.0001	352	Sales	0.0018119	9.348e-05	19.3823	< 0.0001
					intercept	2.58952	0.0597819	43.3162	< 0.0001
Profit	2023	Office Supplies	< 0.0001	1433	Sales	0.0020726	8.272e-05	25.0544	< 0.0001
					intercept	2.07549	0.0347653	59.7	< 0.0001
Profit	2023	Furniture	< 0.0001	432	Sales	0.0021474	0.0001063	20.1929	< 0.0001
					intercept	2.37494	0.0570902	41.5997	< 0.0001

FIGURE 7.87 Output.

Step 9. Here we can observe significant p-values for the overall trend model and individual trend lines as well. This means that our trend model is appropriate.

IV. Power Trend Line

A non-linear (curved) line called the power trendline is helpful when comparing datasets that only show measures that increase at a particular rate. Think about a rushing car, for example, whose acceleration increases every ten seconds. A dataset with zero or negative values cannot be used with a power trendline.

Case Study

Consider the Sample-Superstore data source. Now, suppose we want to analyze the ongoing trend between region-wise sales done and profit earned for the years 2021 and 2022. We will observe the trend by plotting the power trendline and analyzing the values of parameters obtained. The steps are given below:

Step 1. Place dimension "Order-Date" and "Sales" measure to Columns bar, along with "Profit" measure in Rows shelf. Also, drag "Region" to Color under Marks card as displayed in Figure 7.88.

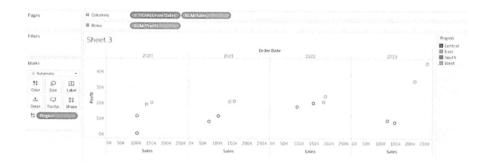

FIGURE 7.88   Output.

Step 2. In the scatter chart, we want to plot all the dimension values in "Sales" and "Profit" measures rather than Sum (Sales) and Sum (Profit). For this, click on the "Sales" quantity in Columns box, and select Dimension. Repeat the same process for Profit measure in Rows shelf. The output will be a set of detailed scatter plots for region-wise sales and profit values in 2020–2023 (Figure 7.89).

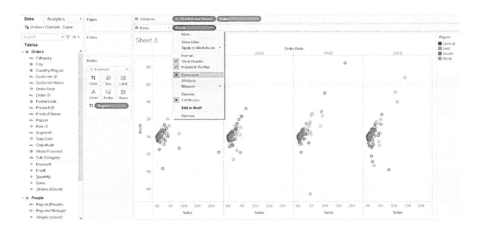

FIGURE 7.89 Output.

Step 3. Browse through Analytics pane and choose to plot Trend Line. Drag trend line over the chart and pick the option for "Power trend" plot as in Figure 7.90.

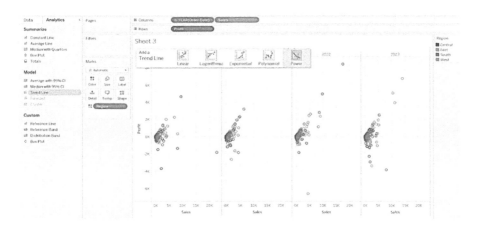

FIGURE 7.90 Output.

Step 4. The output displays power trend lines for each region (Figure 7.91).

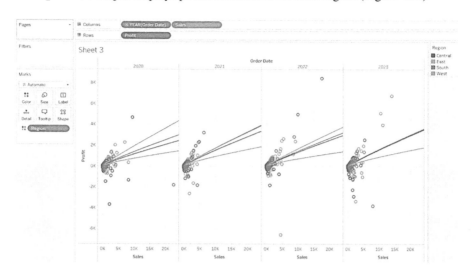

FIGURE 7.91   Output.

Step 5. As per our requirement we need to analyze the trends for years 2021 and 2022 only. So, we **need** apply Filters on years. Drag and drop Order-Date to Filters and select the year option in filter dialog box. Then from the list of years select the years 2021 and 2022 only. Click Ok (Figure 7.92).

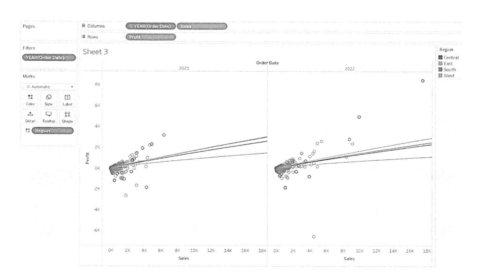

FIGURE 7.92   Output.

Step 6. The output obtained displays the power trend lines for the years 2021 and 2022 only (Figure 7.93).

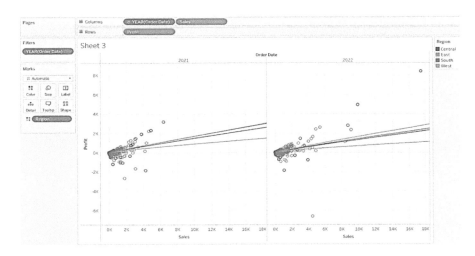

FIGURE 7.93   Output.

Step 7. As we hover above a trendline, we can monitor the power trendline equation along with other significant parameters (Figure 7.94).

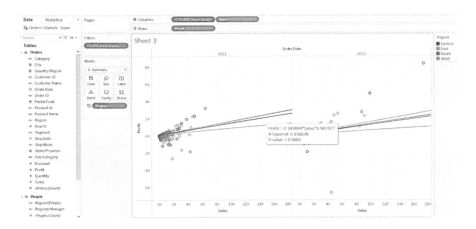

FIGURE 7.94   Output.

Step 8. Choose "Describe Trend Line Model" after right-click on any trend line. It will display all the details related to power Trend lines plotted (Figure 7.95).

Describe Trend Model

Trend Lines Model

A linear trend model is computed for natural log of Profit given natural log of Sales. The model may be significant at p <= 0.05. The factor Region may be significant at p <= 0.05.

Model formula: Region*Year of Order Date*(ln(Sales) + intercept)
Number of modeled observations: 3654
Number of filtered observations: 898
Model degrees of freedom: 16
Residual degrees of freedom (DF): 3638
SSE (sum squared error):   1853.98
MSE (mean squared error):   0.509616
R-Squared: 0.788857
Standard error: 0.713874
p-value (significance):   < 0.0001

Analysis of Variance:

Field	DF	SSE	MSE	F	p-value
Region	12	38.239827	3.18665	6.25305	< 0.0001
Year of Order Date	8	3.2901156	0.411264	0.807009	0.596329

Individual trend lines:

Panes Row	Column	Color Region	Line p-value	DF	Coefficients Term	Value	StdErr	t-value	p-value
Profit	2021	West	< 0.0001	543	ln(Sales)	0.809431	0.0184084	43.9707	< 0.0001
					intercept	-0.651269	0.0823939	-7.90434	< 0.0001
Profit	2021	South	< 0.0001	273	ln(Sales)	0.934286	0.028843	32.3921	< 0.0001
					intercept	-1.16473	0.127031	-9.16883	< 0.0001
Profit	2021	East	< 0.0001	500	ln(Sales)	0.925938	0.0215077	43.0514	< 0.0001
					intercept	-1.09404	0.0948798	-11.5308	< 0.0001
Profit	2021	Central	< 0.0001	311	ln(Sales)	0.907427	0.023152	39.1943	< 0.0001
					intercept	-1.05012	0.106892	-9.8241	< 0.0001
Profit	2022	West	< 0.0001	664	ln(Sales)	0.764625	0.018311	41.7577	< 0.0001
					intercept	-0.493049	0.0812998	-6.06458	< 0.0001
Profit	2022	South	< 0.0001	331	ln(Sales)	0.900305	0.0268888	33.4826	< 0.0001
					intercept	-1.02601	0.121956	-8.41296	< 0.0001
Profit	2022	East	< 0.0001	603	ln(Sales)	0.912243	0.0168714	54.0704	< 0.0001
					intercept	-0.98554	0.0730922	-13.4835	< 0.0001
Profit	2022	Central	< 0.0001	413	ln(Sales)	0.889787	0.0220479	40.357	< 0.0001
					intercept	-0.999534	0.0978456	-10.2154	< 0.0001

FIGURE 7.95 Output.

Conclusion
- The trendline model description window displays significant values of parameters such as p-value (< 0.0001) and R-squared statistic (0.78) for the overall model as well as individual trendlines. This suggests that the generated model is appropriate.

V. Polynomial Trend Line
When data values rise and fall over time, i.e., display continuous fluctuations, we might employ a polynomial trendline. For example, we can use a polynomial trendline to show sales rises and reductions per product category over time in our line chart.

Case Study
We make use of the default Sample-Superstore dataset. Here, we want to study and analyze the ongoing trend of the weekly number of orders of each category with respect to order date. The steps are given below:

Step 1. Bring dimension "Order-Date" to Columns bar, along with Orders measure in Rows shelf. By default, Year (Order-Date) is and CNT(Orders) meaning count or number of orders is displayed. Click on Order-Date under Columns shelf and select Week Number instead of Year to display weekly order details. This will generate a line chart depicting the overall weekly count of orders (Figure 7.96).

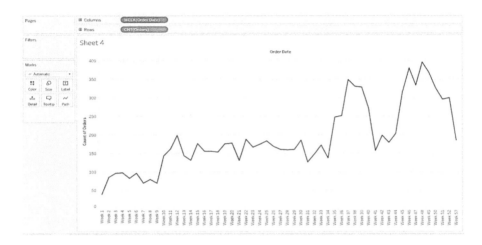

FIGURE 7.96   Output.

Step 2. Go to Analytics pane, and select to plot Trend Line. Drag trend line over the graph, and pick the option for "Polynomial trend" line as in Figure 7.97.

FIGURE 7.97   Output.

Step 3. The output displays a polynomial trend line with default settings for the line chart (Figure 7.98).

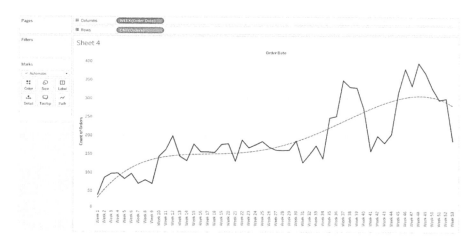

FIGURE 7.98   Output.

Step 4. Let us configure the trendline as per requirements. For this, click right on the trendline and choose option "Edit all Trend lines" (Figure 7.99).

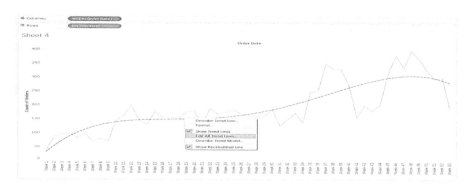

FIGURE 7.99   Output.

Step 5. It will open a configurations window with several options for Trend Line. Here, we can change the degree of polynomial and configure other options to show tooltips, confidence bands, color for each trendlines, etc. So, we set a degree and check to select all the options available for polynomial trendline. Click OK (Figure 7.100).

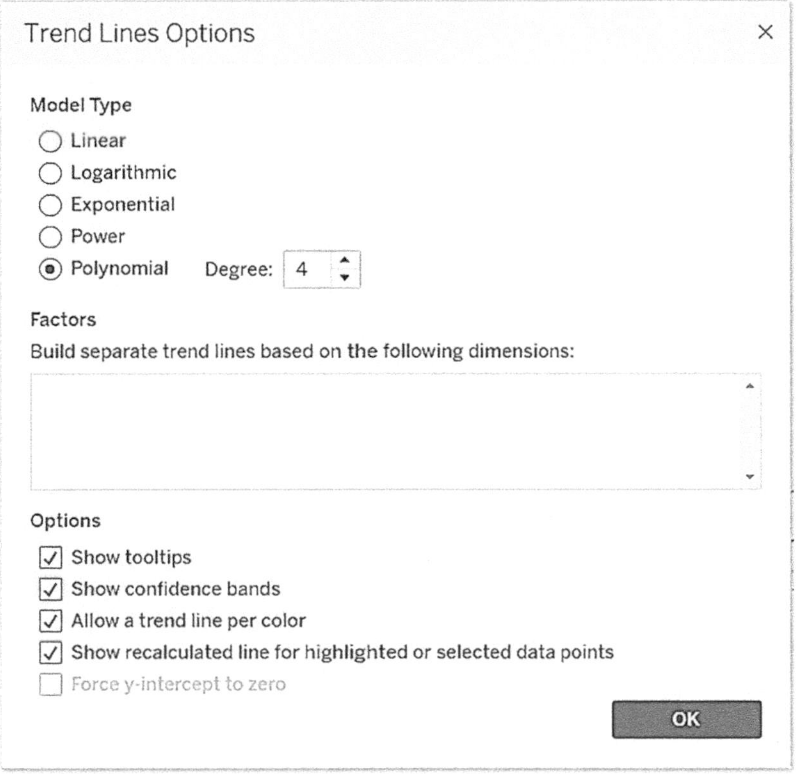

Trend Lines Options   ×

Model Type
○ Linear
○ Logarithmic
○ Exponential
○ Power
◉ Polynomial   Degree: 4 ⬦

Factors
Build separate trend lines based on the following dimensions:

Options
☑ Show tooltips
☑ Show confidence bands
☑ Allow a trend line per color
☑ Show recalculated line for highlighted or selected data points
☐ Force y-intercept to zero

OK

FIGURE 7.100   Output.

The following terms will help understanding the output clearly:
- **Tooltips:** These are simple descriptions about the trendline and related parameter values. It helps users to analyze the performance of trendline.
- **Confidence Bands:** Confidence bands are intervals used to compare estimates or measurements between groups or time periods. They indicate statistically significant differences between groups or time periods. Confidence intervals also assess the precision of estimates, with narrower widths indicating more accurate estimates, and broader bands indicating high inconsistency and less accuracy.

Step 6. The output of the configured trend line is as follows. It displays a trendline along with a confidence band (Figure 7.101).

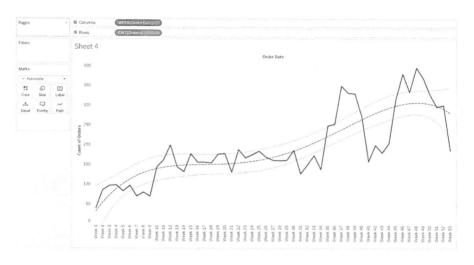

FIGURE 7.101 Output.

Step 7. To view category-wise trends, we need to slide and place the "Category" dimension to Rows bar and also on the Color under Marks card (Figure 7.102).

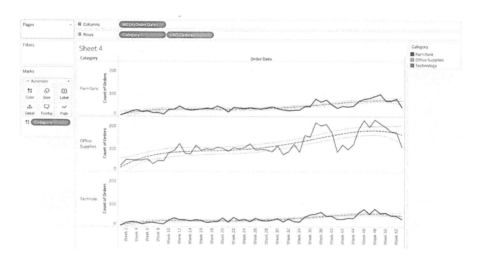

FIGURE 7.102 Output.

Step 8. Also, we can drag CNT (Orders) measure to Label under Marks card and select Min-Max marks to Label and Pane Scope to view the week having maximum and minimum order count per category. Add a suitable title to the sheet (Figure 7.103).

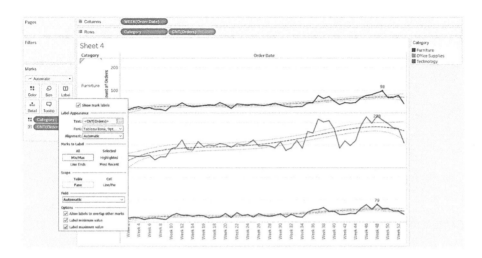

FIGURE 7.103   Output.

Step 9. To view the overall average count of orders per category with 95% CI (Confidence Interval) drag the Average with 95% CI under Model category in Analytics pane and drop it over option Pane as shown below (Figure 7.104).

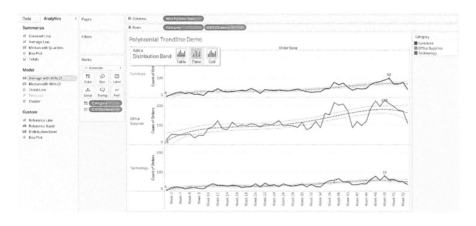

FIGURE 7.104   Output.

Step 10. The output is visible as below (Figure 7.105):.

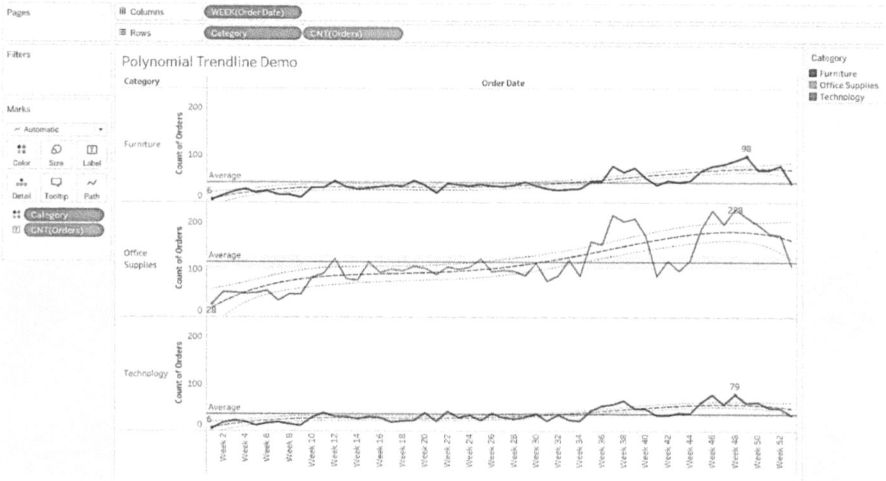

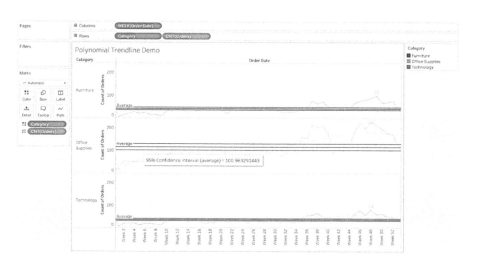

FIGURE 7.105   Output.

Step 11. In the figure, a gray area with the heading "Average" is visible. Clicking on this shaded area shows the Confidence Interval, a region where the average population will fall 95% of the time. The upper and lower lines represent the interval's upper and lower bounds, while the middle line displays the average order count (Figure 7.106).

FIGURE 7.106   Output.

Conclusion

- The dotted lines denote the confidence band surrounding the generated trendline and a shaded region displays the interval in which the typical or average population will be falling 95% of the time.
- The narrow width of the confidence interval for each category indicates more precision and much accurate estimates.
- Week 1 displays the lowest order count for all three product categories. Afterwards, we can visualize an increasing trend in the number of orders placed for each category.
- By week 48, the categories Office Supplies and Technology reach to their peak number of orders while the highest order count can be seen for Furniture category in week 49.

7.3.2 SIGNIFICANCE OF PLOTTED TREND LINE

The degree of goodness of fit of the model is generally evaluated when incorporating a trend line into a perspective, taking into account the importance of each contributing aspect as well as the accuracy of the predictions. The significance of the plotted trend line depends upon some of the critical factors such as p-value, R-squared statistic, and ANOVA table. These factors are described in detail below.

7.3.2.1 p-Value

The statistical significance of observational information is assessed using the p-value. It is always possible that a correlation between two factors that researchers find to be evident may just be a coincidence. One way to assess whether the observed association could be the product of chance is to compute the p-value. Consequently, p-values are important to consider when evaluating the relevance of the model. A model or factor is considered more significant the smaller its p-value (Figure 7.107).

Trend Lines Model

A linear trend model is computed for sum of Profit given Order Date Month. The model may be significant at $p \leq 0.05$. The factor Category may be significant at $p \leq 0.05$. The factor Region may be significant at $p \leq 0.05$.

Model formula:	Category*Region*(Month of Order Date + intercept)
Number of modeled observations:	144
Number of filtered observations:	0
Model degrees of freedom:	24
Residual degrees of freedom (DF):	120
SSE (sum squared error):	3.85351e+08
MSE (mean squared error):	3.21126e+06
R-Squared:	0.590198
Standard error:	1792
p-value (significance):	< 0.0001

FIGURE 7.107   Trend lines model.

P-value, which ranges from 0 to 1, is frequently used to indicate the degree of statistical significance. The "95% confidence" criteria, which states that a p-value ≤ 0.05 is regarded as good fit and is frequently used to determine significance (Figure 7.108).

P-value	Interpretation
P-value > 0.05	The result is not statistically significant. Do not reject the null hypothesis.
P-value < 0.05	The result is statistically significant and does not happen by chance or randomly.
P-value < 0.01	Result is highly statistically significant and not occurred randomly or by chance.

FIGURE 7.108   P-values with their interpretation.

A p-value of <0.05 indicates lesser than 5% chance of seeing extreme results randomly or by chance. A p-value of 0.0345 indicates a 3.45% chance of random results. A high p-value of .9 (90%) suggests that there is a 90% chance that the results are entirely random and unimportant. $P < 0.05$ indicates statistical significance, while $P < 0.001$ indicates highly significant, meaning there is less than a one in a thousand chance of being incorrect.

7.3.2.2   R-Squared Statistic

By expressing how well the data fits the linear model, the R-squared statistic evaluates a statistical model's predictive accuracy. It calculates the percentage of the outcome variable's variance that may be attributed to the forecasts. The fit is better when the R-squared value is nearer "1. " A "0" value indicates no fit, while a 1 value indicates a perfect fit, predicting 100% of the relationship dependent and independent variables. A 0.5 value indicates a 50% prediction.

7.3.2.3   Analysis of Variance

All fields used as factors in the model are listed in the "Analysis of Variance" table, also called the ANOVA table. The p-value is displayed meant for each field together with other values. In this instance, the p-value shows the extent to which that field raises the overall model's significance. A lesser p-value indicates a lesser possibility that the variation in the unexplained variance between models with or without the field may have occurred by chance (Figure 7.109).

Analysis of Variance:					
Field	DF	SSE	MSE	F	p-value
Category	16	3.1319579e+08	1.95747e+07	6.09566	< 0.0001
Region	18	2.6391894e+08	1.46622e+07	4.56586	< 0.0001

FIGURE 7.109   Analysis of variance.

The p-values for fields "Category" and "Region" are both rather minor, as one can notice. In this model, both components are statistically significant.

7.3.3 Forecast for Decision-Making

Using previous data as the main source of knowledge, forecasting is a technique for producing well-informed predictions about future events. Forecasting is a useful tool used by businesses for budget allocation and cost planning in the future. Forecasting algorithms look for a consistent pattern in measurements that they can use going forward. If a scenario has at least one measure and a date variable, we can add a forecast to it.

7.3.3.1 Case Study

Consider the Sample-Superstore data source. In this dataset we have historical data comprising of sales for the years 2019–2022. Based on this information suppose we want to forecast the category-wise sales for the upcoming year. We can do so by using the Forecast option given in analytics pane in Tableau and configure the generated forecast as per requirements. The steps for the same are given below:

Step 1. Place "Order-Date" dimension in columns box and right-click to alter Order-Date to Months detail instead of year detail which is set by default (Figure 7.110).

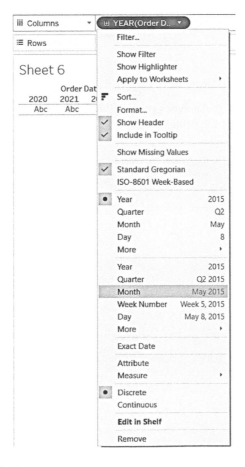

FIGURE 7.110 Output.

Step 2. Drag Sum (Sales) measure and Category dimension to Columns shelf. It will generate a time series chart for sales of each category. Also, drag Category to Color under Marks to generate line plots of different colors for each category (Figure 7.111).

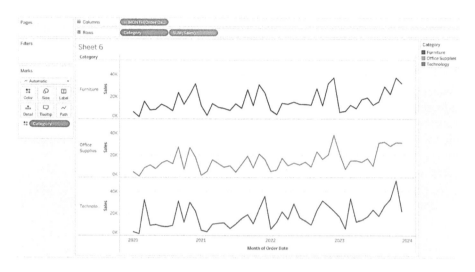

FIGURE 7.111   Output.

Step 3. Browse through Analytics pane and click on "Forecast" option to generate forecasts for future time period (Figure 7.112).

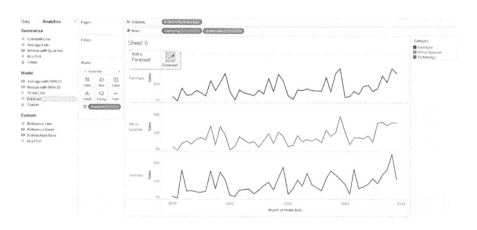

FIGURE 7.112   Output.

Step 4. The output generated is as follows (Figure 7.113).

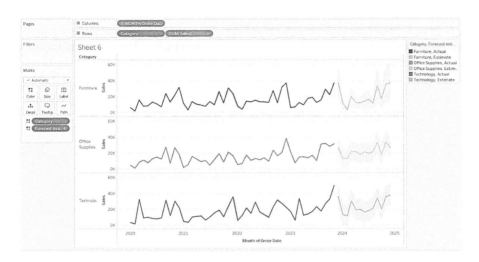

FIGURE 7.113   Output.

The screenshot above shows the projections for the upcoming months. The Estimate is shown as a shaded plot around the Actual forecast at the far right, while the Actual is shown as a dark line.

Step 5. Now we need to configure the generated forecasts. For this either click on Analysis menu -> then click Forecast -> select Forecast options. As an alternate way, right-click on any shaded Forecast area generated -> click Forecast -> select Forecast Options (Figure 7.114).

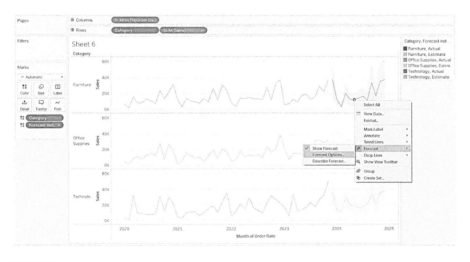

FIGURE 7.114   Output.

Step 6. The value is set to 2 for the next two years once we choose the "Exactly" option in this case. Additionally, look at the "Aggregate by" option, which is followed by a drop-down selection. Years, Quarters, Months, Weeks, Days, Hours, Minutes, and Seconds are among the aggregate metrics that we can use. The Order-Date format is used to pick Automatic (Months) by default (Figure 7.115).

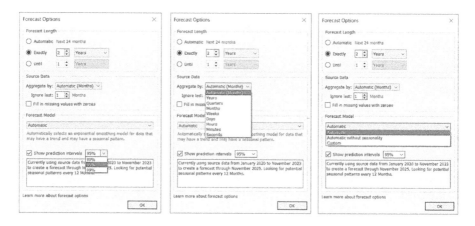

FIGURE 7.115 Output.

Step 7. The "Forecast Model" panel appears in the screenshot above. Three options are available: Automatic, Automatic with Seasonality, and Custom. Take note of what each option does:
- When using the Automatic option, Tableau chooses the best model by itself, taking trend and seasonality components into account.
- Although the Seasonality component may exist in the time series, it is disregarded in the "Automatic without Seasonality" option. It could provide false results.
- The user can choose the Trend and Seasonality components using the custom option.

Step 8. Let us first select the option "Automatic without Seasonality" in Forecast Model section and analyze the output (Figure 7.116).

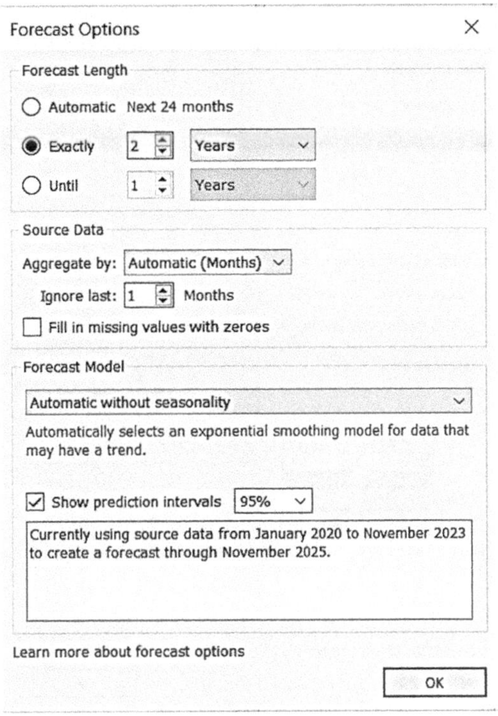

FIGURE 7.116   Output.

The forecast becomes incorrectly constant when we choose the "Automatic without seasonality" option, as can be seen in the screenshot above. Since we consciously choose to overlook the seasonality component, it exists in the time series. This forecast model is therefore inappropriate in this circumstance.

Step 9. As an upgrade, we select the Forecast Model section's Custom option, which gives us the ability to enter the "Trend" and "Season" parameters as desired (Figure 7.117).

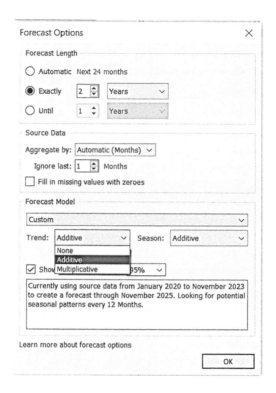

The time series has a constantly moving trend with constant peaks and amplitude of the seasonality component. It is likely an additive time series, summating components over time. The output matches the Tableau generated with the default "Automatic" option. To match the output, we select "Additive" for both Trend and Season sections in the "Additive" section (Figure 7.118).

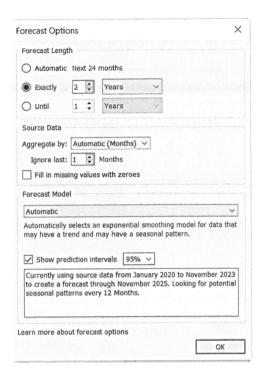

FIGURE 7.118 Output.

Step 10. In Forecast options, we also see a checkbox for prediction intervals along with a drop-down box with 90%, 95%, and 99% values. It refers to the percentage of confidence users require the algorithm to regulate the forecast values. Default interval is 95%.

Step 11. Now to understand the results click on Analysis Menu -> click on Forecast -> select "Describe Forecast" option. The summary tab is open and illustrates that the Quality of the model is "Good" for Category "Furniture" and "Ok" for others (Figure 7.119).

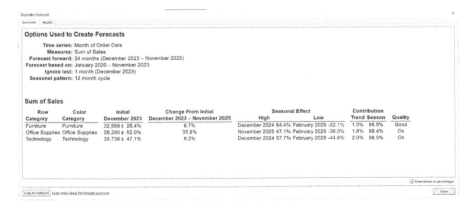

FIGURE 7.119 Output.

Step 12. For further information on the different technical aspects of the mathematical model, visit the "Model" tab (Figure 7.120).

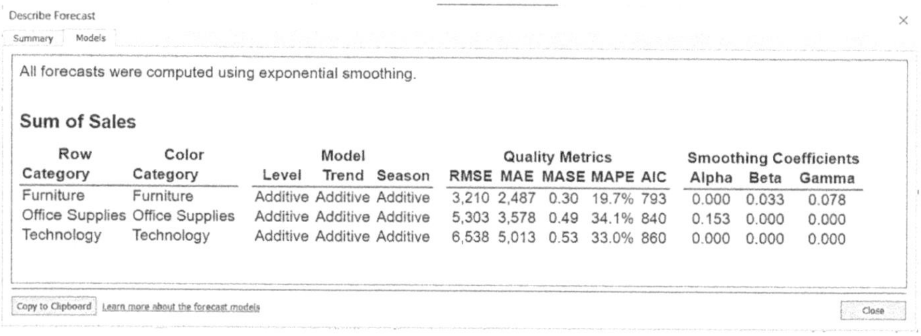

Describe Forecast

Summary   Models

All forecasts were computed using exponential smoothing.

Sum of Sales

Row Category	Color Category	Model			Quality Metrics					Smoothing Coefficients		
		Level	Trend	Season	RMSE	MAE	MASE	MAPE	AIC	Alpha	Beta	Gamma
Furniture	Furniture	Additive	Additive	Additive	3,210	2,487	0.30	19.7%	793	0.000	0.033	0.078
Office Supplies	Office Supplies	Additive	Additive	Additive	5,303	3,578	0.49	34.1%	840	0.153	0.000	0.000
Technology	Technology	Additive	Additive	Additive	6,538	5,013	0.53	33.0%	860	0.000	0.000	0.000

Copy to Clipboard   Learn more about the forecast models   Close

FIGURE 7.120   Output.

The smoothing coefficients for levels, trends, and seasons are alpha, beta, and gamma, respectively. Rapid component changes and a strong reliance on current data are made possible by decreasing leveling or approximations as a smoothing coefficient approaches 1.00.

7.4   STATISTICAL MODELS FOR TREND ANALYSIS

There is no one formula for trend analysis, as the specific methods used to analyze trends can vary depending on the data being analyzed and the goals of the analysis. However, there are several statistical measures that are commonly used in trend analysis to identify patterns and trends in data. Here are a few examples of statistical measures that might be used in trend analysis:

1. **Moving Averages:** A moving average is a statistical measure that is used to smooth out fluctuations in data over time. It is also known as moving mean or rolling mean. A simple moving average (SMA) is calculated by taking the average of a set of data points over a given period, such as the past 10 days or the past 50 weeks. Moving averages can be used in time series to identify trends by smoothing out short-term fluctuations in data and highlighting longer-term patterns.
2. **Linear Regression:** Linear regression is a statistical method that is used to model the relationship between two variables. It can be used to identify trends by fitting a line to the data and determining the slope of the line, which can indicate the direction and strength of the trend.
3. **Correlation:** Correlation is a statistical measure that indicates the strength and direction of the relationship between two variables. A positive correlation means that the variables are moving in the same direction, while a negative correlation means that they are moving in opposite directions. Correlation can be used to identify trends by analyzing the relationship between two variables over time.

In this section, we will discuss about creating moving averages for a dataset for the purpose of trend analysis. The other two measures Regression and Correlation will be discussed in the next chapter.

7.4.1 CASE STUDY FOR CREATING MOVING AVERAGE TREND

We might find it interesting to examine the general trend of sales for the year 2022 using the Superstores dataset. It is challenging to determine the trend of overall data without using moving average. We can create a dual chart for the case, with one line chart computing the moving average and the second line chart returning the aggregates of each data point. Using the moving average makes the trend of this data much more obvious than it would be when utilizing aggregated data points especially when working with large numbers of data points. The steps are given below:

Step 1. Drag dimension Order-Date to the Columns shelf and SUM(Sales) measure to the rows shelf. In this case have filtered data to show sales only for the year 2022 (Figure 7.121).

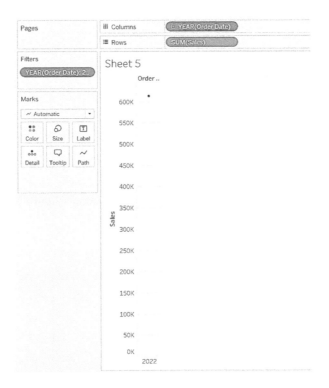

FIGURE 7.121   Output.

Step 2. Click the Order-Date to the Columns shelf and set it as a continuous field showing Exact Date checkmark (Figure 7.122).

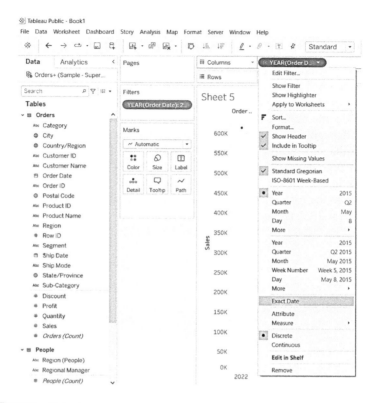

FIGURE 7.122   Output.

Step 3. The output for the date wise is displayed as below (Figure 7.123).

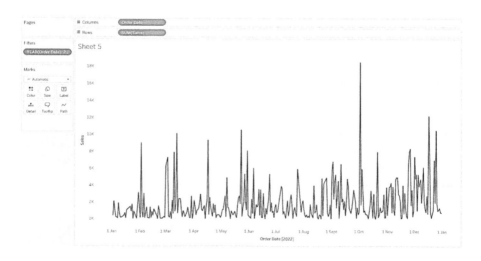

FIGURE 7.123   Output.

Step 4. Now Right-click on the dimension SUM(Sales) to open a list of options available. Click on Quick Table Calculation and select Moving Average (Figure 7.124).

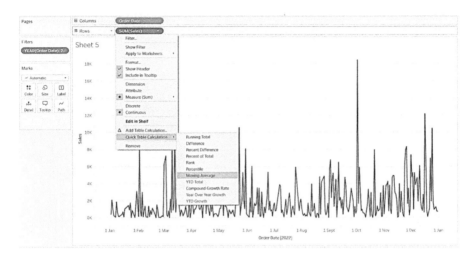

FIGURE 7.124 Output.

Step 5. Please note that by default, Tableau computed the moving average using the previous two data points only. However, we can customize our computation to set the number of data points as per requirement. For this Right-click on the dimension SUM(Sales) and select Edit Table Calculation (Figure 7.125).

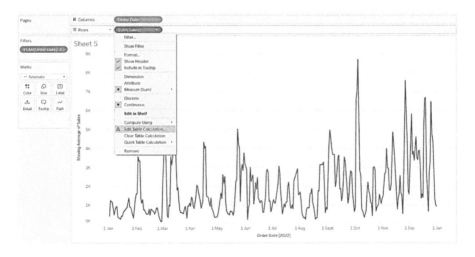

FIGURE 7.125 Output.

Step 6. In the Table calculation dialog box, click the drop-down for Average and set the number of previous values to 30 instead of 2. Make sure Moving Calculation is selected in Calculation type and Current value checkbox is checked (Figure 7.126).

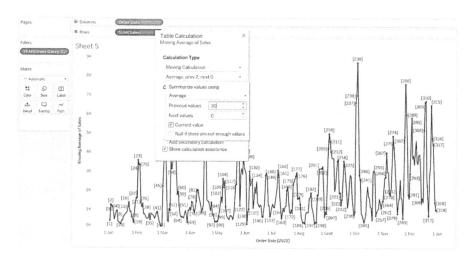

FIGURE 7.126   Output.

Step 7. The output for moving average for previous 30 data values is given below (Figure 7.127).

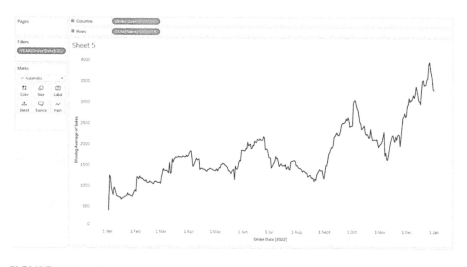

FIGURE 7.127   Output.

Step 8. Drag Sum (Sales) measure to Rows shelf to create a line chart for Sales of 2022 (Figure 7.128).

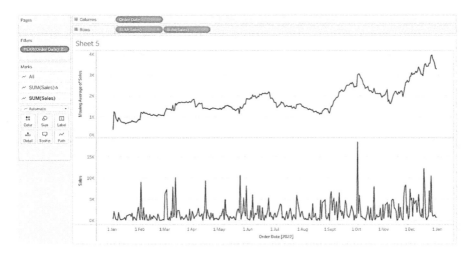

FIGURE 7.128   Output.

Step 9. Under the Marks card we can observe the two headings for Sum (Sales). The first heading for Sum (Sales) with a triangle symbol Δ denotes the quick calculation for moving average trendline while the second Sum (Sales) denotes the sales line chart for the year 2022. We can set the color of the line plot by selecting the Color under option under the desired Sum(Sales) heading (Figure 7.129).

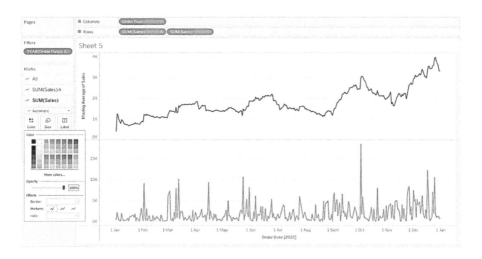

FIGURE 7.129   Output.

Step 10. Now drag the Sales axis and take it to the right of the Moving Average axis to combine both the charts together (Figure 7.130).

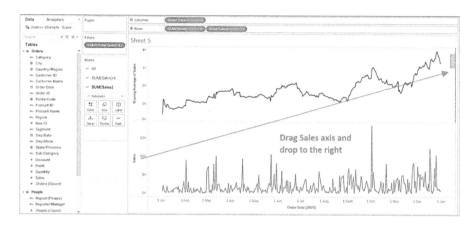

FIGURE 7.130   Output.

The output will be as follows (Figure 7.131).

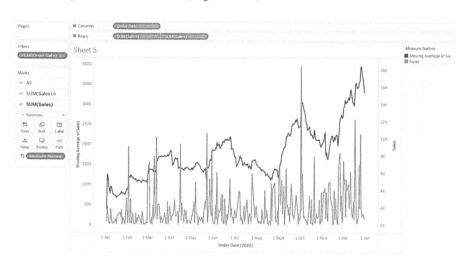

FIGURE 7.131   Output.

Step 11. We can observe that both Moving Average and Sales axis are parallel to each other but the scale of both axis is different. So, we need to synchronize both the axis. For this right-click the Sales axis on the right and select the option to Synchronize Axis (Figure 7.132).

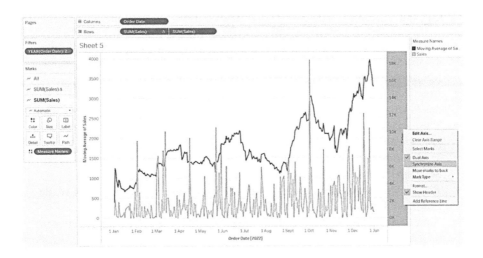

FIGURE 7.132   Output.

Step 12. Now we can observe both Moving Average and Sales axis in sync with each other and display a common scale for comparison (Figure 7.133).

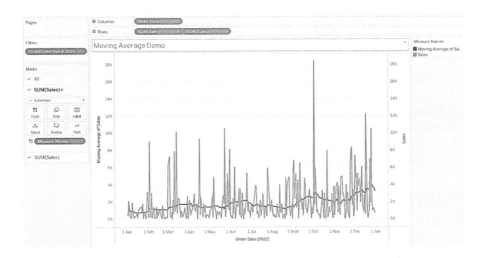

FIGURE 7.133   Output.

Step 13. In the above figure we can analyze the two line plots together. The orange color line plot denotes the overall Sales while the blue line denotes the moving average of sales for the year 2022.

KEY NOTES

- Comparison charts are useful tools for comparing the performance of critical metrics in data. They include text tables, bar charts, column charts, lollipop charts, line charts, and time series and trendlines.
- Line charts, also acknowledged as line graphs or plots, use sequential values to identify trends and forecast future values for better decision-making.
- Time series analysis is a method of in-depth examination of time series data points gathered over a period.
- Time series components are divided into four groups: trend, seasonal variations, and cyclic variations.
- These charts help users identify trends, forecast future values, and make informed decisions based on the data.
- Time series analysis is crucial for understanding the relationship between data and trends.

PRACTICE CASE STUDY

Stock Prices Analysis Dashboard

Users can use NIFTY-50 Stock Market Data (2000–2021) dataset present on Kaggle data repository in public domain. You may use any of the stocks data to compare their values and plot trends for the same. Also, plot forecast for the trends generated. Find the significance of trendlines and trend model.

TEST YOUR SKILLS

1. Discuss the major types of comparison charts in Tableau.
2. Elaborate upon the advantages and shortcomings of comparison charts.
3. Discuss various types of trend lines supported in Tableau.
4. Define time series. Discuss the different components of time series.
5. What are the different statistical models for trend analysis.
6. Differentiate between seasonality and cyclic variations.

REFERENCES

[1] Meier, Marleen. *Mastering Tableau 2023: Implement Advanced Business Intelligence Techniques, Analytics, and Machine Learning Models with Tableau*. United Kingdom, Packt Publishing, 2023.
[2] Munroe, Kirk. *Data Modeling with Tableau: A Practical Guide to Building Data Models Using Tableau Prep and Tableau Desktop*. United Kingdom, Packt Publishing, 2022.
[3] Hwang, Jaejin, and Yoon, Youngjin. *Data Analytics and Visualization in Quality Analysis Using Tableau*. United Kingdom, CRC Press, 2021.
[4] Sarsfield, Patrick, et al. *Maximizing Tableau Server: A Beginner's Guide to Accessing, Sharing, and Managing Content on Tableau Server*. United Kingdom, Packt Publishing, 2021.

[5] Sleeper, Ryan. *Innovative Tableau: 100 More Tips, Tutorials, and Strategies.* United States, O'Reilly Media, 2020.

[6] Milligan, Joshua N.. *Learning Tableau 2019: Tools for Business Intelligence, Data Prep, and Visual Analytics*, 3rd Edition. India, Packt Publishing, 2019.

[7] Loth, Alexander. *Visual Analytics with Tableau.* United States, Wiley, 2019.

[8] Sleeper, Ryan. *Practical Tableau: 100 Tips, Tutorials, and Strategies from a Tableau Zen Master.* United States, O'Reilly Media, 2018.

8 Distribution Charts in Tableau

8.1 INTRODUCTION TO DISTRIBUTION CHARTS

Business scenarios often use average values, such as daily sales, revenue, and sales comparisons, to provide essential information. However, these general queries may overlook other interesting insights and facts in the data. A distribution chart helps visualize data distribution across a range of values, rather than combining them into an average value [1]. This approach allows for a deeper understanding of the data and its distribution across different values, allowing for more insightful exploration. Consider a group of school students among whom we want to choose players for our basketball team. We analyze that the average height of students is 5'4. Apart from this general information, we come across a particular student whose height is 6'6. This is an exceptional yet interesting case because he can serve as the game starter in the team. All we need to do is pass him the ball and no one else will be able to touch it easily! For such scenarios, a distribution enables us to analyze how various students are dispersed into each height range so that any outliers or exceptions can be visualized in the chart. Tableau supports various distribution charts for fast and smart data analysis. It not only helps in finding better insights from data but also enables users to reach the underlying root causes quickly [2]. A list of distribution charts is given below:

- Histogram
- Scatter plot
- Bubble chart
- Radar chart
- Heat map
- Box plot

8.2 HISTOGRAM WITH ITS TYPES AND COMPONENTS

A histogram is an illustration that demonstrates the values of a numerical variable's distribution as a collection of bars [3,4]. Each bar usually represents a class or bin, which represents a range of numerical values; the height of a bar shows how frequently a given value appears in each bin.

Histogram chart symbol ▁▃▅ in "Show Me" in Tableau. A histogram chart's structure can be understood by looking at the graphic below, which shows the distribution of students' overall marks for a particular subject (Figure 8.1).

 DOI: 10.1201/9781003429593-8

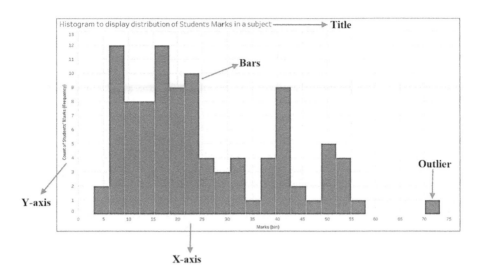

FIGURE 8.1   Illustration of histogram.

Take a close look at the graph's x-axis, which represents the "Marks (bin)" and provides the uniformly sized ranges needed to make a histogram. The frequency or count of occurrences of values inside the bin range is shown by the y-axis. The vertical bars show how many student records fall within each of these ranges. A histogram's bars do not have any space between them, as you can see. Let us take a closer look at the composition of a simple histogram.

8.2.1   STRUCTURE OF HISTOGRAM

- **Caption (Title):** The caption, which condenses all of the data displayed in the histogram into a few words, is the most significant component.
- **Horizontal Axis at Bottom (i.e., x-axis):** The horizontal axis, often known as the x-axis, in a histogram denotes the data categories or bins that the data points have been classified into.
- **Longitudinal or Vertical (i.e., y-axis):** In contrast, the vertical axis (y-axis) represents the frequency with which data points fall into each bin or category. Each bar's height represents the occurrence frequency of all observations that fit into each bin.
- **Plotted Bars:** The data's value is displayed using the bars. Additionally, the height of the bar can be used to calculate the total number of times the values happened inside the interval, while the width of the bar specifies the interval it covers.

8.2.2   CHARACTERISTICS OF HISTOGRAMS

A histogram possesses certain characteristics that must be observed for better data analysis and help to gather more insights from it. These characteristics are discussed below:

A. Shape

Essential information about the characteristics of the data distribution can be obtained from a histogram's shape. This form might be symmetric, tilted to the left or right, unimodal (one peak), bimodal (two peaks), or multimodal (several peaks). The various types of histograms according to their shape are described as follows:

1. Symmetrical Histograms

A symmetrical distribution, also known as a bell-shaped histogram, is a normal distribution with a center (mean) and evenly distributed data points. As the value moves toward the sides from the center, it appears to decrease. The left and right sides of a symmetrical histogram resemble mirror images of each other (Figure 8.2).

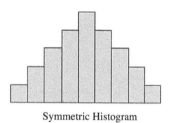

Symmetric Histogram

FIGURE 8.2   Illustration of symmetric histogram.

2. Skewed or Tilted Histograms

The data points in a skewed histogram tend to tilt more to one side. A histogram is referred to as "right-skewed" if there is a "tail" on the right side of the distribution. This type of distribution is sometimes referred to as "Positively" skewed. A histogram is referred to as "left-skewed" if there is a "tail" on the left side of the "distribution." This kind of dispersion is often referred to be "Negatively" skewed at times (Figure 8.3).

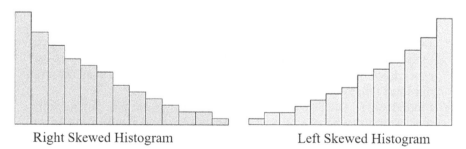

Right Skewed Histogram   Left Skewed Histogram

FIGURE 8.3   Illustration of skewed histograms.

3. Histograms That Have Unimodal, Bimodal, and Multimodal Peaks

A single, noticeable peak, or most common observation, characterizes a unimodal histogram. Yet, multimodal histograms have numerous peaks, and bimodal histograms have two different peaks, signifying two frequent observations (Figure 8.4).

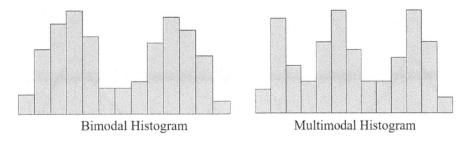

FIGURE 8.4 Illustration of bimodal and multimodal histograms.

4. Uniform Histogram

A histogram is deemed "uniform" if every data point in a dataset appears about equal amounts of times. This kind of histogram frequently has a lot of rectangular bars with no visible peaks (Figure 8.5).

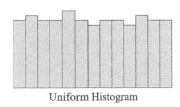

FIGURE 8.5 Illustration of uniform histogram.

5. Random Histogram

If there is absolutely no recognizable pattern in the data, the form of a distribution can be characterized as "random" (Figure 8.6).

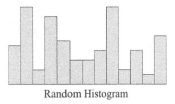

FIGURE 8.6 Illustration of random histogram.

B. Center of Histogram

The median of the dataset, which divides it into two equal halves, is the center point of a histogram. While the mean and median in a skewed distribution are different, they are the same in a symmetric distribution. To determine the predicted "typical" value or general trend from the data, center analysis is essential (Figure 8.7).

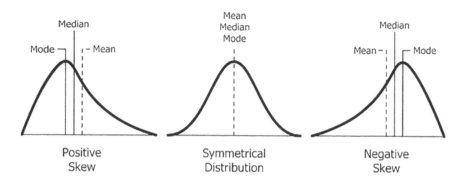

FIGURE 8.7   Mean, median, and mode in histograms.

C. Width of the Bars Represent Class Intervals

The spread in a histogram refers to the data's distribution, encompassing factors like the interquartile range, which represents the middle 50% of the data, the range (the difference between the highest and lowest data points), and the standard deviation (the degree of deviation from the mean) (Figure 8.8).

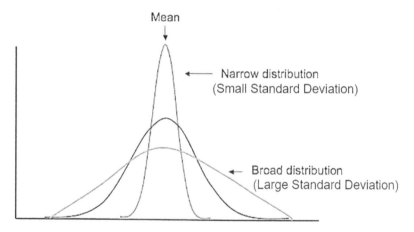

FIGURE 8.8   Demonstrating data distributions in histogram.

- **D. Frequency:** A bar's height in a histogram indicates the frequency.
- **E. Gap between Bars:** Because a histogram is meant to illustrate continuous data within a category range, it does not have a space or gap between any two bars.
- **F. No Reorder Allowed:** The plotted bars are rigid and cannot be rearranged.
- **G. Zero-Valued Baseline:** Plotting histograms requires the use of a zero-valued baseline, which is a crucial component.

H. Choosing Number of Bins: The selection of bin size is inversely related to the number of bins. Larger bin sizes require fewer bins to cover the entire data range, while smaller bin sizes require more. It is recommended to test different bin sizes to observe the distribution and select the plot that best represents the data (Figure 8.9).

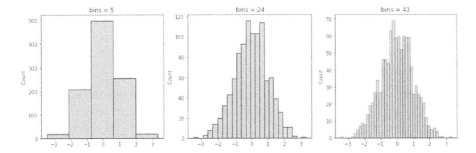

FIGURE 8.9 Illustration of histogram with different bin numbers.

Bins should contain all data, including outliers. Select from 5 to 20 bins; additional bins are needed for larger datasets. Although the number of bins is up to the user, the dataset should be evenly divisible by the number of bins. Let's say you have ten different data points, use five bins instead of six or seven.

I. Unequal Bin Sizes: Histograms typically have equal bin sizes. However, this is not a rigid requirement. Combining bins can lead to mismatched bin sizes in sparse datasets, which complicates interpretation. A histogram's total area denotes the entirety of the data, whereas each bar denotes a component of the data. The vertical axis encodes the frequency as density per unit of bin size when bin sizes become uneven, however this is difficult to understand. Therefore, it is better to have completely equal bin sizes in a histogram (Figure 8.10).

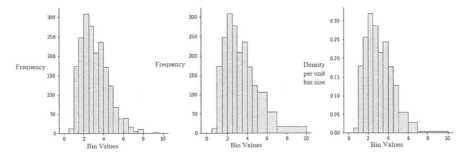

FIGURE 8.10 Illustration of histograms with unequal bin sizes.

Three histograms are displayed in the figure: one is with equal bins, one has unequal bins but incorrect vertical axis units, and one uses density heights in the y-axis rather than frequency.

J. Outliers: Outliers are extreme values that do not fit with other data points, often representing unusual cases or data entry errors. They can be easily identified using a histogram and should be investigated as they can provide valuable insights into the data. We can observe presence of outlier in Figure 8.1.

8.2.3 CASE STUDY

Consider the Sample-Superstore data source. Here we try to analyze the distribution of quantity (i.e., count of orders) placed overall. We also want to observe whether customer segment displays any trend as the number of items in an order increase. This will help to understand the impact of the customer segment on the quantity of orders placed. The steps are given below:

Step 1. Open a new worksheet and connect to the Sample-Superstore data source.

Step 2. To choose the type of histogram chart, drag Quantity to Columns and click Show Me on the toolbar. Please be aware that when a view has just one measure and no dimensions, Show Me can display the histogram chart type (Figure 8.11).

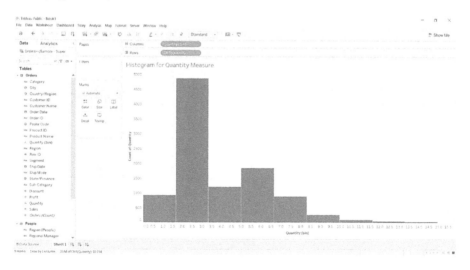

FIGURE 8.11 Output.

Following changes occur once we click the histogram icon in Show Me:
- The perspective shifts to reveal vertical bars with a continuous y-axis (0–5,000) and continuous x-axis (0.0–15.5).

- A continuous quantity (bin) dimension has been added to the Columns shelf in place of the quantity measure that you previously placed there and aggregated as SUM. (The field on the Columns shelf is continuous; this is indicated by its green color.)
- The aggregate shifts from SUM to CNT (Count), and the quantity measure goes to the Rows shelf.

Step 3. Right-click the bin in the Data pane and choose Edit to make changes to it (Figure 8.12).

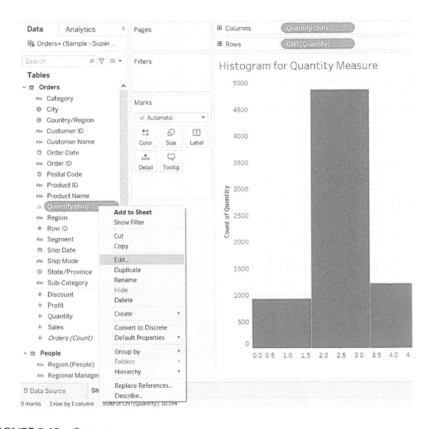

FIGURE 8.12 Output.

Step 4. In the Edit Bins dialog box, we set the bin size to 2 to view a better histogram (Figure 8.13).

Edit Bins [Quantity]   ✕

New field name: Quantity (bin)

Size of bins: 2   ⌄   Suggest Bin Size

Range of Values:

Min: 1   Diff: 13

Max: 14   CntD: 16

OK   Cancel

FIGURE 8.13   Output.

Step 5. The updated histogram is displayed in Figure 8.14.

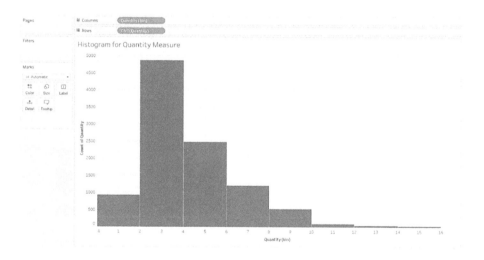

FIGURE 8.14   Output.

Conclusion:
- The quantity measure records how many things there are in a specific arrangement. According to the histogram, around 2,400 orders had four things (the third bar), roughly 4,800 orders had two items (the second bar), and so on.

Step 6. To see whether we can find a correlation between the client segment (consumer, business, or home office) and the number of goods per order, we now take this view a step further and add Segment to Color.

Step 7. To see colored segments within each bar, drag the Segment dimension from the data pane to Color under the Marks card. Next, move the CNT(Quantity) field from the Rows shelf to Label while holding down the Ctrl key. The field is copied to the new position while the Ctrl key presses down, leaving the original location unaltered (Figure 8.15).

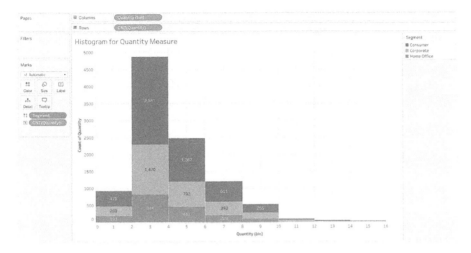

FIGURE 8.15 Output.

Step 8. There isn't a noticeable trend in the colors. Now let's see what percentage of each bar belongs to a specific sector. To accomplish this, right-click the CNT(Quantity) box on the Marks card, select Quick Table Calculation, and then select Percent of Total (Figure 8.16).

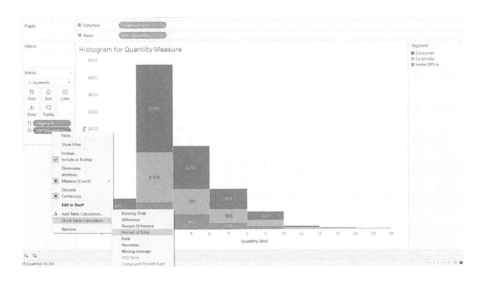

FIGURE 8.16 Output.

Step 9. The colored sections of each bar in the diagram below indicate the corresponding proportion of the overall quantity. But we need the percentages to be on a per-bar basis in order to comply with the criteria (Figure 8.17).

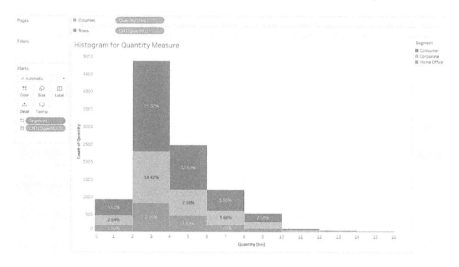

FIGURE 8.17   Output.

Step 10. To do this, right-click the Marks card's CNT(Quantity) field once more, and then choose Edit Table Calculation. Set the Compute Using field's value to Cell in the Table Calculation dialogue box (Figure 8.18).

Table Calculation   ✕
% of Total Count of Quantity

Calculation Type

Percent of Total   ▾

☐ Compute total across all pages

Compute Using

Table (across)
Table (down)
Table
Cell
Specific Dimensions

☑ Segment
☐ Quantity (bin)

At the level

☑ Show calculation assistance

FIGURE 8.18   Output.

Step 11. The output is as follows (Figure 8.19).

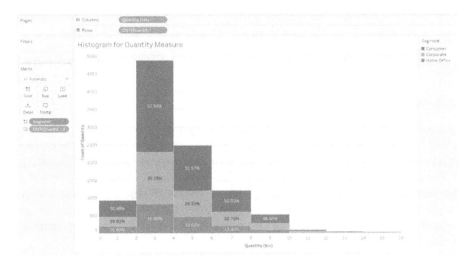

FIGURE 8.19 Output.

Conclusion:
- As the number of items in an order increases, there is still no indication that the percentages by client segment indicate any trend.

8.3 SCATTER PLOT AND MATRIX

Scatter plot, sometimes called scatter chart, is a data visualization technique that shows values for two distinct numerical variables as points or dots [5,6]. The coordinate position of each data point indicates the values corresponding to the measures represented, and it displays data points at the intersection of two measures. Users can visualize data using Cartesian coordinates and examine correlations between variables with the aid of scatter plots. To show the relationship between pairs of variables in a single chart, the independent variable is represented by the x-axis and the dependent variable by the y-axis.

8.3.1 INTERPRETING SCATTER PLOTS

A scatter plot is a visual representation of data, examining the overall pattern and identifying deviations. The pattern can be described by its type, direction, shape, and strength. An outlier point is a significant deviation from the overall pattern, an individual value that stands out from the relationship between variables. Let us discuss the various factors that help to interpret a scatter plot.

8.3.2   Type and Strength of Correlation in Scatter Plot

Correlational studies are common research projects that examine the relationships between variables. To identify correlations, graphical representations like scatter plots are used. These plots show how variations in the independent variable affect the dependent variable, and it's crucial to introduce the term "correlation" in this context.

8.3.3   Calculate Correlation in Scatter Plot

A statistical tool for determining how much two or more variables vary from one another or affect one another is a correlation. The linear relationship between two continuous, quantitative variables is measured by Pearson's correlation coefficient, or "r." The following is the formula for *Pearson's Correlation Coefficient* (Figure 8.20). The value of "r" is a number between −1 and +1, where "0" denotes no relationship. In a positive relationship, the value of one variable raises the value of another; in a negative relationship, the value of one variable decreases the value of another. A value larger than "0" denotes this relationship.

Formula >

$$r = \frac{\sum (x_i - \bar{x})(y_i - \bar{y})}{\sqrt{\sum (x_i - \bar{x})^2 \sum (y_i - \bar{y})^2}}$$

r = correlation coefficient

x_i = values of the x-variable in a sample

$\bar{x}$ = mean of the values of the x-variable

y_i = values of the y-variable in a sample

$\bar{y}$ = mean of the values of the y-variable

FIGURE 8.20   Pearson's correlation coefficient.

8.3.4   Strength of Correlational Relationship

The stronger the correlation or relationship between the two variables, the closer the points are to each other in the cluster. The graph below provides a deeper knowledge of correlation coefficients in scatter plots (Figure 8.21).

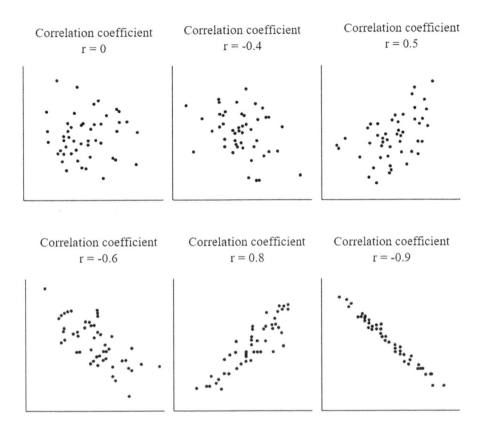

FIGURE 8.21 Scatter plots with correlation coefficients.

Generally, the following rules listed in the table below help in deciding the strength of correlation (Figure 8.22):

Positive and Negative range of Pearson's Correlation Coefficient 'r'	Strength of Correlation
0.1 to 0.3 and -0.1 to -0.3	None or very weak Correlation
0.3 to 0.5 and -0.3 to -0.5	Weak Correlation
0.5 to 0.7 and -0.5 to -0.7	Moderate Correlation
0.7 to 1.0 and -0.7 to -1.0	Strong Correlation
1	Perfect Positive Correlation
-1	Perfect Negative Correlation
0	No Linear Correlation

FIGURE 8.22 Strength of correlation with range values.

When the r-value of a pair of variables is more than 0.7 and approaching 1, it is generally regarded as a strong association.

8.3.5 SHAPE FOLLOWED IN CORRELATIONAL RELATIONSHIP

The contour or shape of the correlation between the two variables is a crucial aspect of a scatter plot (Figure 8.23).

FIGURE 8.23   Shape of scatter plot and correlational relationships.

In general, the three types of patterns created in correlational relationships are as follows:

1. **Linear Correlation:** When one variable grows or decreases at roughly the same pace as the other variables change by one unit, it indicates a linear correlation between the two variables.
2. **Non-Linear or Curvilinear Correlation:** A curvilinear association is said to resemble an inverted U when represented graphically. Because variables with curved relationships are not properly captured by "r," the observed correlation for curvilinear relationships is considered to be close to 0, as the Pearson correlation coefficient only captures linear correlations.
3. **Independent or No Pattern:** Sometimes a scatter plot may demonstrate a relationship without any pattern, i.e., neither linear nor curved shape is formed. Such scatter plots display null correlation.

8.3.6 TRENDLINE, CLUSTERS AND OUTLIERS IN SCATTER PLOT

An illustration of data points connecting two variables is called a scatter plot. It is helpful for determining a relationship between variables that can be applied to forecast future events [7]. On the scatter plot, every item of data is represented by a single, disconnected point (Figure 8.24).

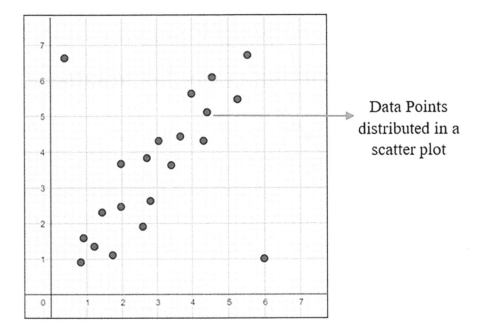

FIGURE 8.24 Data points in scatter plot.

A trend line is a line-of-best fit that accurately describes the data pattern on a scatterplot to estimate unknown outputs for given inputs. It may pass through some points but not all, with about half of the points on either side. The trend line can show a positive or negative trend. However, no trend line can be adequately drawn if there is no relationship. Outliers are usually overlooked or ignored when a trend line is drawn, as shown in Figure 8.25.

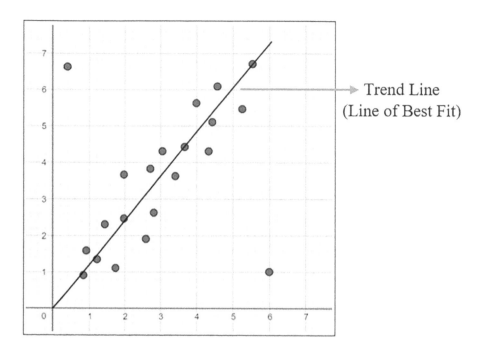

FIGURE 8.25   Trendline in scatter plot.

A scatter plot consists of a cluster of points that follow a general pattern, such as linear or curved. These clusters can contain multiple points. A data point that is outside of the cluster and either too high or too low to fit the pattern is called an outlier. Outliers are points that are zero, one, or more in number that are found in the data and shown on a scatter plot (Figure 8.26).

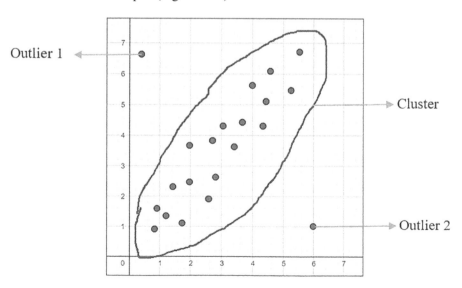

FIGURE 8.26   Outliers in scatter plot.

8.3.7   CASE STUDY

Consider the Sample-Superstore data source. Suppose this time we are supposed to analyze and observe the region-wise sales and profit distribution for each category of products. Also, we want to plot the trendlines for sales of each category and draw insights from the plotted graph. After this we also want to plot reference lines to view the performance of sales and profit values of each data point against the maximum average sales and profit values.

Step 1. Open a new worksheet and the Sample-Superstore data source to create the desired graphic.

Step 2. Move the Profit metric to Columns. Tableau generates a horizontal axis by adding together the measures. Drag the Sales measure to Rows in a similar manner. Additionally, Tableau adds a vertical axis by adding the measure to a sum (Figure 8.27).

FIGURE 8.27   Output.

Continuous numerical data can be used as measurements. Plotting two integers against each other compares them; the resulting chart has x and y coordinates, just like a Cartesian chart. As in the figure above, we now have a one-mark scatter plot.

Step 3. Drag the "Category" dimension of the Marks card to Color. The data is separated into three marks, one for each dimension member, in order to color-encode the markings. The figure below shows three markings. The position of each brand in each category corresponds to the associated sales and profit (Figure 8.28).

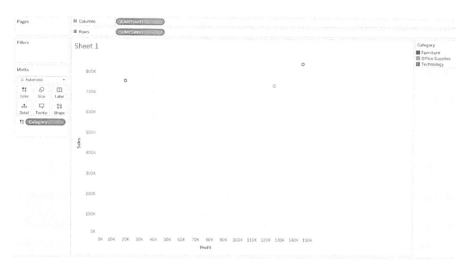

FIGURE 8.28   Output.

Step 4. Within the Marks card, place the "Region" dimension to Detail. There are a lot more marks visible now. The number of marks is determined by multiplying the number of categories (3) by the number of unique regions (4) in the data source. There are 12 points in the scatter plot, all of which are in the standard circle form. Every plotted mark represents a client in a certain area to whom a product of any kind was supplied (Figure 8.29).

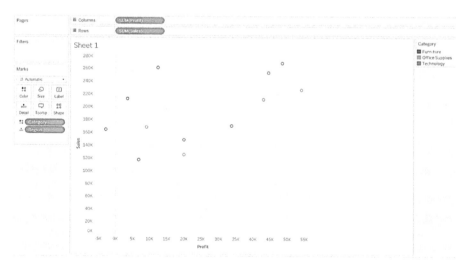

FIGURE 8.29   Output.

Step 5. Within the Marks card, drag the "Region" to Shape detail once more. We can now see that the scatter points have a different form. Each point shows a shape associated with a certain "Region" (Figure 8.30).

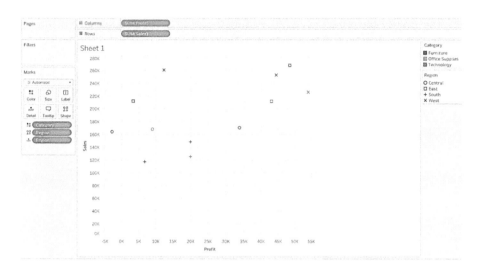

FIGURE 8.30 Output.

Step 6. To add trend lines, choose the "Trend Line" model from the Analytics pane to the display and drop it onto the appropriate model type. A trend line can provide a statistical representation of the relationship between two numerical values (Figure 8.31).

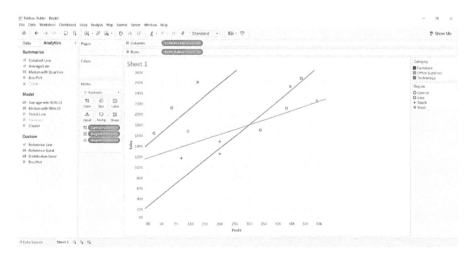

FIGURE 8.31 Output.

To add trend lines to a view, both axes need to contain a field that can be read as a numerical value. For each hue, Tableau inserts three linear trend lines to help differentiate the three categories.

Step 7. The scatter plot that displays here is still the one that plots just the combined sales and profit figures. Dissecting the measurements and charting the data points associated with each sale alongside the profit data record, however, might be fascinating. To do this, select the Analysis menu and click to deselect the Aggregate option, which is selected by default (Figure 8.32).

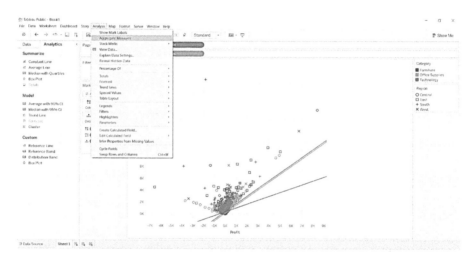

FIGURE 8.32   Output.

Step 8. The segmented scatter plot now has many data points. Furthermore, noted is the fact that the Profit and Sales measurements found on the Columns and Rows shelf are no longer combined by Sum. Additionally, statistical details regarding the model that was used to construct the line are displayed when we move the mouse pointer over the trend lines. Every category exhibits an upward trend that we can see (Figure 8.33).

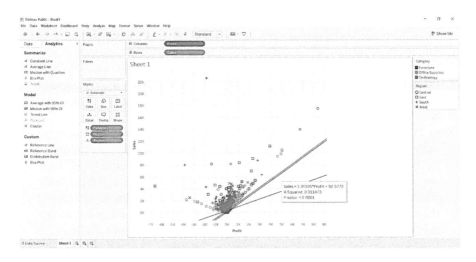

FIGURE 8.33 Output.

Step 9. We can choose to Describe the Trendline Model by right-clicking on any trend line. The statistical measures' output indicates significant values with a P-value of less than 0.0001. Thus, our model is suitable (Figure 8.34).

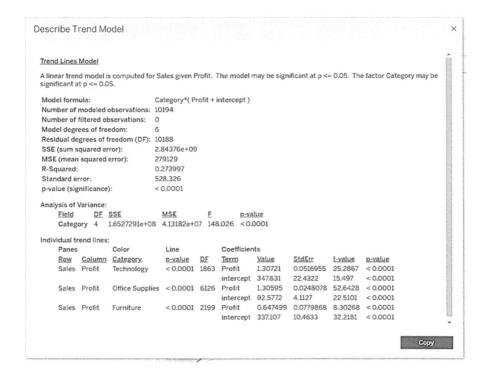

FIGURE 8.34 Output.

Step 10. Reference lines are an important configuration for analyzing Scatter plots. They are horizontal or vertical lines that serve as a baseline for a certain measure against which data points can be compared. To observe how each data point performed in comparison to the average, for example, you can put a reference line on the sales axis if you are analyzing the average sales for multiple product categories. Let's create a reference line for maximum average sales and profit distribution.

Step 11. Now we want to add a reference line for average profit and average sales. So, first we will create a new calculated field and name it as Average Sales. For this click on Analysis Menu -> select Create Calculate Field. Then we need to use a function called WINDOW_AVG(SUM[Sales]). This function will sum up each sale mark plotted in the scatter chart on the screen and then take average of it. This is what WINDOW_AVG() function does when it is a table calculation. Click Apply and Ok. This will add new calculated field Average Sales under Measure Names (Figures 8.35 and 8.36).

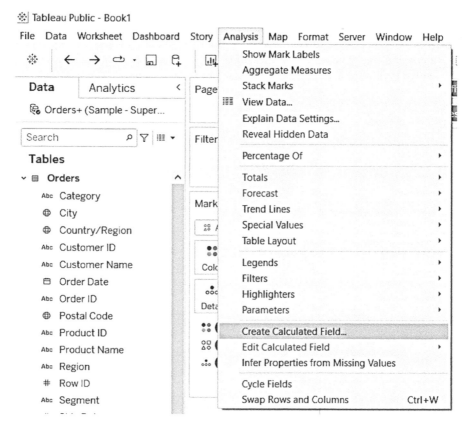

FIGURE 8.35 Output.

FIGURE 8.36 Create calculated field.

Step 12. Place the computed field "Average Sales" to the "Details" section under "Marks Card." After that, select Add Reference Line by right-clicking the Sales axis (Figure 8.37).

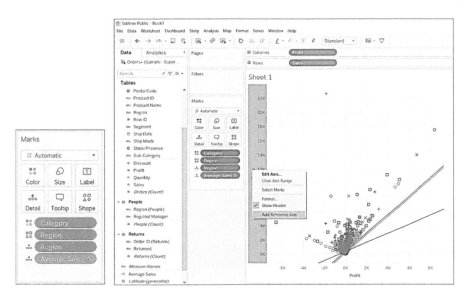

FIGURE 8.37 Output.

Step 13. In the dialog box for "Add Reference Line" under the Line section select "Average Sales" in Value and "Maximum" from adjacent drop down. For Label select "Custom" and give the label as "Average Sales." In Formatting section, choose the desired style and color for Line. Click Ok (Figure 8.38).

FIGURE 8.38   Output.

Step 14. Repeat step four10 to 12 for Profit to create a calculated field Average Profit and add reference line for the same. The output for scatter plot with reference lines for both Average Sales and Average Profit is given below. The Average Sales reference line act as reference to view those data points which are above and below maximum average sales. Similar conclusions can be drawn about Average Profit reference line (Figure 8.39).

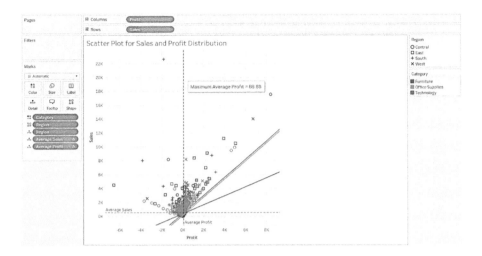

FIGURE 8.39 Output.

8.3.8 SCATTER PLOT MATRIX

A tool for displaying pairwise scatter plots of data variables such as x1, x2, x3, and xn in a single graphic is the scatter plot matrix. Each row and column in it represent a single dimension, and there are n rows and n columns total. Every cell creates a two-dimensional scatter plot. Instead of creating a single overall scatter chart for a case study, a matrix of several scatter charts is made to show the distribution of sales and profit across several categories and regional areas (Figure 8.40).

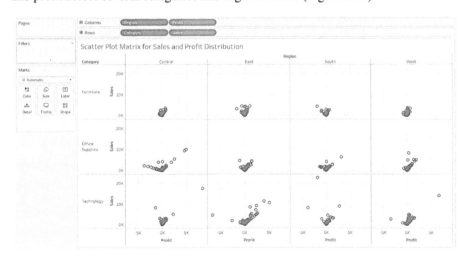

FIGURE 8.40 Output.

8.4 BUBBLE CHART FOR DISTRIBUTION

Scatter plots are a sort of graph where two variables can typically be displayed and the plot will appear as a collection of points, as we learned in the previous section. The bubble chart, an improved scatter plot variant, is supported by Tableau [7, 8]. It may be applied to datasets containing three data variables that must be plotted so that the value of the third variable and a chosen color scheme dictate the size of each bubble in the plot (Figure 8.41).

Bubble Chart for State-wise view of Sales and Profit

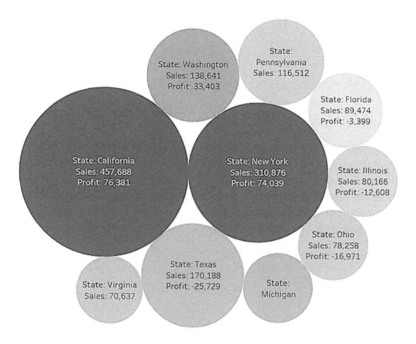

FIGURE 8.41   Illustration of bubble chart.

The term bubble chart implies that the plotted image resembles a group of bubbles. Three or four data dimensions can be shown. Every bubble in the diagram represents a member in the dimension field, and the measure's value is indicated by the bubble's size.

8.4.1 FEATURES OF BUBBLE CHART

- The size of the bubbles in a bubble chart indicates the values of the members or categories within that field.
- The quantity of categories in the field you have chosen will dictate how many bubbles appear in your chart.

- Adding color can offer valuable information and is frequently employed to distinguish between different groups or assess numerical values.
- Labels can also facilitate comparisons and improve the efficacy of communication. It's possible that some of the bubbles aren't big enough to have labels on them. If you feel that you need to view every value, you should think about using a different graphic. Something like a bar chart can communicate without labels because it is self-explanatory.

8.4.2 CASE STUDY

Take into account the Sample-Superstore repository of data. To generate a simple packed bubble chart that displays several product categories' sales and profit data. These are the steps to make a bubble chart:

Step 1. Take into account the Sample-Superstore repository of data. To generate a simple packed bubble chart that displays several product categories' sales and profit data. These are the steps to make a bubble chart (Figure 8.42).

FIGURE 8.42   Output.

Step 2. To draw a bubble chart, select the icon ⣿ for bubble chart from the Show Me tab (Figure 8.43).

From the above screenshot, we can analyze that the size of the bubble representing California State is bigger than the remaining states because there the sales value is higher than the other states.

FIGURE 8.43   Output.

Step 3. Now we want to see the sales and profit values also in the bubble along
with State name so, drag both, the State and Profit measures to the Label
under Marks shelf (Figure 8.44).

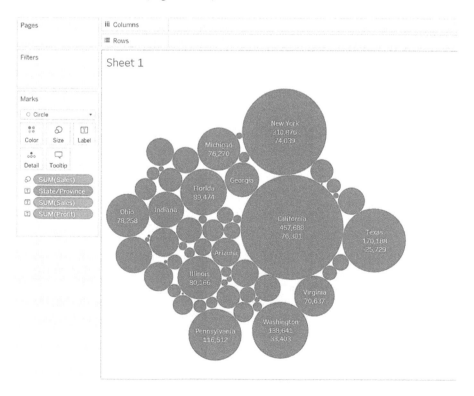

FIGURE 8.44   Output.

Step 4. We can also configure the labels by doing right-click on Label under the Marks shelf. Then click the small box with three dots present on the extreme right side of Text option. This will open the Edit Label dialog box. There we can add desirable label headings each for State, Sales, and Profit for clarity on displayed information. Also, give a suitable title to the sheet (Figure 8.45).

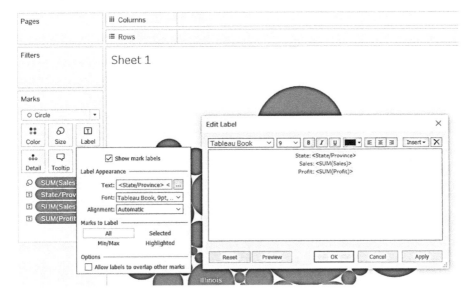

FIGURE 8.45   Output.

Step 5. We can configure the color scheme of bubble chart so that the color intensity (dark or light) for each bubble depends upon the value of Profit measure. For this bring the "Profit" metric to the Color detail underneath Marks shelf (Figure 8.46).

Above displayed bubble chart screenshot shows State name California with the Maximum value of profit measure in Dark Blue and the Least Sales Amount in light orange. Small bubbles do not show any labels to avoid clumsy visualization.

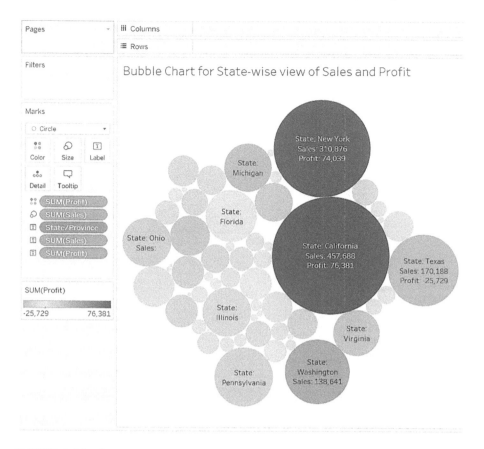

FIGURE 8.46   Output.

Step 6. Suppose we want to sort the bubbles in descending order of Sales, we can do this by selecting sorting option from tool bar (Figure 8.47).

FIGURE 8.47   Output.

This will sort the bubbles and display is updated like below (Figure 8.48).

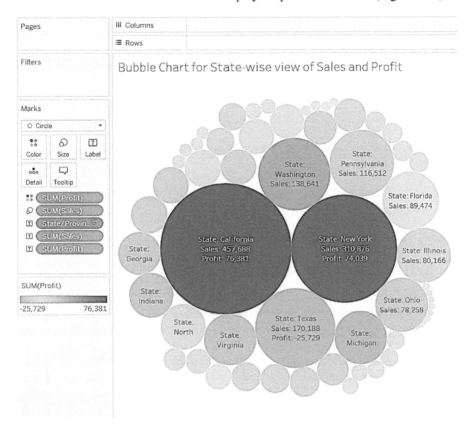

FIGURE 8.48   Output.

Conclusion:

1. The size of bubbles depicts the values of sales amount. Higher the sales means bigger size of bubble, while smaller bubble means low sales.
2. The color variation of bubbles is according to the value of profit measure. Higher profit value is depicted by dark blue color, while decreasing profit values are displayed using lighter shades of blue and orange color.

Step 7. Occasionally, the bubble chart could appear a little crowded and the labels might not appear. So, to improve the display, we must reduce the number of bubbles. According to our case study, we wish to provide the names and profits of the top ten states with the highest sales values. To the Filters shelf we drag the State dimension. Under the By Field option in the Filter settings dialog box, we choose the Sales dimension and Sum method. Afterwards, click OK (Figure 8.49).

The above bubble chart displays the top ten states grossing the highest sales values.

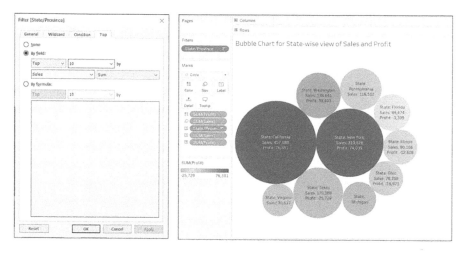

FIGURE 8.49   Output.

8.5   RADAR CHART FOR MULTIVARIATE DATA

A radar chart, also known as a spider chart, is a visual representation of multivariate data with quantitative measures. It is used in statistics to analyze multiple outcomes or observations. Radar graphs can be created for two, three, or more dimensions, depending on the number of comparable variables used. The variables are represented on axes starting from the same points with equal intervals. Number of axes in radar graph depends on number of variables used.

Suppose a team manager had to give performance reviews for his subordinates along seven different variables such as communication, diligence, flexibility, attentive, problem-solving, teamwork, and optimism on a 16-point scale in a pattern of eight grids at a difference of two points each. In this scenario their performance can be compared easily through a radar chart (Figure 8.50).

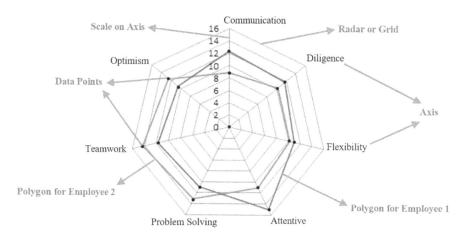

FIGURE 8.50   Illustration of radar chart.

The figure above demonstrates this example where the two polygons demonstrate the performance of each subordinate along the 7-axis where each axis represents a variable. The data points displayed against the values of each axis for each worker are joined to generate these polygons.

8.5.1 Components of Radar Chart

A spider chart includes a few fundamental components that make it easy to grasp even though it might occasionally appear a little confusing:

1. **Grids, the Center, and the Axis:** A spider chart is a visual representation of data, consisting of a central axis, at least three axes representing variables, and grids dividing the graph into different sections.
2. **Labels and Scale:** Axis labels identify the corresponding variable or category, while scales indicate the values for each variable.
3. **Connected Gridlines:** Gridlines connect the scale markings on each axis, helping visualize the distribution and relationship of values across different variables.
4. **Data Representation:** Data points, represented by dots or symbols, plot the actual values of each variable on the corresponding radial axis.
5. **Polygonal Outlines:** Data lines or polygons form closed shapes for easy visual comparison of different categories or dimensions.
6. **Shades and Colors:** The area enclosed by these lines can be filled with color or shading to enhance the visual representation and make comparisons easier. This allows for the comparison of multiple datasets on the same chart.

8.5.2 Mathematical Foundations for Radar Diagram

In order to generate a radar chart, it is necessary to possess a rudimentary understanding of mathematics. Specifically, this involves the polar coordinate system, which indicates the position of a point P in a plane determined by its angle () created between the line segment joining P and the x-axis and its distance (r) from the origin (Figure 8.51).

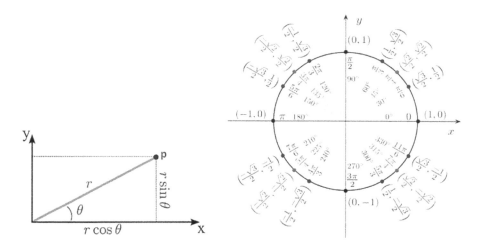

FIGURE 8.51   Mathematical foundations for radar chart.

We need the four measures as given below to plot a point P for every dimension.

1. **Angle Represented by Theta (θ):** The angle θ formed by the X-axis and
   the line that extends from the origin to point P. By default, Tableau prefers
   to utilize radians over degrees. Radians are one of only two units of angular
   measurement used as a standard in mathematics, together with degrees, to
   describe angles. The symbol "θ" represents a center angle's radian measure.
   The angle θ is computed using the formula (Figure 8.52).

Angle (θ) = 360 degrees/ Number of dimensions
Please note that 360 degrees = 2π (in radians)

FIGURE 8.52   Angle (θ) formula.

Any given angle must be multiplied by π/180 to convert it from degrees
to radians (Figure 8.53).

$$\text{Angle in radian} = \text{Angle in degree} \times \frac{\pi}{180}$$

FIGURE 8.53   Angle (radians) formula.

2. **Distance Represented by "r":** The measurement of the distance that separates data point "P" from the origin (center).
3. **X-axis:** Location of point "P" on the x-axis. The cosine of the angle (θ)
   must be multiplied by the distance (r) to obtain the x-axis. It is calculated as
   (Figure 8.54).

X= r. cos θ

FIGURE 8.54   Position on x-axis.

4. Y-axis: Location of point "P" on the y-axis. The y-axis must likewise be multiplied by the sine of the angle (θ) and distance (r). It is calculated as (Figure 8.55).

$$Y = r. \sin \theta$$

FIGURE 8.55 Position on y-axis.

8.5.3 Case Study

Think about the superstore sample data source. Assume for the moment that we wish to examine the total sales for the entire year, as these will serve as the axes and spokes of the radar chart. The steps are given as below:

Step 1. Generate a new calculated field by utilizing DATENAME() function on Month of Order Date to return only the month name as string from Order Date.

DATENAME("month," [Order Date])

For this, click on Analysis Menu and select the Create Calculate Field option (Figure 8.56).

FIGURE 8.56 Output.

Step 2. As we learned in the above section, to create a radar chart we need to perform four calculations: the angle calculation, distance "r" and data points on X-axis and Y-axis. Let us create the angle calculation that will divide our radar chart into 12 parts for 12 months of a year.

Step 3. The angle θ is determined by the number of dimensions/segments you would like to plot. Which can be computed as follows (360°/Number of dimensions). As we know, $360° = 2\pi$ (in radians). A RUNNING_SUM calculation is added to this computation to count distinct Months and plot the 12 increments of data points around the polygon. Then it adds 90°, i.e., PI()/2 to orient December toward the top of polygon. The Angle θ in this case is computed as follows (Figure 8.57).

Angle (θ) = RUNNING_SUM(2*PI())/MIN({COUNTD([Month])})+PI()/2

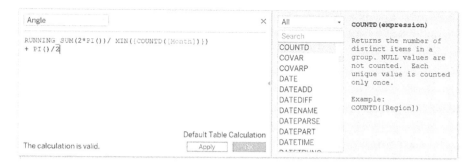

FIGURE 8.57 Output.

Step 4. Let us now create second calculation for Distance "r" from the center. It will be simply the Sum (Sales) in our case (Figure 8.58).

Distance		×	All	▾	**SUM(expression)**
SUM([Sales])			Search		Returns the sum of all the values in the expression. SUM can be used with numeric fields only. Null values are ignored.
			SIZE		
			SPACE		
			SPLIT		
			SQRT		
			SQUARE		
			STARTSWITH		Example: SUM([Profit])
			STDEV		
			STDEVP		
			STR		
The calculation is valid.	Apply	OK	SUM		
			TAN		

FIGURE 8.58 Output.

Step 5. The following computations are made for the X and Y axes. To get the X-axis, distance "r" must be multiplied by the cosine of angle (θ) (Figure 8.59).

X_axis		×	All	▾	**COS(angle)**
[Distance]* COS([Angle])			Search		Returns the cosine of an angle. Specify the angle in radians.
			ATTR		
			AVG		
			BUFFER		Example: COS(PI()/4) = 0.707106781186548
			CASE		
			CEILING		
			CHAR		
			COLLECT		
			CONTAINS		
			CORR		
The calculation is valid.	Apply	OK	COS		
			COT		

FIGURE 8.59 Output.

To find the y-axis, by the sine of angle (θ) (Figure 8.60).

FIGURE 8.60   Output.

Step 6. Now bring the dimension Month to the detail shelf. Also, place the measure Angle to the Detail block and Right-click the Angle calculation -> click on Compute Using -> Select dimension Month that we created in Step 2 (Figure 8.61).

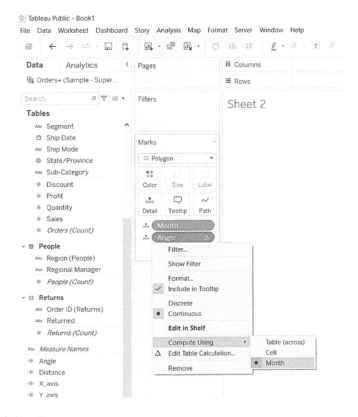

FIGURE 8.61   Output.

Step 7. Add the measures Y_Axis and X_Axis to the rows and columns blocks, respectively. Additionally, switch the markings card's Automatic setting to Polygon. Next, drop the measure Angle to the Path beneath Mark's shelf by dragging it (Figure 8.62).

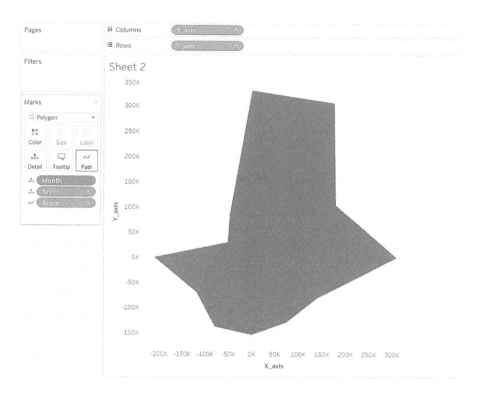

FIGURE 8.62   Output.

Here in the above figure, we can observe the polygon being formed.

Step 8. Drag Order Date to Color under Marks shelf and set the detail as Year (Order Date). This will generate multiple polygons for each year as according to our dataset a.d these polygons will be differentiated by colors (Figure 8.63).

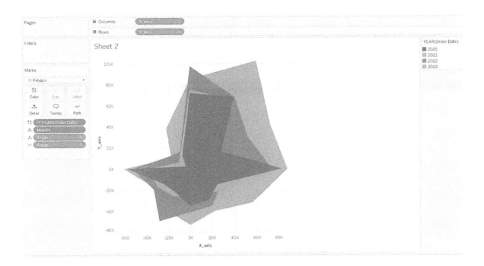

FIGURE 8.63   Output.

Step 9. Click on Color detail under Marks shelf and reduce the Opacity value to 50% or as per choice. This will lighten the color intensity for each polygon (Figure 8.64).

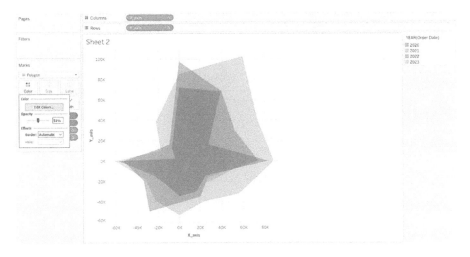

FIGURE 8.64   Output.

Step 10. To create dual axis for radar chart and segregate data polygon by month for each year we apply the following steps:

a. Drag X_Axis to Columns shelf in order to simply duplicate the view (Figure 8.65).

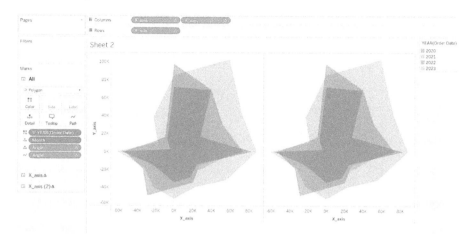

FIGURE 8.65   Output of step 10 (a).

b. Change the Marks card of the second view to Shapes (Figure 8.66).

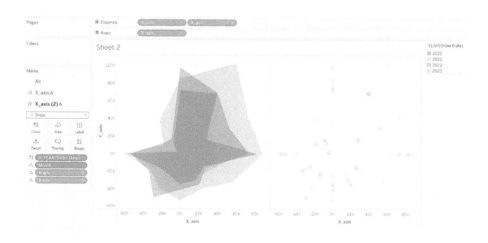

FIGURE 8.66   Output of step 10 (b).

c. Add the dimension Month to the label shelf of the second view (Figure 8.67).

FIGURE 8.67 Output of step 10 (c).

    d. Right-click x-axis of second polygon and select Dual Axis to combine both polygons. This is done to make the view dual axis and synchronize the axes (Figure 8.68).

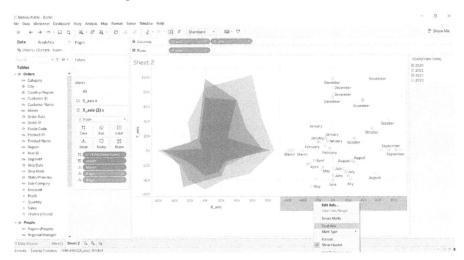

FIGURE 8.68 Output of step 10 (d).

        This will create a dual-axis chart by merging axis.

    e. Right-click on the graph's horizontal x-axis and select "Synchronise Axis" to synchronize the dual axis that was generated previously (Figure 8.69).

FIGURE 8.69   Output of step 10 (e).

f. To filter the polygons year-wise we drag "Order-Date" to Filters block and set the details as Year (Order Date). Also, right-click the filter created for Year (Order Date) and click on Show Filter option to view the checkboxes for years (Figure 8.70).

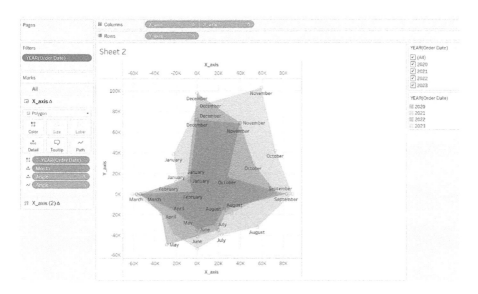

FIGURE 8.70   Output of step 10 (f).

> **Step 11.** Now we can select the compare the monthly sales of any two years or
> more as per requirement. Suppose we select years 2022 and 2023 to create
> their respective Radar charts for comparison (Figure 8.71).

FIGURE 8.71   Output.

Step 12. We can also configure the view to display Month name, monthly sales and Profit percentage in the polygon data points (Figure 8.72).

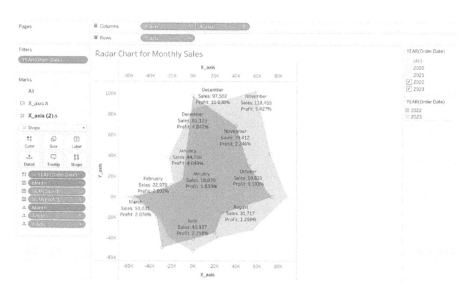

FIGURE 8.72   Output.

Step 13. Now we want to a grid structure for better view of radar chart. For this copy the Sales and Month columns from data source to a blank MS Excel workbook (Figure 8.73).

FIGURE 8.73   Output.

Step 14. Go to "Data" Menu and click on "Consolidate" option from Toolbar menu options. In the Consolidate Dialog box choose both the columns in "Reference" and mark the checkbox for "Top Row" under Use labels section. Click Ok (Figure 8.74).

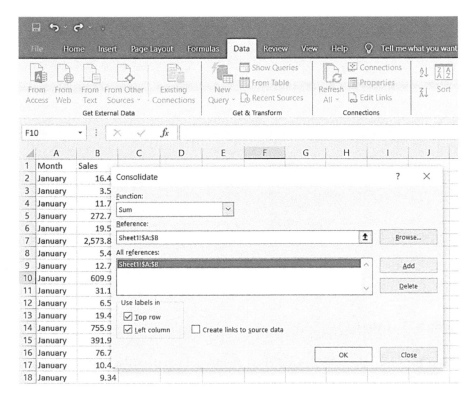

FIGURE 8.74 Output.

Step 15. This creates a consolidated list of Sales for each Month. Now click on Insert Menu and expand the list of Recommended charts to select desired radar chart from a list of offered charts in the "Insert Chart" window (Figure 8.75).

We can observer three options for Radar charts—Basic radar chart, Radar chart with Markers, and Filled Radar chart. We can select any of these as per choice.

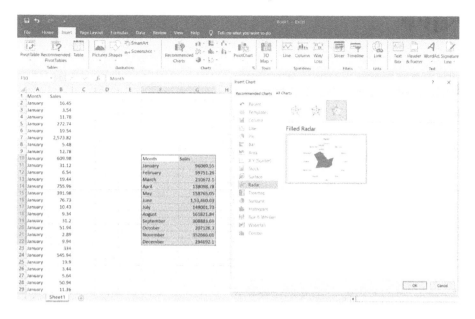

FIGURE 8.75   Output.

Step 16. Now select the desired chart elements to extract the grid structure (Figure 8.76).

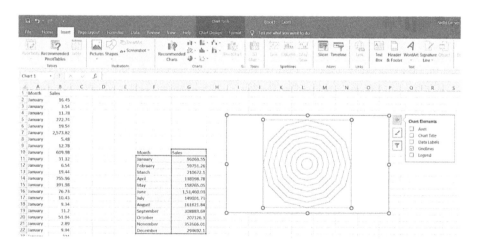

FIGURE 8.76   Output.

Step 17. We can also choose any style for the grid and copy the figure and paste in any image processing tool like MS Paint and save a JPEG image of the figure (Figure 8.77).

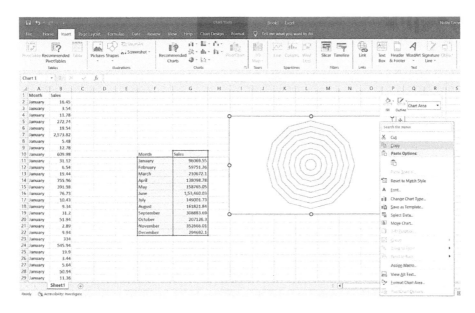

FIGURE 8.77   Output.

Step 18. To import the saved image in Tableau, go to Map menu and click on Background Image and select the Data source (Figure 8.78).

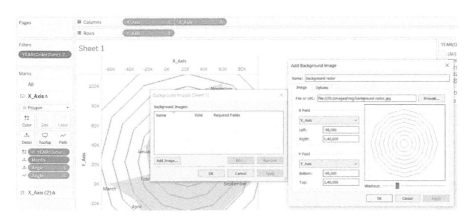

FIGURE 8.78   Output.

Step 19. Now we can view a perfect Radar grid chart that compares the monthly Sales and Profit percent of Total for years 2022 and 2023 (Figure 8.79). Users can study the monthly comparison and draw insights from analysis.

FIGURE 8.79   Output.

8.6   HEAT MAP WITH COLOR VARIATIONS

A *Heat Map*, sometimes referred to as an *Intensity Map*, is a type of data visualization where the density or concentration of data points in a given area is represented by color intensity. Heat maps receive their name from the way they appear to get "brighter" or "hotter"—that is, from light to dark color tones as values rise. With the use of color, heat maps make it simple to spot patterns and trends in our data. If we wish to analyze patterns using the density or population of data points, we can set the heat map's mark to the "Density" type. Heat maps can also be useful for identifying too many or too few data points in the visualization (Figure 8.80).

Heat Map

						Order Date						
Sub-Category	January	February	March	April	May	June	July	August	September	October	November	December
Accessories												
Appliances												
Art												
Binders												
Bookcases												
Chairs												
Copiers												
Envelopes												

FIGURE 8.80   Illustration of heat map.

Tableau allows us to construct a heat map by selecting one continuous measure from the Columns shelf and one dimension or measure from the Rows shelf (or vice versa). We can then bring one measure to the Marks card to represent size variation and, additionally, place another measure to specify color variations. These graphs are an effective tool for exploring a large dataset with several data points and are particularly helpful in various scientific research.

8.6.1 FEATURES OF HEAT MAP

Detailed below are some of the reasons why you should be using heat maps for representing your data:

- Visual clarity: Heat maps use color coding to represent the concentration of data points, making it easy to identify areas of high and low density immediately. This allows you to spot patterns and outliers in your data quickly.
- Versatility: Heat maps can be applied to various data types, from geographical to categorical data. This makes them highly adaptable and useful across different industries and use cases.
- Efficiency: By combining multiple data points into a single view, heat maps can convey a large amount of information in a compact and digestible format. This makes it easier to understand a huge dataset and make informed decisions based on your findings.

8.6.2 CASE STUDY

Take into account the Sample-Superstore data source. Here, we want to assess the sales of each product sub-category in the dataset according to the month of the order in order to look for any seasonal patterns. The actions are listed below:

Step 1. Place "Order-Date" in Columns shelf aggregated by Month detail and Sales metric to Rows area. Also, bring "Sub-category" dimension to Color under Marks block (Figure 8.81).

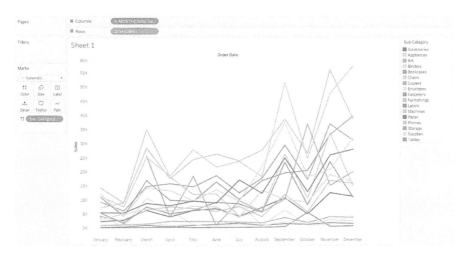

FIGURE 8.81 Output.

In the figure above, we can observe that Tableau created a default line chart containing several lines and each line displays monthly sales pattern for a product sub-category. However, this graph is a little jumbled and unclear. A number of the sub-categories at the bottom are on a much smaller scale than the others, and there is a lot of overlap due to the various lines drawn. It becomes difficult to obtain pertinent ideas as a result. Making a heat map might be a preferable choice in this situation.

Step 2. To generate a Heat Map, click on "Show Me" tab and select Heat Map

icon (Figure 8.82).

FIGURE 8.82   Output.

Step 3. The resulting heat map created is given below (Figure 8.83).

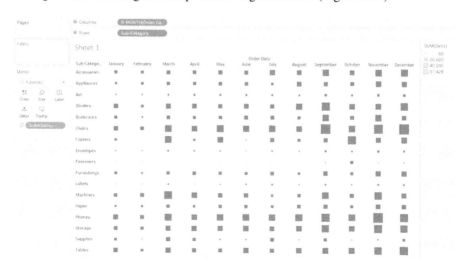

FIGURE 8.83   Output.

Step 4. We can observe above that all blocks differ by size. Big size blocks represent high sales while small blocks represent less sales. However, the color attribute of each block displays same color. So, we drag the Profit dimension to Color so that variations in color intensity displays difference in Profit values (Figure 8.84).

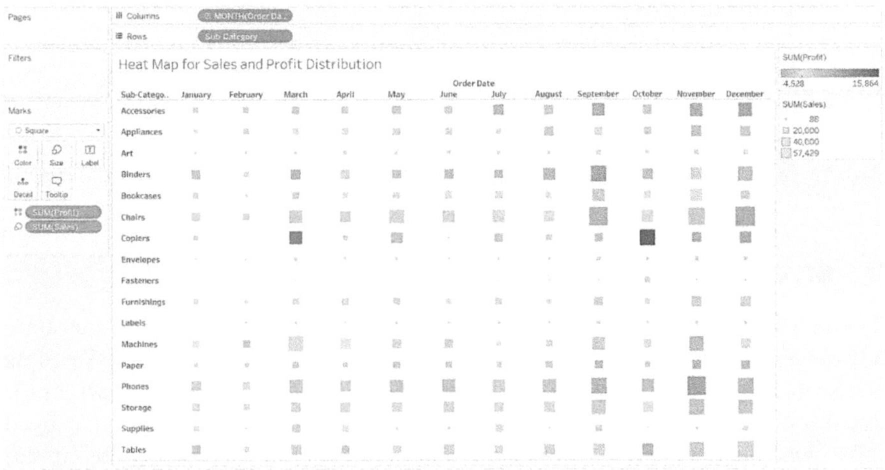

FIGURE 8.84   Output.

Step 5. We can modify the square shape of blocks as per requirement. For this under Marks shelf select a shape such as Circle instead of Automatic (Figure 8.85).

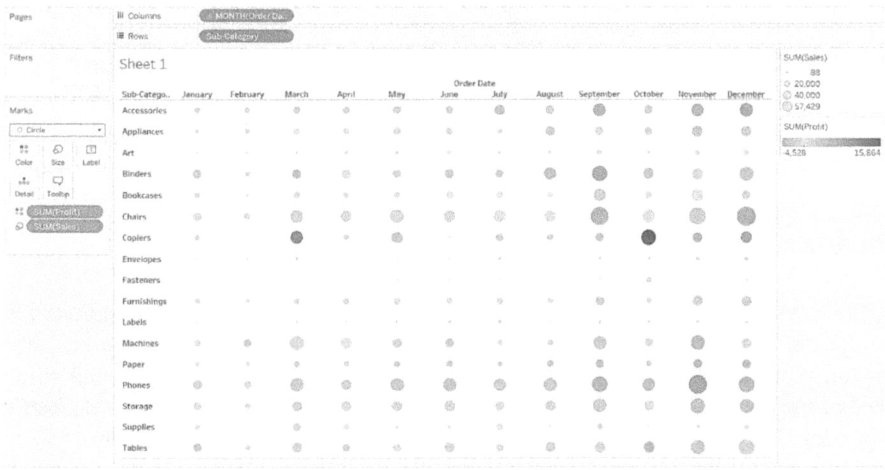

FIGURE 8.85   Output.

Conclusion:

- We determine that circles of a larger size and more vibrant colors indicate that the sales and earnings for this product sub-category were higher in the given year.
- Large, light-colored circles indicate higher sales but lower profitability for the sub-category.
- The product sub-category with smaller, more intensely colored circles had higher profits in that specific year, although having fewer sales.
- Small, light-colored circles indicate lower sales and profitability for the Sub-category in question.
- For every category, more insights about patterns in sales, etc., can be obtained.

8.7   BOX PLOT AND QUARTILES

A box plot, also referred to as a boxplot, is a popular chart form in explanatory data analysis. Another term for it is a box and whisker plot. In box plots, the skewness and distribution of the numerical data are graphically represented by the quartiles (or percentiles) and averages of the data. Five numerical summary values are displayed in box plots: the lowest, first (lower) quartile, median, third (upper), and maximum scores (Figure 8.86).

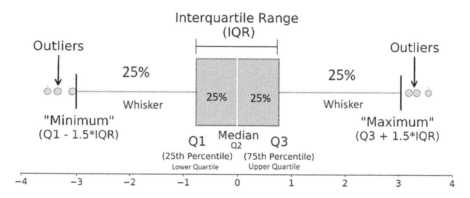

FIGURE 8.86   Illustration of box plot.

Plotting outliers—observations that stand out from the rest—as separate points is one option. More statistical data can be displayed on a single chart using a box and whisker plot than usually possible to implement. It gives researchers a visual summary of the data that makes it easy to spot skewness, mean values, and the dataset's dispersion. It divides the data into portions, each of which contains roughly 25% of the whole data. The different components of box plot are as follows:

1. **Least Score:** When outliers are excluded, the lowest score is shown at the end of the left whisker.
2. **Lower Quartile:** Data is split into four equal ranges by quartiles. They fall into the first, second, third, and fourth quartiles, respectively. The first

quartile Q1, or 25 percent of scores, is the value that is below the lower quartile.

3. **Median:** The median, also known as the second quartile, or Q2, is the middle of the data, represented by the line that divides the box in half. This quantity is over or equal to half of the scores, and the other half are less.

4. **Upper Quartile:** Seventy-five percent of the scores fall below the upper quartile, or third quartile, or Q3. As a result, 25% of the data surpass this cutoff.

5. **Maximum Score:** The maximum score, indicated at the right whisker's end, omitting outliers.

6. **Whiskers:** Scores outside of the center 50% are represented by the upper and lower whiskers, representing the lower 25% and upper 25% of scores, respectively.

7. The Interquartile Range (or IQR): The range between the 25th and 75th percentiles. IQR is calculated as: IQR = Q3-Q1.

8. **Outliers:** The data points that go outside of the lower and upper bounds are known as outliers. The lower and upper bound is calculated in the formula below (Figure 8.87).

$$Lower\ Limit = Q1 - 1.5*IQR$$
$$Upper\ Limit = Q3 + 1.5*IQR$$

FIGURE 8.87   Outlier points in box plot.

The data points plotted below and above these bounds are considered as outliers or anomalies.

8.7.1 CHARACTERISTICS OF BOX PLOT

A. **Display Median:** Box plots are helpful because they give a summary of the average score for data collection. A dataset's median or average value is shown as the line that divides the box in half. Scores that are bigger than or equal to the median are found on the right side of the median line, while scores on the left side are less than the median.

B. **Data Skewness:** Since they display a dataset's skewness, box charts are helpful. A statistical dataset's box plot shape will indicate whether it is skewed or regularly distributed. The skewness observed in box plots are of following three types:

  I. Left skew or negative skew: When the median is closer to the top of the box and the whisker is shorter on the higher end of the box, the distribution is negatively skewed, or skewed left (Figure 8.88).

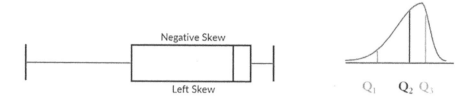

FIGURE 8.88 Left data skew.

II. No skew or Symmetric Plot: The distribution is considered symmetric when the whiskers on either side of the box are roughly equal and the median is situated in the middle of the box (Figure 8.89).

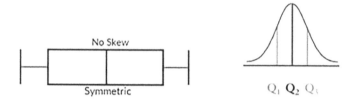

FIGURE 8.89 No data skew.

III. Right Skew or Positive Skew: The three main features of right-skewed data are the prolonged tail on the right side, the median tilting toward the left side of the box, and the unequal whisker lengths. This shows that the distribution is skewed to the right because most of the data is concentrated on the left and there are a few high numbers on the right (Figure 8.90).

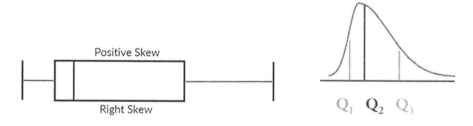

FIGURE 8.90 Right data skew.

C. **Dispersion of a Dataset:** In statistics, dispersion—also referred to as variability, scatter, or spread—denotes how much a distribution is stretched or compressed. The values at the ends of the "whiskers" are the lowest and largest, and they are useful in providing a visual depiction of the range, or spread, of values. The interquartile range (IQR), represented by the box plot showing the middle 50% of scores, can be calculated by subtracting the upper quartile from the lower quartile (Q3–Q1).

D. **Display Outliers within a Dataset:** An observation that deviates significantly from the rest of the data numerically is called an outlier. A data point outside the box plot's whiskers is referred to as an outlier when examining a box plot. For instance, outside of the interquartile range that is 1.5 times greater than the upper quartile (Q3 + 1.5 * IQR) and below the lower quartile (Q1 – 1.5 * IQR).

8.7.2 COMPARISON GUIDELINES FOR BOX PLOTS

Box plots are a helpful tool for displaying variations among samples or groups. They can access a wide variety of statistical data, including ranges, medians, and outliers. When utilizing boxplots to compare different sets of data, it is typically advised to carefully consider each individual characteristic. The following suggestions might be useful.

1. Look at and compare the corresponding median for each box plot. If the median line of a box plot is beyond the comparison box plot's box, then most likely is a difference between the two groups (Figure 8.91).

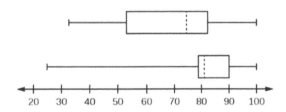

FIGURE 8.91 Comparing lengths of box plots.

2. Compare the box lengths or the interquartile ranges to look into how the data were distributed among each sample. The larger the box length, the more widely spread the data are. The lesser the data, the less varied the data is.
3. Examine for aspects of skewness in data (Figure 8.92).
4. Seek out any possible deviations or outliers.

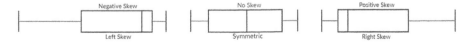

FIGURE 8.92 Viewing data skewness using box plots.

8.7.3 CASE STUDY

Take into account the Sample-Superstores dataset, which we wish to use to show the Overall Distribution of Sales for each Product Sub-Category. We want to observe different statistical parameters and find if any outliers are present in the dataset. The steps are given below:

> **Step 1.** Move and place dimension "Sub-Category" to the Columns block.
> **Step 2.** Bring metric "Sales" to the Rows block. By default, "Sales" metric is aggregated by SUM() function. The below figure displays a simple bar chart comparing sales for each sub-category (Figure 8.93).

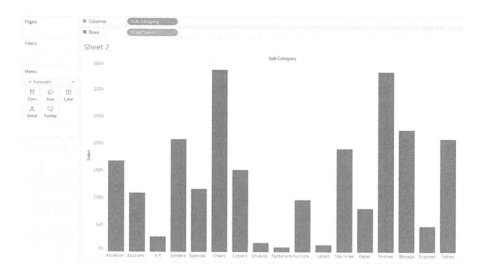

FIGURE 8.93   Output.

> **Step 3.** Pick "Box-and-whisker-plots" under the "Show Me" menu to produce box plots rather than bar charts. A breakdown of the statistic is displayed when we move the cursor over the box (Figure 8.94).

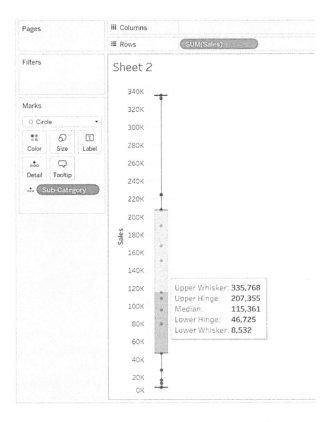

FIGURE 8.94   Output.

Step 4. The generated chart, when viewed at the Sub-Category summary level, displays the sales distribution. We want to compare the distribution of sales across all sub-categories and notice how it is distributed within each Sub-Category. In this instance, drag the dimensions Sub-Category to the Columns shelf. Additionally, we need to disaggregate the data, so select the Analysis menu's "Aggregate measures" option and uncheck it (Figure 8.95).

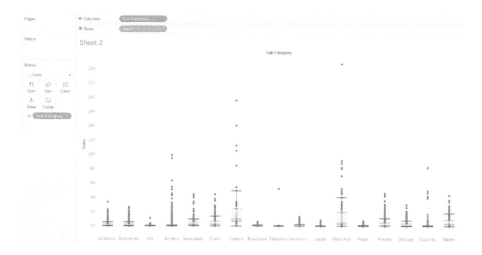

FIGURE 8.95   Output.

Conclusion:

- Each sub-category's box and whisker plots are shown in the above picture. Simple statistical insights are readily apparent, such as the sales distribution across various product sub-categories.
- By looking at the interquartile range, for instance, we may determine that the machines and copiers in the sub-category of machines have the highest sales distribution, while the distribution of fasteners is the lowest.
- Additionally, we can see that several sub-categories have outliers.

KEY NOTES

- Instead of aggregating the data into an average value, a distribution chart is a tool for visualizing the data's distribution across a range of values.
- Distribution charts come in a variety of forms, such as heat maps, box plots, radar charts, bubble charts, histograms, and scatter plots.
- The distribution of the values of a numerical variable is plotted as a series of bars in a histogram.
- Values for two distinct numerical variables are represented by points or dots in a scatter plot.
- All pairwise scatter plots of variables are displayed on a single figure in a scatter matrix.
- Tableau supports an enhanced variation of scatter plot known as bubble chart.
- A radar chart uses quantitative metrics to depict data that has three or more dimensions.
- Heat maps show the density or concentration of data points in a certain area using color intensity. Boxplots are frequently used in explanatory data analysis.

PRACTICE CASE STUDY

Marketing Campaign Dashboard

   Create a marketing campaign dashboard for Superstore Marketing Campaign Dataset which can be downloaded from Kaggle or any other public domain data repository. Assume that the superstore wants to determine the various elements that influence the customer's response and forecast the possibility that the consumer would respond favorably. To determine these parameters, you must first examine the available data. Then, you must develop a trend model to determine the likelihood that a consumer will respond favorably.

TEST YOUR SKILLS

1. What are the benefits and shortcomings of using distribution charts in Tableau?
2. Discuss different types of histograms with respect to peaks and skewness.
3. How a scatter plot helps in finding correlation among different data values?
4. Elaborate the different types of trend lines and their mathematical equations.
5. How forecasting helps stakeholders in the process of decision-making?
6. Discuss the significance of p-value and R-squared statistic in assessing trends.

REFERENCES

[1] Meier, Marleen. *Mastering Tableau 2023: Implement Advanced Business Intelligence Techniques, Analytics, and Machine Learning Models with Tableau.* United Kingdom, Packt Publishing, 2023.

[2] Munroe, Kirk. *Data Modeling with Tableau: A Practical Guide to Building Data Models Using Tableau Prep and Tableau Desktop.* United Kingdom, Packt Publishing, 2022.

[3] Sarsfield, Patrick, et al. *Maximizing Tableau Server: A Beginner's Guide to Accessing, Sharing, and Managing Content on Tableau Server.* United Kingdom, Packt Publishing, 2021.

[4] Sleeper, Ryan. *Innovative Tableau: 100 More Tips, Tutorials, and Strategies.* United States, O'Reilly Media, 2020.

[5] Milligan, Joshua N. *Learning Tableau 2019: Tools for Business Intelligence, Data Prep, and Visual Analytics*, 3rd Edition. India, Packt Publishing, 2019.

[6] Loth, Alexander. *Visual Analytics with Tableau.* United States, Wiley, 2019.

[7] Costello, Tim, and Blackshear, Lori. *Prepare Your Data for Tableau: A Practical Guide to the Tableau Data Prep Tool.* Germany, Apress, 2019.

[8] Sleeper, Ryan. *Practical Tableau: 100 Tips, Tutorials, and Strategies from a Tableau Zen Master.* United States, O'Reilly Media, 2018.

9 Part-to-Whole Relationship
Composition Charts

9.1 INTRODUCTION TO COMPOSITION CHARTS

Composition in literature refers to the process of assembling parts to create a coherent and meaningful description [1]. It involves understanding the different parts that make up a whole and visualizing how these elements come together to form a single entity. Charts are used to compare parts to a whole, usually in percentages [1,2]. All these graphs fall under one of the two categories discussed below:

1. Charts that illustrate the static alignment of the data:
   a. Pie chart and donut chart
   b. Waterfall charts
   c. Tree maps
2. Charts that demonstrate variations in the overall composition with time:
   a. Stacked charts
      Let us discuss each of these in detail.

9.2 CHARTS FOR STATIC COMPOSITION

Static composition charts display the data's stable composition, without any change or progression over time [3]. These charts are used for comparisons with reference to a single point in time, such as the top ten states with the highest sales in a specific year. Examples of static composition charts include pie charts, donut charts, waterfall charts, and tree maps.

9.2.1 PIE CHART FOR CATEGORIES

To show numerical problems, a statistical graphic is divided into sectors or parts and shown as a pie chart, also called a circle chart [2]. A proportionate percentage of the entire is represented by each sector. In place of other graphs like bar graphs, line plots, and histograms, pie charts are frequently used to show the composition of something [4]. They portray the total using a circle, and other categories are represented by slices of that circle or "pie" (Figure 9.1).

DOI: 10.1201/9781003429593-9

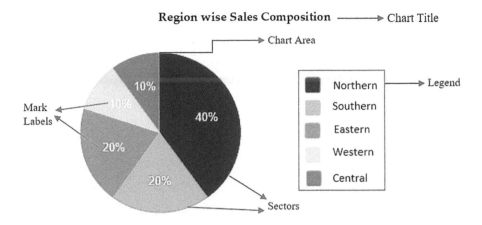

FIGURE 9.1 Illustration for pie chart.

This kind of chart allows the viewer to compare the relationships between several dimensions (people, products, categories, countries, etc.) within a certain context. On a chart, the numerical data (measure) is usually shown as a percentage of the total sum. Every slice should be measured as a representation of the proportion of the value that it represents.

9.2.1.1 Interpreting a Pie Chart

A pie chart is a spherical graph that illustrates information arranged according to angle, arc length, and area [4, 5]. It should start with the biggest component and work down to the smallest for simple interpretation. The colors of the segments should match the matching blocks in the legend. The circle symbolizes the values of all its components, and the overall angle created at its center is 360°. The angle at the center that corresponds to an observational component can be determined as shown in Figure 9.2.

$$\text{Angle of a component at center} = \frac{\text{Value of the component}}{\text{Total value}} \times 360°$$

FIGURE 9.2 Formula for angle of a pie slice at center.

If component values are to be stated as percentages, the center angle for each component is provided as shown in Figure 9.3.

$$\text{Angle of a component at center} = \frac{\text{Percentage value of component}}{100} \times 360°$$

FIGURE 9.3 Alternate formula for angle of a pie slice at center.

The following are the fundamental components of a pie chart (Figure 9.4).

Mark type:	Pie
Color:	Dimension
Angle:	Measure

FIGURE 9.4   Fundamental components of pie chart.

9.2.1.2   Case Study

Consider the default Superstore data collection. Suppose we want to observe the region-wise sales composition in percentage for each product category:

Step 1. Move the "Region" dimension to the Rows block and the "Sales" metric to the Columns block. Tableau adds up the "Sales" metric values and shows a bar chart by default (Figure 9.5).

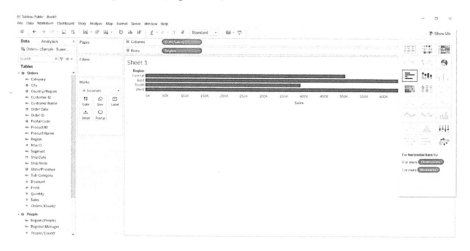

FIGURE 9.5   Output.

Step 2. Pick the pie chart category by choosing from the "Show Me" option. Pie charts must have at least one or more measures and at least one or more dimensions (Figure 9.6).

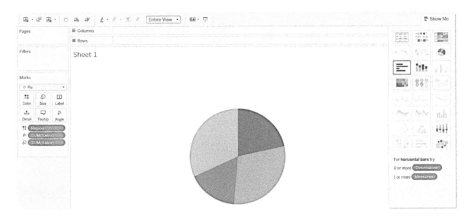

FIGURE 9.6   Output.

Step 3. Now, since we want to view region-wise sales for each product category, so we must create separate pie charts for each product category. For this, drag Category dimension to Columns shelf (Figure 9.7).

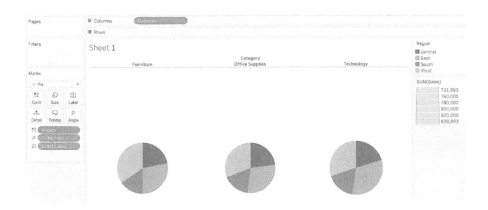

FIGURE 9.7   Output.

Step 4. We can observe separate pie charts created for sales across regions for each category. But the pie charts are blank. So, we will label them with relevant information. For this, drag Region dimension and Sales measure to Label under Marks shelf (Figure 9.8).

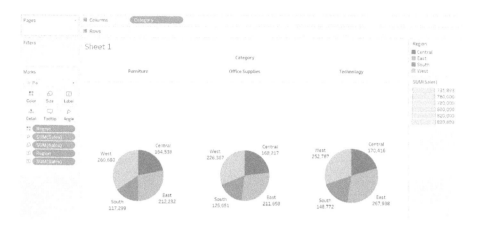

FIGURE 9.8   Output.

Step 5. For a better view of the chart, we may want to see mark labels inside the pie chart in each sector rather than outside. For this, simply drag and drop each mark label to its respective sector inside the pie chart (Figure 9.9).

FIGURE 9.9   Output.

Step 6. Now, in each sector, we can see big numbers marked for sales values. But we want to see the percentage of sales for each sector in each pie chart, so for this, we click on the label Sum (Sales) under the Marks panel, pick "Quick table calculation," and choose the "Percent of Total" option in calculation type (Figure 9.10).

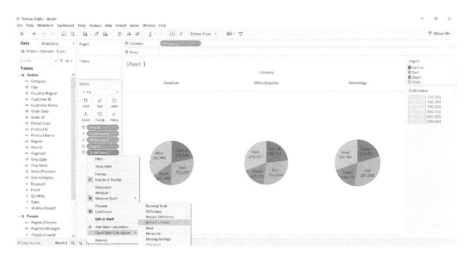

FIGURE 9.10   Output.

Here, output will be modified as follows (Figure 9.11).

FIGURE 9.11   Output.

Step 7. Choose the "Sum (Sales)" label under the Marks shelf and opt for
"Edit table calculation" to determine the sales percentages individually for
each column type. Choose "Cell" under the "Compute Using" component
of the dialog box. This will display the correct sales percentages. When
adding percentages in each pie chart, an absolute 100% total is obtained
(Figure 9.12).

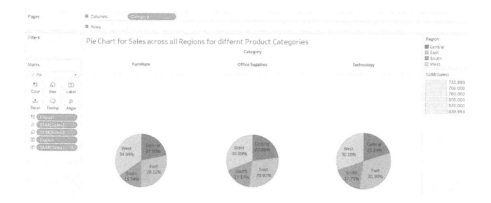

FIGURE 9.12 Output.

Conclusion:

- We can very well observe the composition of Sales percentage across all regions for different product categories and draw relevant insights from it.
- The general trend shows that all product categories have higher sales percentage in the Western region while lowest and almost equivalent sales percentage in the Southern region.

9.2.1.3 Pie Chart Best Practices for Visual Analysis

A pie chart is a useful tool for visual analysis, allowing for comparison of categories within a single dimension. It can be used to create a "whole" by dividing categories into distinct slices. To effectively use a pie chart, follow certain guidelines for optimal visual analysis:

- Each pie slice should be labeled with the correct amount or percentage and organized rendering to size for easy comparison, either smallest to biggest or biggest to smallest.
- If a chart has more than five slices, consider using an alternative chart style, but if a pie chart is chosen, use legend, list, or table for more context.
- Use a pie chart to visualize data when:
  - The entire quantity can be split into 2–5 sections.
  - The proportions of each group differ significantly.
- Pie charts should be avoided if:
  - The chosen dimension has an excessive number of categories.
  - Values inside the selected dimension have similar percentages or numbers between them.
  - The data does not represent a steady "whole" or the percentages do not sum up to 100%.
  - There are complex or negative fractions in the selected measure value.
- Pie graphs can be effectively replaced with bar charts and stacked bar charts.

9.2.2 Donut Chart for Multiple Data Series

The Tableau Donut chart, a type of pie chart, is shaped like a donut and resembles pie charts with a hole in the middle. It divides the outer periphery into segments proportional to related values. It shifts focus from area to arc length, making it easy to calculate. Donut charts resemble stacked bar charts coiled around themselves (Figure 9.13).

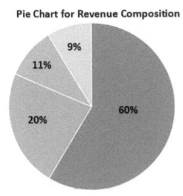

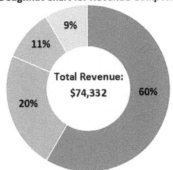

FIGURE 9.13 Pie chart vs donut chart.

Donut charts are popular due to their smaller size and higher data-intensity ratio, while pie charts require more space. The middle hole displays additional details like arc labels, data points, or parameters for quick comparisons.

9.2.2.1 Case Study

In this section, we follow the same case study that we analyzed in the above section for a pie chart using Sample-Superstore data source. Here again, we want to observe the region-wise sales composition in percentage for each product category using a donut chart instead of a pie chart. The steps are given below:

Step 1. Open a new worksheet after connecting to the Sample – Superstore data source.

Step 2. Create a simple pie chart as we did in the above case study for the pie chart (Figure 9.14).

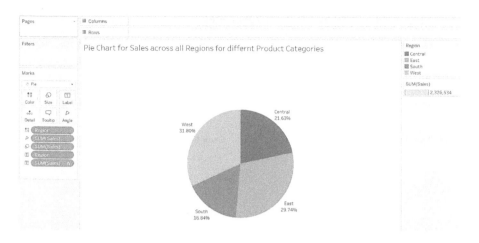

FIGURE 9.14   Output.

Step 3. Double-click on the Rows shelf and type avg(0). Please note that 0 is numeric zero in parenthesis. Repeat this step and again type avg(0) to create a duplicate pie chart. The resulting view is given below (Figure 9.15).

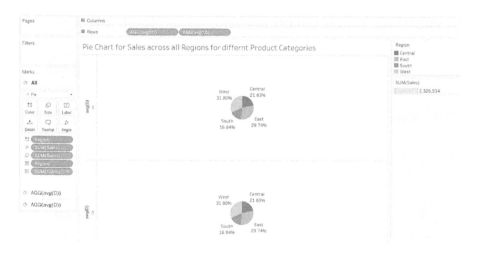

FIGURE 9.15   Output.

Step 4. In the "Marks" card on the left, under the heading "AGG(avg(0))," we might see a few new entries. These are the two blank placeholders that we made in the step above. Click on the first instance of "AGG(avg(0))" in this window, and then choose the pie chart from the drop-down menu. Make sure the "Region" dimension is present in the Colors card and the "Sales" dimension is present in the Angle card (Figure 9.16).

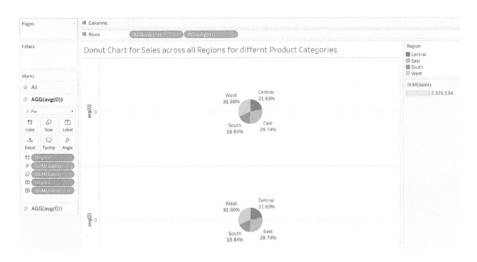

FIGURE 9.16   Output.

Step 5. Under the Marks card, select the second "AGG(avg(0))" option. Follow the instructions below after selecting the Circle chart from the drop-down option.

a. Remove Region dimension from Color and Sum(Sales) from the Size card.

b. Click the Color card, select "white," and then select "black" for the border. We shall designate this as the donut chart's hole.

c. Click on the size card and reduce the size.

d. Remove "Region" from the label and drag "Sales" measure to the Labels card.

e. For better view, drag the Sales label inside the circle (Figure 9.17).

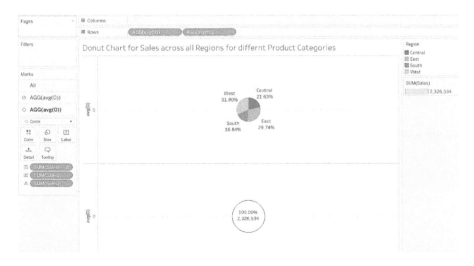

FIGURE 9.17   Output.

Step 6. Under the Rows shelf, right-click the AGG(avg(0)) pill and select dual-axis (Figure 9.18).

FIGURE 9.18   Output.

Step 7. Now, we can observe that both graphs—pie chart and circle—super-impose each other. We can increase or decrease the size of each of them to form an exact donut shape (Figure 9.19).

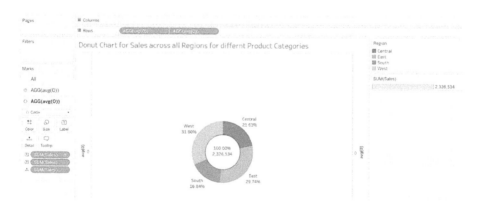

FIGURE 9.19   Output.

Conclusion:

- We can compare the donut chart created with the pie chart created in the previous section to analyze structural differences.

Step 8. To view category-wise sales donut charts, we can drag Category to Columns and view a donut created for each (Figure 9.20).

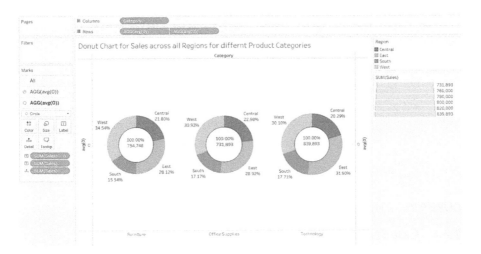

FIGURE 9.20 Output.

9.2.2.2 Which One to Choose—Pie or Donut?

The donut chart is a variation of the pie chart, displaying categories as arcs and having a hole in the center. Both charts create part-to-whole relationships and are easily understandable. When choosing between pie and donut charts, ensure data is used for comparative analysis only. The number of categories to compare is a good criterion. If more than 4 or 5 categories are needed, pie charts are suitable. If 2–4 categories are needed, donut charts can be used. Donut charts can also be used for displaying additional information.

9.2.3 WATERFALL CHART TO ANALYZE VALUE CHANGES

A waterfall chart shows a running total of field values, allowing for the observation of how each category's positive value increases the total value and vice versa [6]. This allows for the analysis of how individual elements contribute to achieve a total value, unlike normal running totals that do not (Figure 9.21).

The waterfall chart is named after its shape which resembles a waterfall. The above visual representation of a waterfall graphic displays how each sub-category in the Sample-Superstore dataset contributes to total profit. It begins with a zero-bar representing the baseline value, followed by a series of floating bars, rising and falling, and a final bar representing the ultimate quantity of the chosen measure.

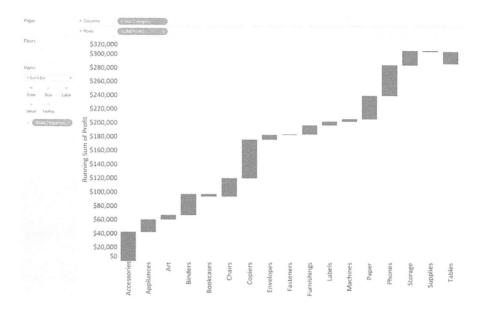

FIGURE 9.21   Illustration of waterfall chart.

9.2.3.1   Case Study

Consider the Sample-Superstore data source. Here, we want to plot the Running Profit of the Superstore over years, indicating whether profit values dip or rise continuously and by how much amount. We plot a waterfall chart to analyze the cumulative effect of the profit measure and see how it increases and decreases. The steps are given below:

> **Step 1**. Place the "Sales" measure to the Rows block and the "Sub-Category" dimension to the Columns block (Figure 9.22).

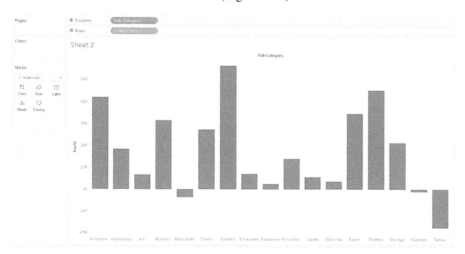

FIGURE 9.22   Output.

Step 2. Choose "Quick Table Calculation" from the menu that appears by right-clicking the metric and choose the "Running Total" option (Figure 9.23).

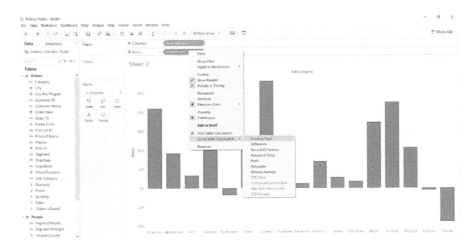

FIGURE 9.23 Output.

Step 3. The output with Running Total of profits is as follows (Figure 9.24).

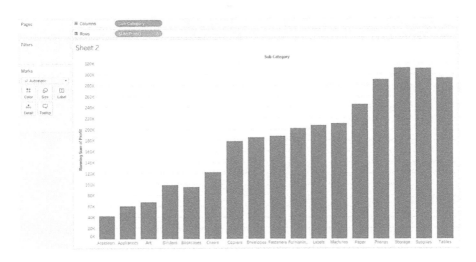

FIGURE 9.24 Output.

Step 4. Place the "Profit" metric to the Color under the Marks panel. Then, choose "Gantt Bar" from the mark type drop-down (Figure 9.25).

FIGURE 9.25   Output.

Step 5. Choose the "Create Calculated Field" option from the Analysis menu. Use the name "Profit Sizes" to create a new calculation for negative profit values (i.e., loss value). The calculation is given as: *-sum([Measure])* (Figure 9.26).

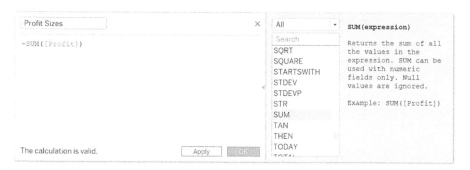

FIGURE 9.26   Output.

Step 6. Drag and place the "Profit Sizes" calculated field onto the Size card under the Marks shelf to generate a view depicting the required waterfall effect (Figure 9.27).

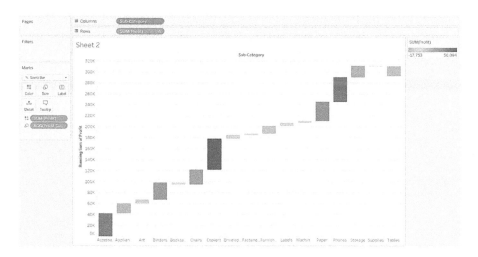

FIGURE 9.27 Output.

Step 7. Right-click the metric placed on the Rows block and choose "Edit Table Calculation" from pop-up drop-down. Select the "Specific Dimensions" option under the "Compute Using" section, and then tick the box next to the "Sub-Category" dimension. Close the window for table calculations (Figure 9.28).

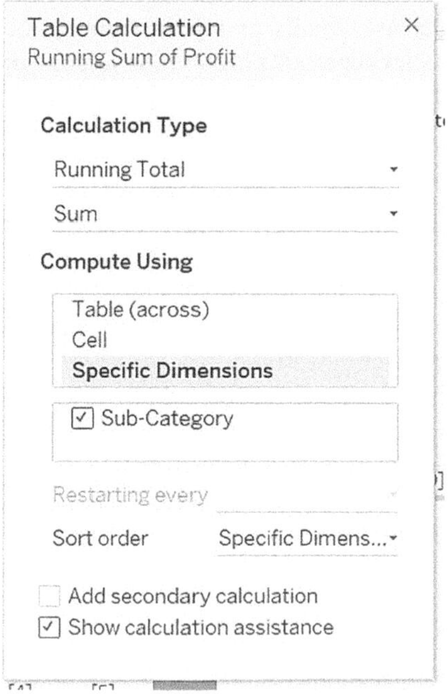

FIGURE 9.28 Output.

Step 8. Move the Profit measure to the Label card under the Marks shelf. The following is the waterfall chart that results, which displays the Running Total of Profit for each of the subcategories (Figure 9.29).

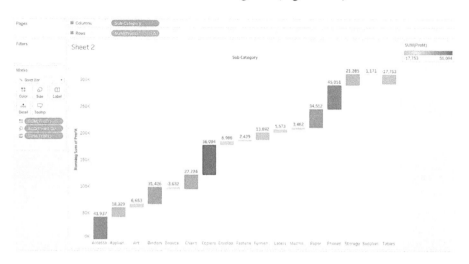

FIGURE 9.29   Output.

Conclusion:

- The waterfall chart above displays how the profit for each category increases or decreases finally giving the running total of profit values.
- The dark blue color represents high profit value, while deep orange and shades of orange represent drop in profits.

9.2.4   TREE MAPS

The tree map is a visual representation of nested rectangles that makes use of a hierarchy to depict categories within a dimension [7]. The tree map design was created by computer science professor Ben Shneiderman at the University of Maryland to make the best use of the space that was available while allowing for comparison and display of data and trends (Figure 9.30).

The Tableau Treemap structure is determined by dimensions, with each rectangle's size and color determined by Measures [7,8]. For example, the Sales and Profit compositions for each product sub-category in the Sample-Superstore dataset are displayed. Tree maps are visually appealing and are ideal for displaying cumulative totals for working data. They can be labeled with information like date, time, name, revenue, and budget.

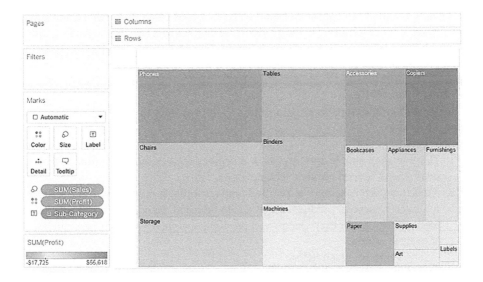

FIGURE 9.30 An illustration for tree map.

9.2.4.1 Building Blocks and Design Strategies for Treemap
The following are the fundamental components of a tree map (Figure 9.31).

Mark type:	Automatic or Square
Color:	Dimension or Measure
Size	Measure
Label or Detail:	Dimension(s)

FIGURE 9.31 Fundamental components of tree map.

Tree maps are useful when visualizing many related categories. However, if definite values should be prominently demonstrated, then a bar chart may be a better alternative to a tree map. A good tree map will possess the following characteristics:

- **Scalable Hierarchical Structure:** Tableau Treemap is a powerful tool for handling large amounts of data due to its scalability and hierarchical structure.
- **Easy to Interpret:** Its focus on highlighting major contributors is easy to interpret, with larger rectangles or bold colors making it a great option for linking and interpreting multiple marks in a single view.
- **Efficient Space Utilization:** Tree maps also allow efficient space utilization, with packed rectangles that can be nested to show additional parts-to-whole.
- **Distinct Value:** Each rectangle block represents distinct numerical values and a distinct hierarchy but does not display negative values.

At times, a tree map can appear cluttered with numerous categories, labels, and similar values, potentially leading to the need for alternatives like bar charts. Additionally, the number of components can cause the rectangles to become small, affecting the overall presentation.

9.2.4.2 Case Study

Consider the Sample-Superstore data source. Here, we want to display two scenarios using a tree map:

1. The tree map should initially show a segment-by-segment examination of sales across several product subcategories.
2. After that, apply changes to the tree map such that it now shows total sales sums across several product categories. In addition, we would like to see the profit variations for each category of products together with their percentage of overall values.

   The steps are given below:

   Step 1. Launch a new worksheet after connecting the default Superstore dataset.

   Step 2. For displaying a horizontal axis that shows product categories, place the "Sub-Category" dimension to Columns. Bring the "Sales" measure to Rows as well. Tableau provides a vertical axis and aggregates the measure as a total by default (Figure 9.32).

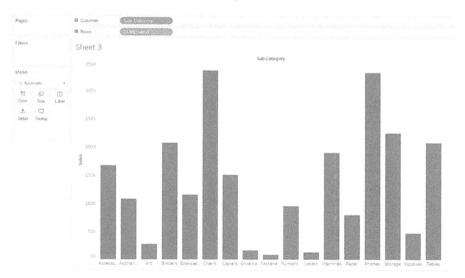

FIGURE 9.32 Output.

Step 3. Pick the "Treemap" type of graph after clicking "Show Me" on the toolbar to display a tree map rather than a bar chart (Figure 9.33).

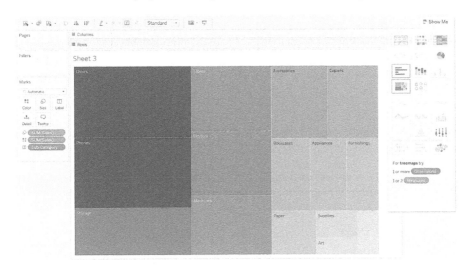

FIGURE 9.33 Output.

The amount of sales determines both the color and size of each rectangle; the higher the total sales for a category is, it is depicted by a darker shade along with a large box size.

Step 4. To implement the first scenario, drag the Segment dimension to the Color card and drag Sales to the Label card under the Marks shelf (Figure 9.34).

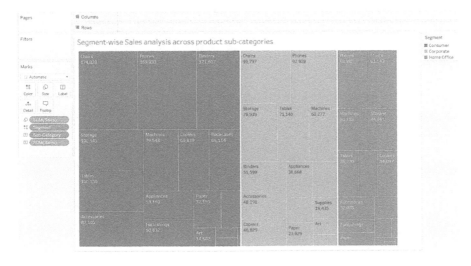

FIGURE 9.34 Output.

The tree map above displays three big colored blocks representing customer, corporate, and home office segments. Within each segment, we can observe nested blocks representing different subcategories varying by size.

Step 5. In addition, we wish to use color to differentiate between subcategories within each segment. On the Marks card, pick Color by placing the label icon to the left of "Sub-Category" (Figure 9.35).

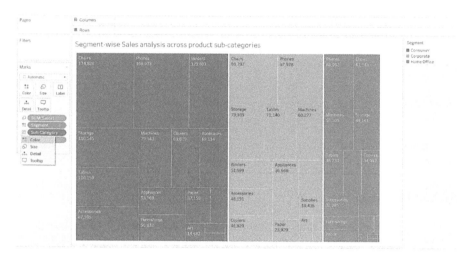

FIGURE 9.35   Output.

Final output for the first scenario is given below (Figure 9.36):

FIGURE 9.36   Output.

Step 6. Now, for implementing the second scenario, we drag the Profit measure to the Color card and to Label under the Marks shelf. Make necessary configurations for labels such as adding text "Profit," "Sales" before their numeric values and changing size, color, font of label, etc. (Figure 9.37).

FIGURE 9.37 Output.

The tree map above shows the color variation for profit values and size variation for sales value across each sub-category of products.

Note: Tree maps are primarily based on size and color, with measures placed on these variables. They can accommodate any number of dimensions, including one or two on color, but expanding beyond that divides the map into several smaller rectangles difficult to interpret.

9.3 CHARTS FOR DYNAMIC COMPOSITION OVER TIME

A dynamic composition chart is the one that shows change over time, i.e., we have a progression of change happening throughout the time. As learnt in the previous section, static composition charts focus on only one point in time, whereas in dynamic composition charts, we make comparisons over time. It is recommended to utilize stacked bar or column charts if there are a few time intervals involved. Give stacked area charts priority if there are a large number of timespans.

9.3.1 STACKED AREA CHARTS

An area chart, that demonstrates cumulative totals over time, is a standard line chart with a highlighted region between the line and axis. Stacked area charts, similar to area charts, allow comparison of data series by stacking group values on top of one another [8]. They highlight relative and absolute differences between categories and track changes in total values across various categories over time. Two distinct sorts of area charts are available in Tableau:

1. Continuous area plots
2. Discrete (or distinct) area plots

Since a continuous area plot does not have individual values, it is always measured. Conversely, because a discrete area plot looks at each value independently, it always counts every value within a category. The continuous area charts (or stacked area chart) are represented by the icon [icon], while discrete area charts are represented by the icon [icon] in Show Me in Tableau (Figure 9.38).

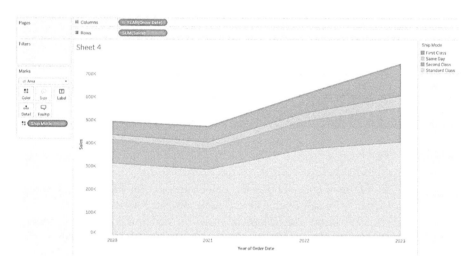

FIGURE 9.38   An illustration for stacked area chart.

A stacked area chart is useful for understanding the trend of variables and their breakdown by categories or groups [9]. It allows comparison of each subgroup's contribution to the total value over time. It works best with more than two series, but a simple chart can be created with only one series. Moderation is needed in the number of series to maintain legibility. While generating a stacked area plot, remember to use only data with positive values and try not to use too many groups to avoid plots from overlapping [9, 10].

9.3.1.1   Case Study

Consider the Superstore data collection. Here, we want to plot stacked area plots (continuous) and discrete area plots to view the part-to-whole composition of sales over the years 2019–2023 across multiple shipping modes with stacked layers for each product category. The steps are given below:

Step 1. Launch a new worksheet.

Step 2. Tableau advises utilizing a date field when creating an area chart. So, we begin by placing the "Order-Date" dimension onto the Columns block. Additionally, place the measure "Sales" to the Rows block (Figure 9.39).

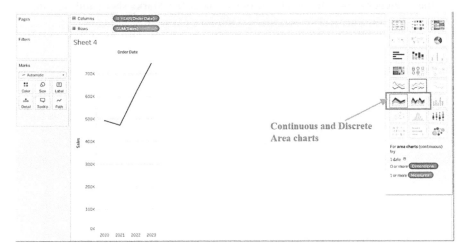

FIGURE 9.39 Output.

Step 3. By default, we can see a line plot created for sales over time. However, we need to plot a continuous stacked area plot for this scenario. So, choose the continuous stacked chart from the Show Me tab.

Now, drag the "Ship Mode" field from Data Pane to Color under the Marks panel (Figure 9.40).

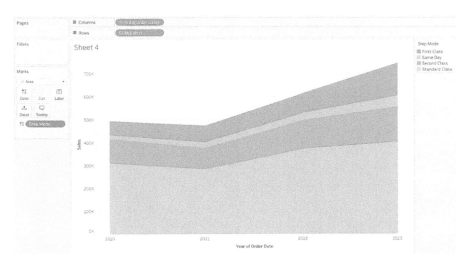

FIGURE 9.40 Output.

The chart is divided into four shipping modes: same day, first class, standard class, and second class with the x-axis representing 2020–2023 and the y-axis indicating the total sales scale.

Step 4. To view internal stacked area coverage for each product category, place the "Category" field to the Detail block under the Marks shelf, adding thin lines for furniture, office sales, and technology (Figure 9.41).

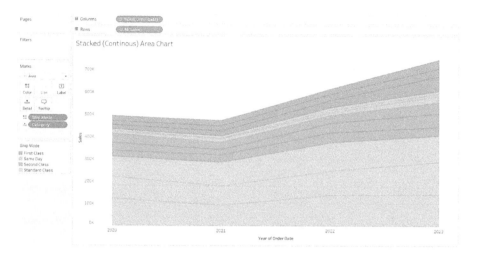

FIGURE 9.41   Output.

Step 5. Let us choose the discrete area chart, the second form of area chart, from Show Me. To do this, we return to the visualization window and choose Area charts (discrete) (Figure 9.42).

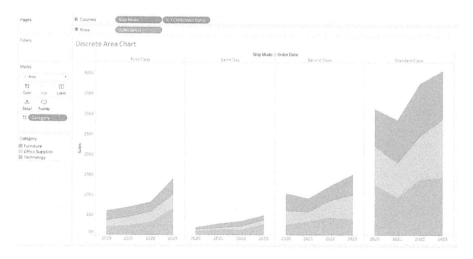

FIGURE 9.42   Output.

The discrete area chart divides the chart space into four sections, displaying separate charts for the four shipping fmodes, as shown in the screenshot above.

Conclusion:

- The cursor can be hovered on specific area segments to access information about it over a 4-year period.

KEY NOTES

- Composition involves understanding the components of a whole and visualizing how they come together.
- The choice between a pie or donut chart depends on the number of categories to compare. Pie charts have more than 4 or 5 categories, while donut charts have 2–4 categories.
- Waterfall charts show a running total, tree maps have nested rectangles, and area charts have a colored shaded area between lines and axis.
- Stacked area charts, like area charts, allow comparison of data series by stacking group values on top of one another.

PRACTICE CASE STUDY

E-Commerce Sales Performance Dashboard

Create an E-Commerce Sales Performance Dashboard using the E-Commerce Data containing records for actual transactions from UK retailers. This dataset is present on the Kaggle and UCI data repository.

TEST YOUR SKILLS

1. What are the different types of composition charts?
2. Differentiate between pie chart and donut chart.
3. How the waterfall chart is helpful in plotting business use-cases?
4. Differentiate between tree map and heat map.
5. How stacked charts are helpful in displaying dynamic composition over time?
6. Discuss the benefits of using area chart over other composition charts.

REFERENCES

[1] Jamsa, Kris. *Introduction to Data Mining and Analytics with Machine Learning in R and Python*. United States, Jones & Bartlett Learning, LLC, 2020.
[2] Ohmann, Ashley, and Floyd, Matt. *Creating Data Stories with Tableau Public*. United Kingdom, Packt Publishing, 2015.
[3] Wexler, Steve, et al. *The Big Book of Dashboards: Visualizing Your Data Using Real-World Business Scenarios*. Germany, Wiley, 2017.

[4] Milligan, Joshua N. *Learning Tableau 2019: Tools for Business Intelligence, Data Prep, and Visual Analytics*, 3rd Edition. India, Packt Publishing, 2019.

[5] Loth, Alexander. *Visual Analytics with Tableau*. United States, Wiley, 2019.

[6] Costello, Tim, and Blackshear, Lori. *Prepare Your Data for Tableau: A Practical Guide to the Tableau Data Prep Tool*. Germany, Apress, 2019.

[7] Sleeper, Ryan. *Practical Tableau: 100 Tips, Tutorials, and Strategies from a Tableau Zen Master*. United States, O'Reilly Media, 2018.

[8] Khan, Arshad. *Jumpstart Tableau: A Step-By-Step Guide to Better Data Visualization*. United States, Apress, 2016.

[9] Acharya, Seema, and Chellappan, Subhashini. *Pro Tableau: A Step-by-Step Guide*. United States, Apress, 2016.

[10] Murray, Daniel G. *Tableau Your Data! Fast and Easy Visual Analysis with Tableau Software*. Germany, Wiley, 2016.

10 Project Management with Evaluation Charts

10.1 INTRODUCTION PROJECT AND PROJECT MANAGEMENT

The attempt to implement actions necessary to accomplish a specific goal given a finite number of resources and time can be summed up as a project. With the aid of a project team, project managers can use the process of project management to plan, carry out, monitor, and complete projects [1]. To do this, they must guide team members through each step of the project lifecycle using project management principles, methodologies, and tools (Figure 10.1).

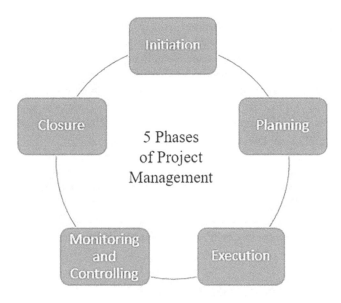

FIGURE 10.1 Various stages in the project management process.

The five stages of the lifecycle process of project management are as follows:

1. **Project Initiation:** The project's conceptualization phase starts with the idea and creating a business case document. The feasibility is checked in terms of costs, timeline, and resources. If approved, a statement of work (SOW) for the project is formulated, discussed, and signed, while finalizing the budget.

DOI: 10.1201/9781003429593-10

2. **Project Planning and Design:** Phase two of the project management process is underway. This phase involves creating a comprehensive project plan. This plan includes the tasks, necessary materials, due dates, expenses, etc. More preparation is done for requirements prioritization.

3. **Project Execution:** The phase of finalizing the project idea and preparation has begun, necessitating the application of earlier planning. The planning is crucial to this phase's success. Project managers adhere to procedures like assigning tasks, allocating resources, holding daily meetings, and compiling a status report based on the advancement of the project. The execution is better when the plan is executed well.

4. **Project Monitoring and Control:** The monitoring phase, which occurs simultaneously with the execution phase, aims to ensure execution follows the plan and adheres to timelines and costs. Key performance indicators (KPIs) are set, progress reports are compared to the project plan, deviations are reduced, KPIs are redefined, plans are updated to meet deadlines, budget utilization is monitored, and project quality is assessed. This phase ensures the project is completed according to plan.

5. **Project Completion and Closeout:** It is critical to release a project to the client or market after it's finished. This entails carrying out the deployment strategy from the planning stage, which entails delivering deliverables, informing stakeholders of closure, approving business documents, releasing team members, completing contracts, submitting payments and paperwork, maintaining knowledge acquired, and establishing support and maintenance structures. The project's success and a smooth transfer for subsequent initiatives are both guaranteed by this procedure.

To plan, carry out, and monitor projects, project management system is necessary. With just one web tool, the project manager can make use of functions like scheduling, monitoring deadlines, budgets, resources, and team synchronization [2]. It creates project schedules and assigns work based on real-time resource availability using visualization approaches such as Gantt charts, Pareto charts, Pert charts, and Risk Matrix [2,3].

10.2 PROJECT MANAGEMENT CHARTS

Project Management involves planning and executing a project to achieve organizational goals. Project managers deliver all project components using tools and techniques to move work forward on time and within budget. Visual charts, such as flowcharts, network diagrams, and bar charts, simplify complex ideas into easily understandable resources for project planning [3]. The commonly used charts in Project Management are listed below:

1. Gauge charts
2. Bullet chart
3. Gantt chart

4. Resource assignment matrix (RAM)
5. Pareto chart

Let us discuss each of these charts in detail.

10.2.1 Gauge Charts to Visualize Metrics

A Tableau Gauge chart, also known as a Tableau speedometer graph, is a quantitative visualization style that displays the minimum, current, and maximum values of a single measure or data field [4]. It is commonly used by administrators to monitor the development of multiple departments or critical data fields. The chart is simple to understand, with a scale divided into segments with different colors representing different values (Figure 10.2).

FIGURE 10.2 An illustration for Gauge chart.

A Tableau Gauge chart consists of three main components: the Gauge Dial, a numeric needle pointer, and a pivot point. The Gauge Dial displays the range of information, the needle points to a specific value, and the pivot point is the center point where the user can view the default needle value.

10.2.1.1 Use Cases for a Gauge Chart

Tableau gauge charts are useful in various scenarios with multiple data fields due to their simplicity. They can show step-by-step information, compare sales with targets, manage projects, visualize statistical data in finance or economics, create administration reports, and implement parameters for competitive studies or product comparisons.

10.2.1.2 Case Study

Consider the Sample-Superstore data source. Here, we are going to create a Gauge chart to indicate the percent sales for each year and a combination of years given the total sales for all 4 years from 2020 to 2023. The steps are given below:

Step 1. Establish connection to the Sample-Superstore data and open a new worksheet.

Step 2. To construct a dummy calculated field, double-click on the Rows section, input 0, and press the "Enter" key. Create a second calculated field following the same process again. This will produce a blank sheet without any values (Figure 10.3).

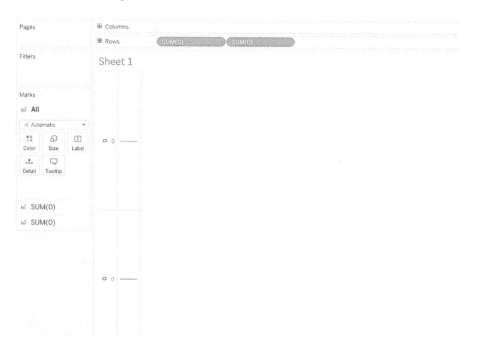

FIGURE 10.3 Output.

Step 3. Select the Dual-Axis option from the drop-down menu of the second dummy field (Figure 10.4).

FIGURE 10.4 Output.

Step 4. The output is given below (Figure 10.5).

FIGURE 10.5 Output.

Step 5. Next, select "Pie" from the Marks card to alter the chart type. Remove the Measure Names as well as the "All" Marks section (Figure 10.6).

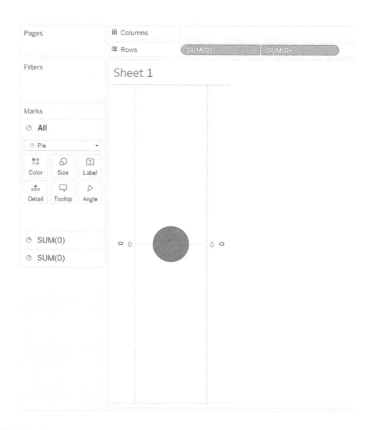

FIGURE 10.6   Output.

Step 6. To match the backdrop color, change the second Pie (SUM(0))'s color to white (Figure 10.7).

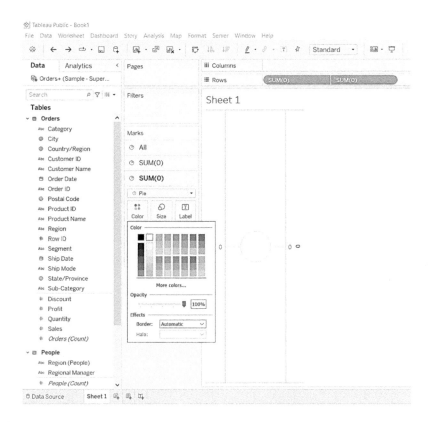

FIGURE 10.7 Output.

Step 7. Reduce the second Pie (SUM(0))'s size as well to generate a donut chart. Switch the sheet's view to "Entire View" and spread the donut across the interface (Figure 10.8).

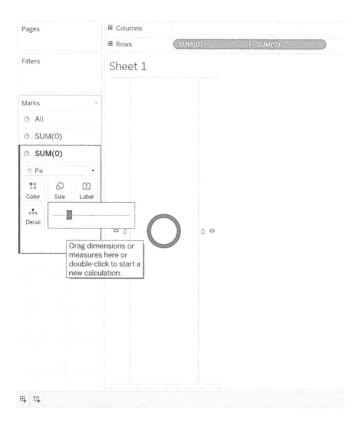

FIGURE 10.8 Output.

Step 8. In the subsequent phases, we will segment our donut chart according to the proportion of values taken from the Sales dimension. Choose the Create Calculated Field option under Analysis in the menu (Figure 10.9).

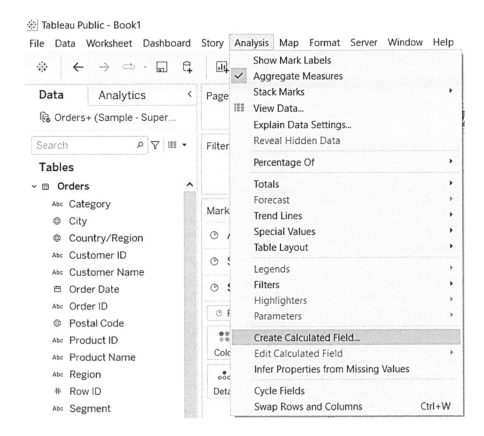

FIGURE 10.9   Output.

Step 9. First, we will create a calculated field named "PercentSales," using Fixed LOD to depict percentage of Sales per year against total Sales. This value will be used later in our chart to act as an indicator for Year sales (Figure 10.10).

FIGURE 10.10   Output.

Step 10. Create another Calculated Field which will store this percent value and will be used to create necessary indicators for our Gauge chart (Figure 10.11).

FIGURE 10.11   Output.

Step 11. These calculated fields enable to get angles and colors for all the slices. The idea is to color the donut slices according to the value of the %.
   a.   If the value is less than 35%, it will be red.
   b.   If the value is between 35% and 65%, it will be yellow.
   c.   If the value is more than 65%, it will be green.

Step 12. The first field is "Value_Red" to Color the 1st Half of Gauge. The descriptive diagram for explanation along with the code written in calculated field is (Figure 10.12).

Portion of
First Half

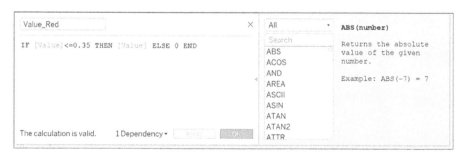

FIGURE 10.12   Output.

Step 13. The first field is "Value_Yellow" to Color the 1st Half of Gauge. The descriptive diagram along with the code written in calculated field is as follows (Figure 10.13).

FIGURE 10.13   Output.

Mark the slice in yellow color if VALUE is between 0.35 and 0.50, else if VALUE is between 0.5 and 0.65, then mark only slice till 0.5(or 50% of Gauge) as yellow. Rest, we will create another calculated field to mark part between 0.5 and 0.65 as yellow.

Step 14. The next calculated field is "Value_Green" to Color the 1st Half of Gauge. The descriptive diagram is (Figure 10.14).

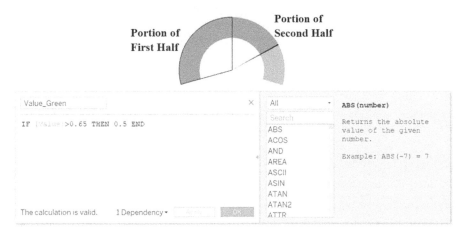

FIGURE 10.14   Output.

Mark the 1st half slice as complete Green if VALUE is greater than 0.65% or 65%. The part in the 2nd half also shows Green in the descriptive diagram because of another calculated field created later to color the 2nd half.

Step 15. The other calculated field is "Value_Grey" to color the first half of Gauge. Mark the remaining slice after VALUE as Grey, and if VALUE is greater than 0.5, then do not mark any part as gray for now. The code written in calculated field is (Figure 10.15).

The code written in the calculated field is:

FIGURE 10.15   Output.

Step 16. The next calculated field is "Value_Yellow2" to color the 2nd Half of Gauge. Mark the remaining part between VALUE and 0.5 as Yellow. (Whole 1st half slice till 0.5 was already colored Yellow in the "Value_Yellow" calculated field for VALUE>0.5 condition) (Figure 10.16)

FIGURE 10.16   Output.

Step 17. Now create another calculated field "Value_Green2" to color 2nd Half of Gauge. If VALUE greater than 0.65, Mark the remaining part between VALUE and 0.5 as Green (As we know, whole 1st Half was already Green from "Value_green" calculated field logic) (Figure 10.17).

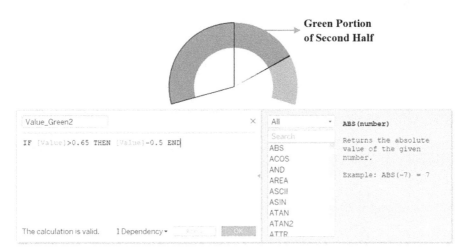

FIGURE 10.17 Output.

Step 18. The other calculate field we create is "Value_Grey" to color 2nd Half of Gauge. This enables to mark the remaining part in the second part of the slice as gray (Figure 10.18).

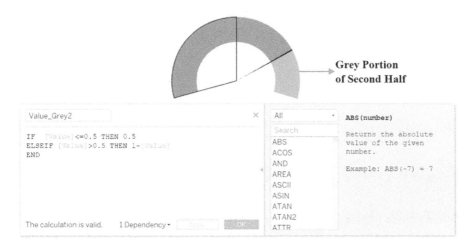

FIGURE 10.18 Output

Step 19. The next calculated field called "Value_White" to color 3rd Half of Gauge. This decides the width of the 3rd part of the Gauge chart. If we kept the value as.50, the shape would have been an entire semi-circle. The descriptive diagram with code written in the calculated field is as follows (Figure 10.19).

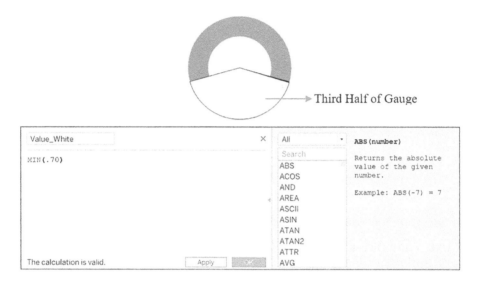

→ Third Half of Gauge

FIGURE 10.19   Output.

Step 20. Now we create Needles for the first and second Half of our Gauge chart. The next calculated field is "Needle1" for first half and "Needle2" for second half (Figure 10.20).

FIGURE 10.20   Output.

The calculated field for "Needle2" (Figure 10.21).

FIGURE 10.21   Output.

After this the list of all calculated fields as can be seen in the section of Measure Names (Figure 10.22).

FIGURE 10.22   Output.

Step 21. Under the "All" card in Marks shelf, drag Measure Names to "Color" and Measure Values to "Angle" to get the respective angles according to the logic used in calculated fields. Edit Filter for Measure Names and select only the ten Cal Fields (excluding "PercentSales" and "Values" fields) that we created above. Also, we can change the colors of slices accordingly (Figure 10.23).

FIGURE 10.23   Output.

Step 22. Our Gauge chart will now start taking shape. But, if you notice, it is tilted to the right side. This happens because, in Tableau, pie charts usually start from 90° (vertical top) and move clockwise. So, 1st Half of the Gauge starts from the vertical top instead of the left side from where we want. So, all slices must be arranged similarly, like below (Figure 10.24).

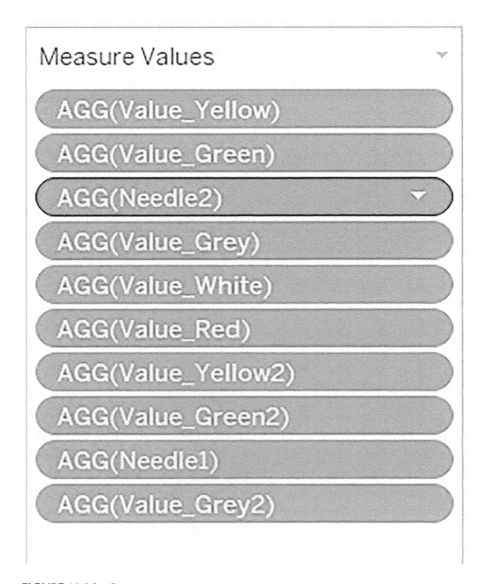

FIGURE 10.24 Output.

Step 23. We need the 2nd smaller pie chart of our Donut to vanish, to get the correct shape of our Gauge chart. For this, we'll create a dummy Cal Field, with value as "dummy," put it on the 2nd pie chart, and make it similar to the background color, white in our case (Figure 10.25).

FIGURE 10.25   Output.

Step 24. Drag the calculated field "Dummy" to the Detail card of the second pie and then modify that to Colors (Figure 10.26).

FIGURE 10.26   Output.

Step 25. Next, open the Color section for the 2nd Pie represented by the second Sum(0) under Marks shelf, and double-click each item to change the color of all fields to White and just the color of both Needles to Black (Figure 10.27).

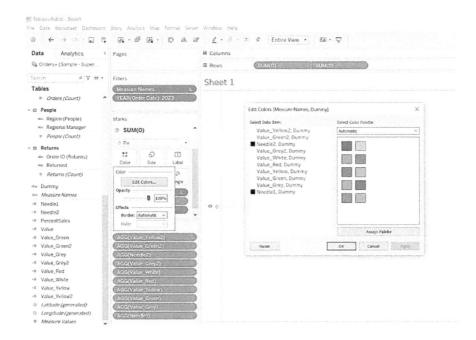

FIGURE 10.27 Output.

Step 26. Now click Color under the first "Sum(0)" in Marks shelf. Change the color of each field as specified in their name itself like change "Value_Red" to Red color, "Value_Green" and "Value_Green2" to Green color etc (Figure 10.28).

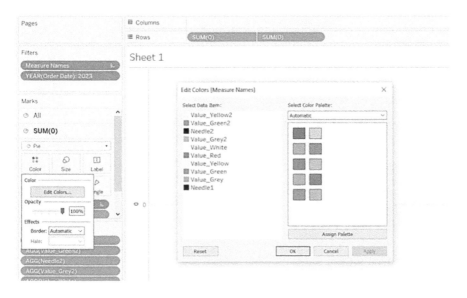

FIGURE 10.28 Output.

Step 27. Drag Order-Date to Filters and right-click it to select the option "Show Filter." Now we can select any year that we want to view (Figure 10.29).

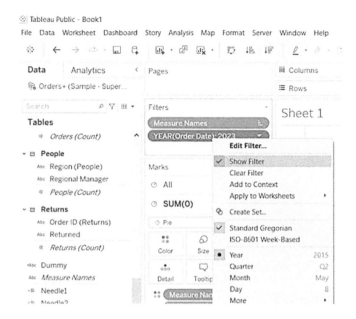

FIGURE 10.29   Output.

Step 28. Now the final Gauge chart with selected years is as follows (Figure 10.30).

FIGURE 10.30   Output.

Step 29. Now we want to add labels for better explanation of the gauge pointer value. So, drag the PercentSales calculated field to the Label card of first pie represented by first Sum(0) under Marks shelf (Figure 10.31).

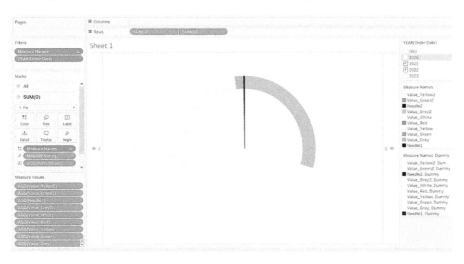

FIGURE 10.31 Output.

Step 30. Click on Label under first Sum(0) and click on three dots present in front of Text to open Edit Label window. Here add the necessary text and required formatting as per choice and close the window. Also, select "Highlighted" option under Marks to Label section (Figure 10.32).

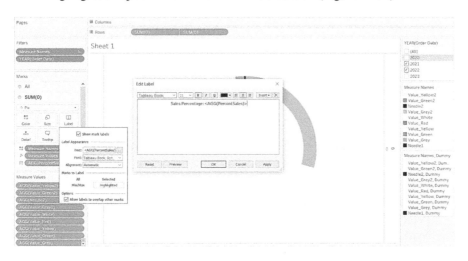

FIGURE 10.32 Output.

Step 31. Now as we select the highlighted area of Gauge chart, we can see the label but it disappears when we remove selection. So to solve this, select the highlighted area of the Gauge chart and right-click on the label visible. Then click on Mark Label option and select "Always Show" option (Figure 10.33).

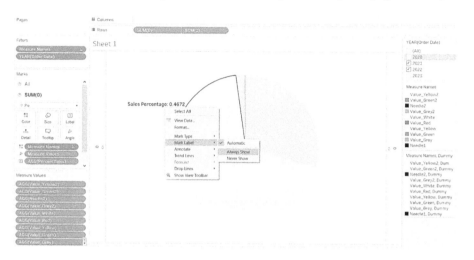

FIGURE 10.33   Output.

Step 32. Here we observe that actual percentage value is not visible. So, we create another calculated field named LabelSalesPercentage and calculate percentage value from PercentSales calculated field (Figure 10.34).

FIGURE 10.34   Output.

Step 33. Finally drag LabelSalesPercentage calculated field instead of PercentSales calculated field under Label card of first pie Sum(0) under Marks shelf (Figure 10.35).

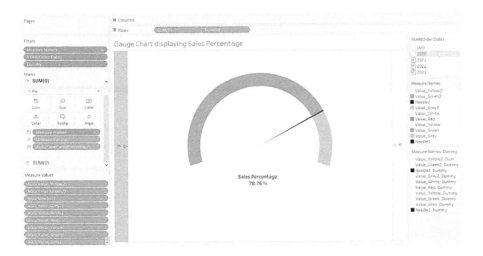

FIGURE 10.35   Output.

Conclusion:
* In a single view using Gauge chart, we can observe in which year sales was below 35% mark in red color and when it was between 35% and 65% in yellow color while more than 65% sales are represented in green color.

10.2.2   CALENDAR REPORTS

Calendars can be useful in reports to show the trend in metrics like ongoing sales, profits, customers, etc. given by each day of a selected month. It can also be used in Dashboards as a filter for other reports by showing relevant data for a selected number of days. A project management calendar is a tool used to plan, organize, and execute a project's tasks [5]. It provides information on the tasks to be completed, their start and end dates, the task responsibilities, and critical milestones. Calendars for projects, tasks, and resources can be used by project managers.

10.2.2.1   Case Study

To implement a simple calendar report here we are using the Superstore Dataset and building a calendar view based on the Order Dates. The steps are given below:

Step 1. Connect to Sample-Superstore and open a new worksheet.
Step 2. First, we will apply the Order-Date as a filter to view data only for 1 month say March month. We can right-click the Month (Order-Date) filter and select Show Filter to select any month as per choice. A Calendar View requires the Date attribute both on the Row and Column shelf of Tableau (Figure 10.36).

FIGURE 10.36 Output.

> **Step 3**. Now, change the column Order-Date to Weekday and the row
> Order-Date to Week Number by clicking on the drop-down of each Date
> attribute and selecting the respective option. This will give us the view of a
> Calendar by aggregating all days in the Column to Weekday level (Sunday
> to Saturday) and aggregating all days in the Rows to Week Number level
> (the number of the particular week in that year) (Figure 10.37).

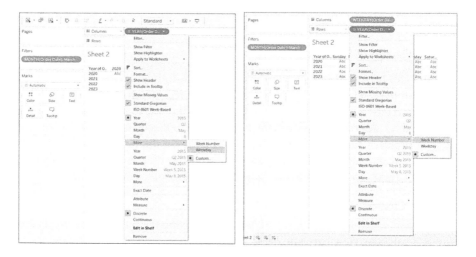

FIGURE 10.37 Output.

The view created after selecting Entire View settings and implementing
above changes is given in Figure 10.38.

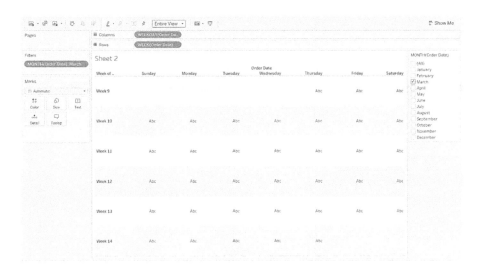

FIGURE 10.38   Output.

Step 4. Drag Order-Date dimension to Filters again. This time create filter for Year (Order-Date) and right-click the filter to select Show Filter option. Now we can select to view calendar for any year and its specific month. Figure 10.39 filter March, 2022.

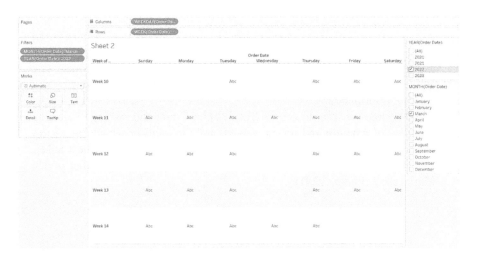

FIGURE 10.39   Output.

Step 5. Next, we want the respective dates to appear on the Calendar instead of the default string "Abc." For this, we will again pull the Order-Date attribute, drag it to Text tab. Now click this Year(Order-Date) label and change its format to display only Day (by selecting the appropriate option from the drop-down) (Figure 10.40).

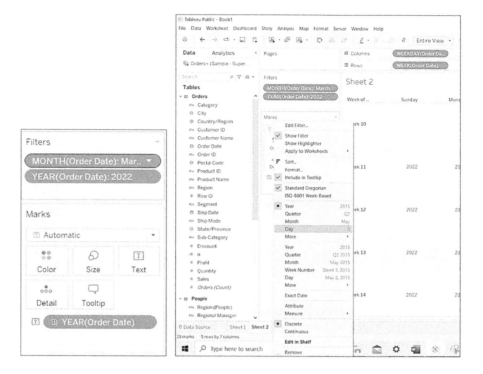

FIGURE 10.40   Output.

Thus, we got our calendar view. But this does not make much sense yet as there is no data displayed on the calendar, so it is not of much use yet. In the next step we will start adding some data and format to display the relevant information.

Step 6. Suppose we want to see the Total Order Count and Average Sales for each day of a month and format this visually to analyze which day of the week usually receive the greatest number of orders and make highest Sales. For this drag Orders (Count) and Sum (Sales) measures to Label under Marks shelf (Figure 10.41).

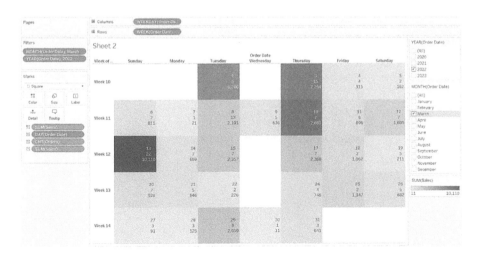

FIGURE 10.41   Output.

Step 7. Also, we want to display the calendar as a Heat Map to show the trend
in Sales measure across the entire month. For this we drag the Sum(Sales)
to "Color" Mark. Also, change the visualization from Automatic to Square
from the drop-down in Marks shelf to get the Heat Map color for the entire
cell and not just the text (Figure 10.42).

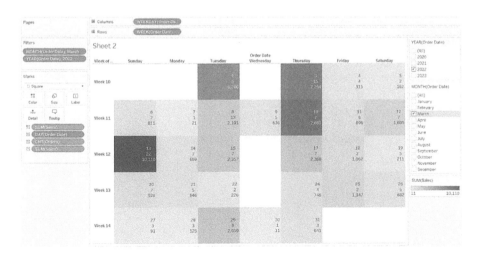

FIGURE 10.42   Output.

Step 8. We update the labels to better understand the output. For this click on
Label under Marks shelf and click on three dots present in front of Text to
open Edit Label window. We add necessary text before every value such as
Date, Order Count, and Total Sales (Figure 10.43).

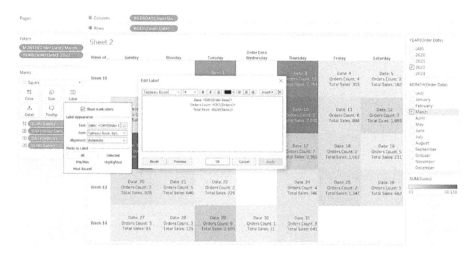

FIGURE 10.43   Output.

Step 9. The final out of the Calendar is as follows (Figure 10.44).

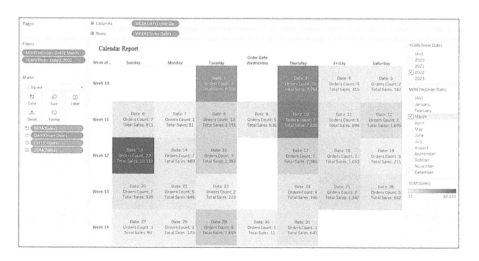

FIGURE 10.44   Output.

Conclusion:

- Here, as the color shade gets darker, it represents higher sales on that day compared to days with lighter color Shade.
- This type of Calendar Report can be very useful to analyze day-wise figures for each month, compare the performance and discover any trend between the metrices and any day of the week.

10.2.3 Bullet Graph in Tableau

A bullet chart is a sophisticated bar chart that allows for comparison of two measurements on a single bar [6,7]. It features a main dark bar on the front, with a reference line beneath it. The reference line can be divided into segments like 50%, 80%, and 100%. Bullet charts are highly informative due to their smaller size and more detailed information. For example, comparing actual and predicted sales as different metrics (Figure 10.45).

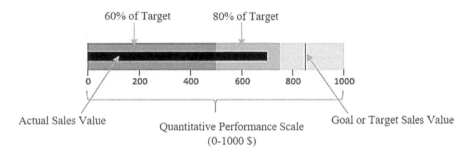

FIGURE 10.45 An illustration for bullet chart.

The example uses a bullet chart to display actual sales and predicted sales on a single bar. The solid black line represents actual sales, while the grey reference line represents predicted sales. This visualization allows for a comparison of actual sales against predicted sales values and assesses progress. The bullet chart serves as a gauge or measure visualization, allowing for easy comparison and assessment of progress.

10.2.3.1 Use Cases for Bullet Chart

- One type of visual aid that shows the objective goal, the current dataset, and the past datasets all at once is the bullet graph.
- One should not use it to analyze distribution, flow, part-to-whole, or change over time. Rather, comparisons are made between forecasts and actual data using bullet graphs.

- They are used by business analysts to check if teams or departments are on track, healthcare systems to gauge capacity, and nonprofits to measure fundraising progress.
- They also help gauge quantitative measures in relation to qualitative ranges, such as production levels, network usage, and marketing campaigns.
- A bullet graph can also be used to measure customer frequency, store attendance, or a daily goal.

10.2.3.2 Case Study

Step 1. Launch a new worksheet after connecting to the Sample-Superstore data source.

Step 2. Press Ctrl key and select Sub-category dimension field with two other measures Sales and Profit. Click on Show Me option to access the visualization pane. Then, we select the bullet graph option with icon ≡ from the visualization pane (Figure 10.46).

FIGURE 10.46 Output.

Step 3. The result is a bullet chart with bars that have blue lines in the foreground and grey lines (reference lines) in the background. The field that is displayed on the Marks section's Detail card is the reference line field. In the figure, the reference field is "Sales," while the main field is "Profit" (Figure 10.47).

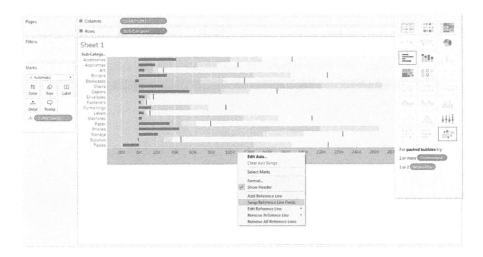

FIGURE 10.47 Output.

Step 4. To obtain a different viewpoint, we can modify or swap both fields. Right-click on the x-axis and select "Swap Reference Line Fields" option. Additionally, switch from Standard to Entire View in the view type (Figure 10.48).

FIGURE 10.48 Output.

Step 5. Right-click on the X-axis and choose "Add Reference Line" to add a reference line for each unique category. Replace Value with "SUM(Sales)" and set the aggregation type for the line as "Average" For the Label set the "None" value. The most significant modification is the switch from "Per Pane" to "Per Cell" for the Scope radio button (Figure 10.49).

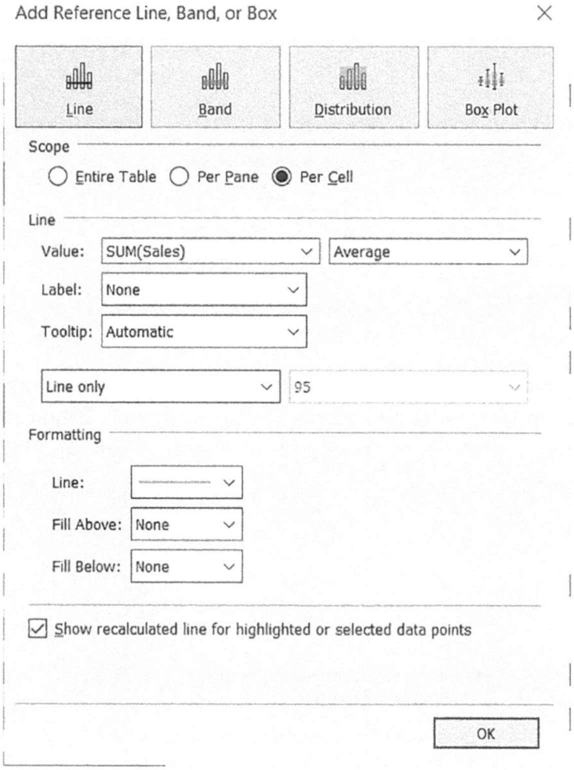

FIGURE 10.49   Output.

The output after doing above settings in given below (Figure 10.50).

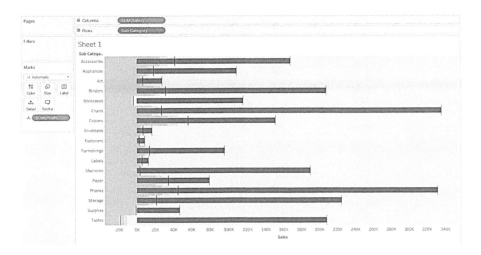

FIGURE 10.50 Output.

Step 6. To observe which categories are exceeding the bar of 60% or 80% of the average Profit, right-click the X-axis once more, pick Edit Reference Line, and then click 60% or 80% of Average Profit (Figure 10.51).

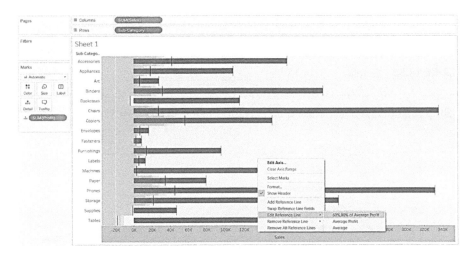

FIGURE 10.51 Output.

Step 7. We choose Scope as "Per Cell" and Label as None in the Edit Reference Line dialog box. The configurations we chose are depicted in the following image (Figure 10.52).

FIGURE 10.52 Output.

Step 8. The final bullet chart is displayed as below (Figure 10.53).

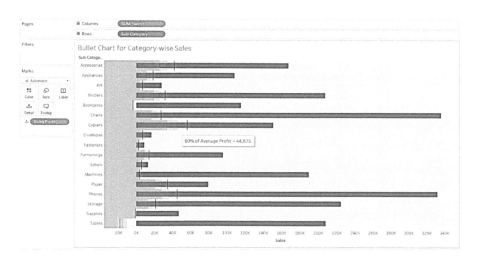

FIGURE 10.53 Output.

Conclusion:

- Thus, our final bullet chart showing sales and profit values for each electronics sub-category or brand is ready.
- The reference line splits into three segments when the percent average option is used. We will initially notice a 60% Average Profit mark with the value when the cursor is over the reference line.
- 80% of the Average Profit mark with the value is located further up the reference line. Thus, we can see the key values on the solid blue bar and more specific figures on the reference line.

10.2.4 GANTT CHART FOR PROJECT PLANNING

When presenting different tasks against time in project management, a Gantt chart is a helpful tool. It shows a time scale at the top and a list of activities on the left, with a horizontal bar for each activity [7]. The start, duration, and finish dates are reflected in the bar's position and length. Gantt charts can provide detailed representations of data values in various timeframes, including yearly, quarterly, monthly, weekly, or daily. This provides an overview of the project's activities, their start and end dates, their scheduled duration, overlaps with other activities, and the overall project's start and end dates (Figure 10.54).

FIGURE 10.54   Output.

As in the above figure, Gantt charts display durations of activities, such as average delivery time for products, with distinct colors assigned for each year, month, or quarter. They are useful for tracking data trends and displaying activities and schedules. They can be used to display data in detail, allowing for easier tracking of value over time.

10.2.4.1 Case Study

Use the data source Sample-Superstore as an example. Following these instructions will help you produce a Gantt chart that displays the typical number of days that pass between the order date and the ship date.

Step 1. Move the Order-Date dimension to Columns shelf. Tableau automatically groups dates by year and provides column headings with year labels. But we'd like to examine durations on a weekly basis. Consequently, pick Week Number by clicking the Year (Order-Date) drop-down arrow on the Columns shelf (Figure 10.55).

FIGURE 10.55   Output.

After this change the view that is displayed is as follows (Figure 10.56).

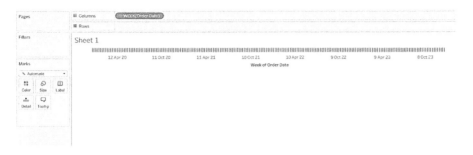

FIGURE 10.56   Output.

The heads for the columns change. Since there are 208 weeks in a 4-year period, the view does not display labels for individual weeks; instead, it displays tick marks.

Step 2. At this point place the Sub-Category and Ship Mode dimensions over to the Rows shelf. To the right of "Sub-Category," place the "Ship Mode." This creates a two-level hierarchical structure of dimensions along the left axis (Figure 10.57).

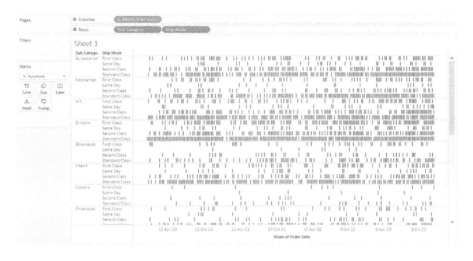

FIGURE 10.57   Output.

We will resize marks based on the interval between the order date and the ship date by creating a calculated field.

Step 3. In the toolbar menu, click on Analysis and select Create Calculated Field (Figure 10.58).

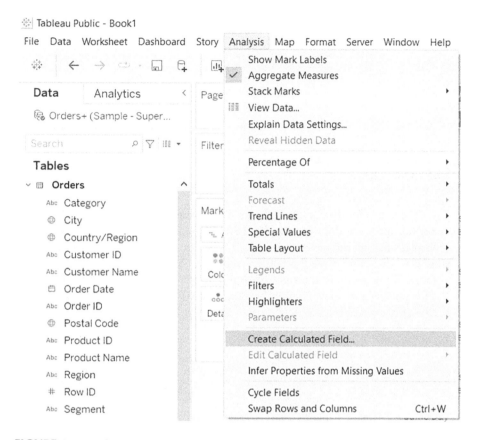

FIGURE 10.58   Output.

Step 4. Name the calculated field "OrderShipDifference" in the calculation dialog box. Insert the following formula in the Formula box, and finally hit OK.

DATEDIFF("day," [Order Date], [Ship Date])

The formula provides a unique measurement that records the days-long difference between the values of the Order-Date and Ship Date (Figure 10.59).

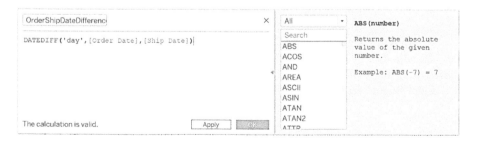

FIGURE 10.59   Output.

Step 5. On the Marks card, move the "OrderShipDateDifference" measure to Size. The default aggregation is Sum, but in this instance
averaging the variables makes more sense. For this, right-click the
SUM(OrderShipDateDifference) field on the Marks card, choose Measure
(Sum), and then click the option "Average" (Figure 10.60).

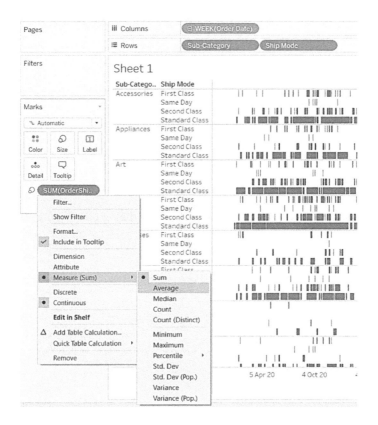

FIGURE 10.60   Output.

Step 6. At this moment, the Order-Date filter can be applied to limit the Gantt
chart to a certain period. Therefore, while holding down the Ctrl key, move
the Week(Order-Date) field from the Columns shelf to the Filter shelf
(Figure 10.61).

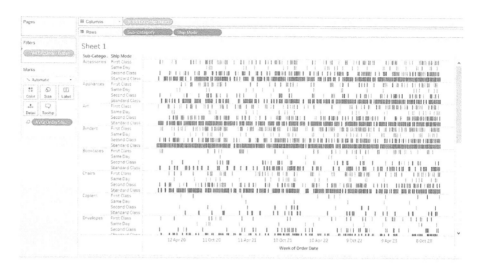

FIGURE 10.61   Output.

Pick the Range of Dates option in the filter dialog box (Figure 10.62).

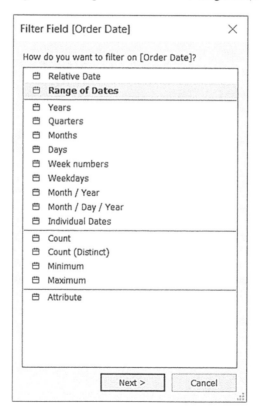

FIGURE 10.62   Output.

Step 7. Select a three-month time frame for the range, such as 01/31/2022 to 03/30/2022, or January to March 2022, and then click OK (Figure 10.63).

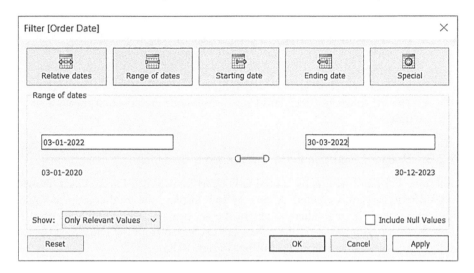

FIGURE 10.63   Output.

Step 8. On the Marks card, drag the Ship Mode dimension to Color. Now, your view provides plenty of data on the delay between order and ship timings (Figure 10.64).

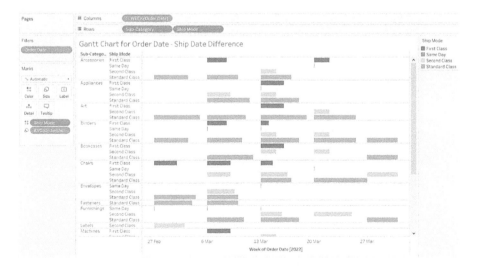

FIGURE 10.64   Output.

Conclusion:

- Here, the "Same Day" ship mode has the lowest lag time while the "Standard Class" ship mode is more prone to greater lag periods.
- In general, the following sub-categories have long lag times:
  - Art
  - Binders
  - Fasteners, Furnishings, and Tables.
- The lag times for "Standard Class" ship mode are constant throughout time.

10.2.5 Pareto Chart for Event Significance

Combining bar and line graphs, a dual-axis chart known as a Pareto chart (named after Vilfredo Pareto) is created. A curving line displays the total combined value, while bars reflect the individual values in the set of data. The cumulative total is shown by the curving line, and the values are expressed from the longest bar to the smallest bar, with individual values falling (Figure 10.65).

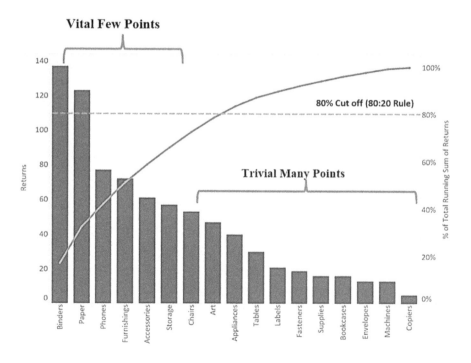

FIGURE 10.65   An illustration for Pareto chart.

The Pareto principle—also referred to as the 80/20 rule, states that 20% of causes account for 80% of effects in occurrences [7, 8]. This idea is used in a Pareto chart to demonstrate how the running total values of the few most significant categories contribute most to the total. The cumulative % line shows which categories to target for overall improvement, and the initial bars are the tallest, suggesting the most significant product categories with greater running total values. Let us discuss the components of Pareto chart:

1. **Bar Chart (Vertical):** A vertical bar chart is a visual tool used to represent various factors or categories, with each bar's height representing the frequency, magnitude, or relevance of the category.
2. **Organized Descending Order:** The bars are organized in descending order, with the most important category on the left.
3. **Line with Cumulative Percentage:** A cumulative percentage line is superimposed on the bar chart, illustrating the cumulative percentage of each category's overall contribution.
4. **Labels for Axis:** The chart uses axis labels to represent the frequency or magnitude of each category, and category labels to indicate the associated category.
5. **Labels for Category:** Each bar on the graph is labeled to illustrate the category it belongs to.
6. **Emphasis on Vital Few:** Pareto charts emphasize the "80/20" concept, suggesting that a large amount of influence can be tracked to a small number of factors, helping to prioritize resources and attention to the most important areas for improvement.
7. **Decision-Making with Careful Analysis:** The chart also aids in decision-making by visually demonstrating the importance of different factors, enabling the identification of main causes and resolution of those to achieve desired results.

10.2.5.1 Case Study

Consider the Sample - Superstore data source. Here, we want to plot a Pareto chart between product sub-categories and the percentage of the total running sum of sales. We wish to examine which products represented by the Sub-Category dimension represent the greatest share of overall sales. The steps with detailed description are given below:

Step 1. Open a new worksheet and connect to the Sample-Superstore data source.

Step 2. Subsequently, make a bar graph that displays Sales by Sub-Category. Drag Sub-Category to Columns from the Data window, then Sales to Rows (Figure 10.66).

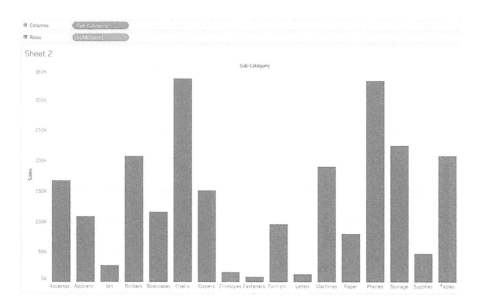

FIGURE 10.66   Output.

Step 3. Look for the "Descending Order" option from the toolbar menu to sort the bars in that order (Figure 10.67).

FIGURE 10.67   Output.

As we note, the products are now arranged from highest to lowest sales (Figure 10.68).

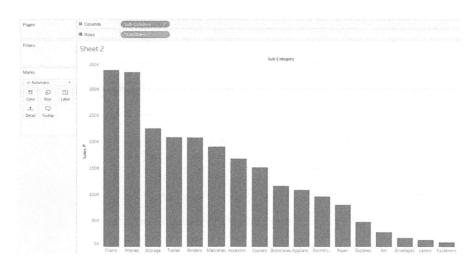

FIGURE 10.68   Output.

Step 4. In this step we want to insert a line chart depicting Sales by Sub-Category. So, move "Sales" measure to the extreme right of the screen where dotted line is now visible (Figure 10.69).

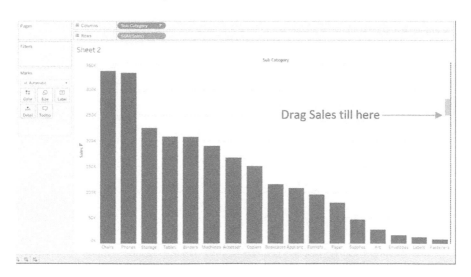

FIGURE 10.69   Output.

The dotted line chart is created as given below (Figure 10.70).

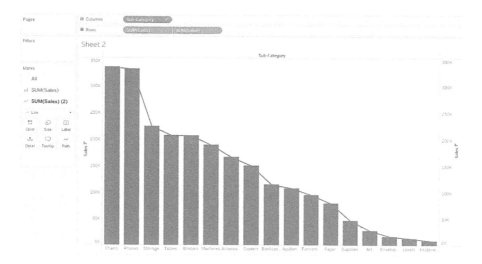

FIGURE 10.70   Output.

Step 5. Switch the mark type from Automatic to Bar on the first SUM (Sales) under the Marks shelf. The mark type should then be changed to Line in SUM(Sales) (2) on the Marks card. Following is the final perspective (Figure 10.71).

FIGURE 10.71   Output.

Step 6. To demonstrate sales by Sub-Category as a running total and as a percentage of total, add a table calculation to the line plot. Choose Add Table Calculation after selecting the second instance of SUM(Sales) on Rows (Figure 10.72).

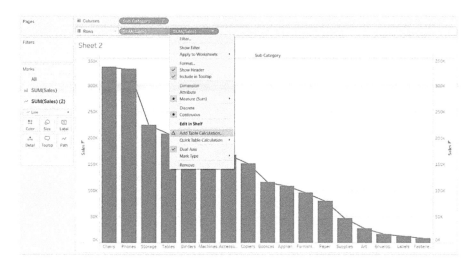

FIGURE 10.72   Output.

Step 7. Select the "Add Secondary Calculation" checkbox by clicking it. We choose "Running Total" from the computation Type menu in the Primary Calculation Type and choose "Sum" as the computation. To display the data as a percentage of the total, add a secondary table calculation. Select "Percent of Total" as the Secondary Calculation Type. Close the table calculator window (Figure 10.73).

Table Calculation	✕
% of Total Running Sum of Sales	

Primary Calculation Type	Secondary Calculation Type
Running Total ▼	Percent of Total ▼
Sum ▼	☐ Compute total across all pages

Compute Using	**Compute Using**
Table (across)	Table (across)
Cell	Table (down)
Specific Dimensions	Table
	Cell
☑ Sub-Category	**Specific Dimensions**
Restarting every ▼	☑ Sub-Category
	At the level ▼

☑ Add secondary calculation

FIGURE 10.73   Output.

Step 8. Click the Color card under Marks shelf and select the line path. This is our final Pareto chart (Figure 10.74).

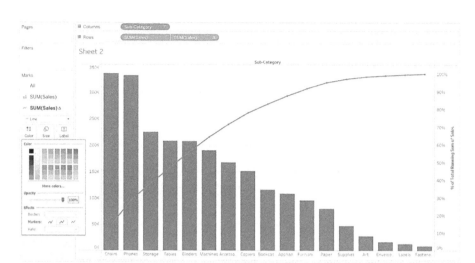

FIGURE 10.74 Output.

Conclusion:

- The Chairs and Phones categories are most significant ones that impact most to the percentage of total running sum of sales.
- The categories Storage, Tables and Binders can be focused for improvement as they are still contributing better to the overall percentage of running sum of sales.
- Together, Chairs, Phones, Storage, Tables, and Binders make up the 20% of percentage of overall running sum of sales. The remaining 80% of categories are those that do not significantly impact the proportion of total running sum of sales.

10.2.5.2 Use Cases of Pareto Chart

The Pareto chart is a useful tool in various aspects of a company, including inventory control, sales, customer service, production control, and human resources.

- It is based on the Pareto principle, which suggests that 20% of items in a warehouse generate 80% of inventory movements. This helps in identifying the most important items for inventory management, ensuring that 20% of the most loyal customers generate 80% of total profits.
- The chart also helps in prioritizing the optimization of product failures, which represent 80% of customer complaints.
- It also aids in production control, identifying 20% of defects that lead to 80% of negative consequences, and identifying Human Resources problems like absenteeism, as 80% of absences are attributed to 20% of candidates.

10.2.6 RESPONSIBILITY ASSIGNMENT MATRIX (RAM)

An efficient approach for determining the responsibilities and tasks of heterogeneous team members, eliminating uncertainty, and cutting down on delays is the Responsibility Assignment Matrix (RAM). Task assignments are delineated, along with who will perform what in a team. Project managers employ the matrix to elucidate the roles and responsibilities of cross-functional teams within the project and its procedures. When answering a Request for Proposal (RFP), it is occasionally necessary. RAM, an acronym for the RACI matrix, stands for responsible, accountable, consulted, and informed. The details are as follows:

- **Responsible:** This individual oversees carrying out the task or work and bears direct responsibility for it.
- **Accountable:** Individual who has final authority over the assignment or job.
- **Consult:** Someone who clarifies doubts and confusion and offers support when needed.
- **Inform:** Individual in charge who must be informed that a decision or action has been made.

An example of RACI chart (Figure 10.75).

Task ID	Task / Role	Team Member1	Team Member2	Team Member3	Team Member4
1	Requirement Analysis	A	R	C	I
2	System Design	R	C	A	I
3	Application Coding	I	C	R	I
4	Code Testing	C	A	I	R

FIGURE 10.75 An example of RACI chart.

The RACI chart aims to clarify team member roles in project tasks by providing detailed information in a matrix. This tool ensures clarity for all members, as multiple people are involved in each task, and ensures a clear understanding of their responsibilities.

10.3 FOCUS ON PROJECT MANAGEMENT ACTIVITIES

The planning of the project, determining the product's scope, estimating costs in various currencies, scheduling work, etc. are just a few of the numerous operations that make up software project management. These are the activities with details on the list:

1. **Planning and Tracking Project:** It is a group of several procedures, including idea perception, planning, and creating prototype designs prior to the beginning of the product's development.

2. **Administration of Resources:** Supervising the resources required for project completion including manpower and technical infrastructure.
3. **Managing the Scope:** Scope management is crucial since it outlines the project's horizon or scope and makes it obvious what strategies will and won't work.
4. **Estimates or Cost Management:** Since we calculate the size (number of lines of code), effort, time, and cost of software before we start developing it, this is about more than just cost estimation.
5. **Managing Schedule and Calendar:** Software scheduling management is the process of tracking the completion of all the tasks in the designated sequence and during the allotted amount of time.
6. **Managing Risks and Hazards:** Identification, analysis, and planning for both predictable and unforeseen risks in the project are all included in risk management.
7. **Supervising Project Interaction and Communication:** Effective communication is critical to the project's success. The client, the business, the team, and other project stakeholders like the hardware suppliers are all connected through it.
8. **Handling Project Configurations:** Configuration management's main goal is to regulate software changes, including those related to requirements, design, and product development. The primary goal is to work harder while making fewer mistakes.

KEY NOTES

- Project management software is crucial for planning, executing, and tracking projects, utilizing features like scheduling, tracking timelines, resources, costs, and team synchronization.
- Tableau Gauge charts display the minimum, current, and maximum values of a single metric or data field.
- Calendars show trends in metrics like sales, profits, and customers.
- Bullet charts compare two measurements on a single bar, while Gantt charts display activities against time.
- Pareto charts combine bar and line graphs, named after Vilfredo Pareto.
- The Responsibility Assignment Matrix (RAM) helps identify the roles and duties of diverse team members, preventing ambiguity and delays.
- Overall, project management software is essential for effective project management and success.

PRACTICE CASE STUDY

Download a project management report dataset available in public domain repositories.

Create an interactive project management dashboard to track and manage the budget, expenses, and other project activities and metrics.

TEST YOUR SKILLS

1. How visualization makes the task of overall project management easier for managers.
2. Create a Gauge chart in Tableau for the product-wise number of units sold across the interval 2020 to 2023 using Sample-Superstore dataset. Use color scheme of your choice.
3. Discuss the pros and cons of developing bullet charts.
4. Is Pareto chart a combinational chart? Elaborate with example case study using a business-relevant dataset.
5. List the activities involved in Project Management tasks that must be stressed upon in the project progression.

REFERENCES

1. Hyman, Jack A. *Tableau for Dummies*. United Kingdom, Wiley, 2023.
2. Sankhe-Savale, Shweta. *Tableau Cookbook - Recipes for Data Visualization*. India, Packt Publishing, 2016.
3. Jones, Ben. *Communicating Data with Tableau: Designing, Developing, and Delivering Data Visualizations*. Germany, O'Reilly Media, 2014.
4. Sarsfield, Patrick, et al. *Maximizing Tableau Server: A Beginner's Guide to Accessing, Sharing, and Managing Content on Tableau Server*. United Kingdom, Packt Publishing, 2021.
5. Sleeper, Ryan. *Innovative Tableau: 100 More Tips, Tutorials, and Strategies*. United States, O'Reilly Media, 2020.
6. Milligan, Joshua N. *Learning Tableau 2019: Tools for Business Intelligence, Data Prep, and Visual Analytics*, 3rd Edition. India, Packt Publishing, 2019.
7. Loth, Alexander. *Visual Analytics with Tableau*. United States, Wiley, 2019.
8. Costello, Tim, and Blackshear, Lori. *Prepare Your Data for Tableau: A Practical Guide to the Tableau Data Prep Tool*. Germany, Apress, 2019.

11 Maps in Tableau

11.1 INTRODUCTION TO MAPS

Tableau enables the visualization of data on Maps for geographic analysis, providing an appealing and dynamic way to display demographic information like population census, income, housing, and household rates [1]. Map charts offer a simple-to-understand and dynamic advantage over other Tableau charts, making them an excellent choice for presenting demographic or geographic data [2,3]. Some reasons for displaying data on a map are as follows:

1. Maps are beneficial to use in case the data source has some geographic information.
2. Sometimes, users may believe that using a map visualization would really make the data stand out and create the necessary appeal.

Both these are adequate reasons for opting to develop a map visualization, but it is critical to remember that maps, like other visualizations, have a specific function, i.e., they provide answers to spatial queries. Some examples of such spatial questions may be:

- Which state has the largest number of electronic markets?
- Which areas in the nation have the highest obesity rates?
- Which train station in the country's east has the busiest schedule?
- What is the Pacific region's storm movement over time?
- Which areas and destinations have the highest rates of cab bookings?

A map display is a useful method for resolving spatial queries, provided it accurately and visually represents the data [1,2]. However, misleading or lack of insight can lead to incorrect interpretation. The Tableau visualization tool can be used to create various types of maps.

    I. Maps with proportional symbols
    II. Filled maps (or choropleth maps)
   III. Distribution maps of points
   IV. Heatmaps or density maps
    V. Path maps or flow maps
   VI. Origin-destination maps, often known as spider maps
        Let us discuss each type of map in detail in the following sections.

DOI: 10.1201/9781003429593-11

11.2 PROPORTIONAL SYMBOL MAPS

A symbol map is a tool used for interpreting numerical values over geographic locations. It uses individual skills to represent data variations in size, shape, or color [4]. The symbols are scaled to represent the value of the measured field at a specific location. For example, a symbol map can help identify cities with hurricane damage, help communities relocate, or illustrate the impact of climate change on coastal communities. This helps in understanding the data and addressing its implications.

11.2.1 CASE STUDY

Let us consider the Sample-Superstore dataset. Here, we want to analyze sales values for each State/Province and plot the same on a proportional symbol map. The steps are given below:

Step 1. Establish a connection to the Sample-Superstore dataset and launch a new worksheet.

Step 2. It is necessary to give the field in the dataset a corresponding geographic role to map a geographic dimension, such as a country or state. In the sidebar, right-click the dimension and select a geographic role like in Figure 11.1.

FIGURE 11.1 Output.

After this, the corresponding latitude and longitude coordinates are generated automatically by the Tableau server once the geographic role is assigned to the selected field.

Step 3. Double-click on the State field to view a blank map (Figure 11.2).

FIGURE 11.2   Output for step 3.

Also, select Map instead of "Automatic" from drop-down in the Marks shelf (Figure 11.3).

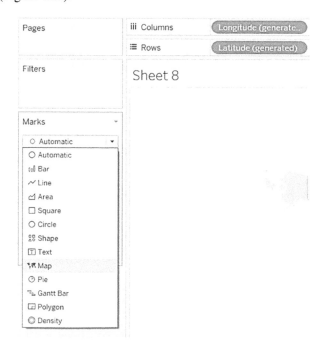

FIGURE 11.3   Second output for step 3.

Step 4. Drag Sales measure to Size card under the Marks shelf. Click on Show-Me and select the symbol map icon (Figure 11.4)

FIGURE 11.4   Output.

Step 5. Also, drag sales measure to Color under the Mark shelf (Figure 11.5).

FIGURE 11.5   Output.

Step 6. Drag State to Label to display state names along with proportional symbols (Figure 11.6).

FIGURE 11.6   Output.

Conclusion:

- Large blue symbols depict higher sales value for that region.
- Small red symbols depict lesser sales value for that region.

Step 7. We can change the shape of the symbol. For this, select the Shape option from drop-down under the Marks shelf (Figure 11.7).

FIGURE 11.7   Output.

11.3 TABLEAU CHOROPLETH MAPS (FILLED MAPS)

Filled maps in the tableau are like symbol maps but with more data points. They draw a polygon around the entire border, showing multiple geographic regions colored based on a measure or dimension, unlike symbol maps which draw a symbol at each latitude and longitude pair [5].

For the same case study as we completed for the Proportional symbol map in the previous section, if we choose the option of filled map icon ⬛ from the Show Me tab, then we will get the following output (Figure 11.8).

FIGURE 11.8 Illustration for filled map.

11.4 POINT DISTRIBUTION MAPS

Tableau offers advanced point distribution maps, which help users identify visual clusters and demonstrate data point distribution based on geographical locations [5,6]. These maps also aid organizations in analyzing data point sharing, providing approximate locations and data clusters. To create a data distribution map, the data source must include latitude and longitude coordinates.

11.4.1 CASE STUDY

Here, we consider the hail storm dataset for the year 2015 from Kaggle data repository. Users are suggested to download the hail storm dataset from severe weather data inventory on Kaggle or any other repository as per choice. The steps to create a point distribution map are as follows:

Step 1. Download the hailstorm dataset from Kaggle data repository (Figure 11.9).

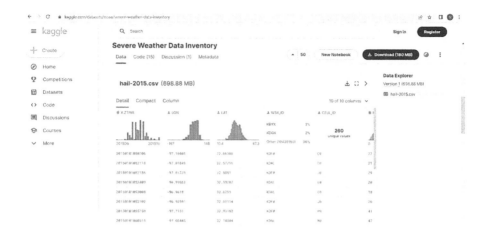

FIGURE 11.9 Output.

Step 2. Connect to the.csv file downloaded in Tableau (Figure 11.10).

FIGURE 11.10 Output.

Step 3. Open a new worksheet (Figure 11.11).

FIGURE 11.11   Output.

Step 4. Allocate the geographic role of "Latitude" to LAT field and "Longitude" role to the LON data field (Figure 11.12).

FIGURE 11.12   Output.

Step 5. Double-click the LAT field (i.e., Latitude) and the LON field (i.e., Longitude) to add them to Rows and Columns, respectively (Figure 11.13).

FIGURE 11.13   Output.

Step 6. Click AVG(LON) and AVG(LAT) on the column and rows shelf and change it to dimension settings (Figure 11.14).

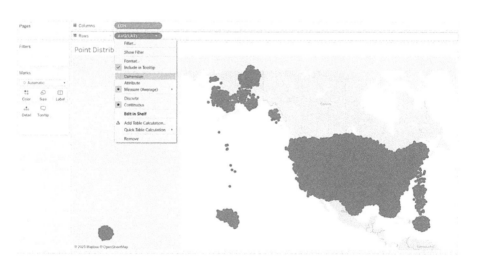

FIGURE 11.14   Output.

Step 7. Drag the "severprob" field, i.e., severity of probability of hail storm occurrence onto the Filters shelf. Set the range of values from 0 to 20 in the Filter dialog box. This restricts our analysis to severity values from 0 to 20 (Figure 11.15).

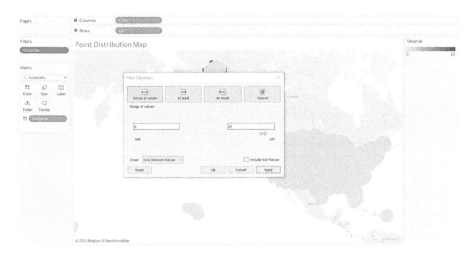

FIGURE 11.15 Output.

Step 8. Click on Severprob on the Filters shelf and change it to Dimension settings (Figure 11.16).

FIGURE 11.16 Output.

Step 9. Press ctrl key and drag Severprob from the Filters shelf to Color card in the Marks shelf. This will keep a copy of the Severprob field on Filters and Color shelf. Also, minimize the size of points to minimum (Figure 11.17).

FIGURE 11.17   Output.

Conclusion:

- We can see a few dark blue points on the map highlighting high severity of hail storms on the scale of 0–20.

Step 10. We can change the scale for severity by updating the range in filters. For example, the below figure is for severity range from 10 to 20 (Figure 11.18).

FIGURE 11.18   Output.

This type of map shows the movement of hail storms all over the continent as per desired severity range.

11.5 FLOW MAPS (PATH MAPS)

Flow maps or path maps are created in Tableau Desktop to depict a path over time [7]. They are ideal for demonstrating events like storm routes or cyclone paths across the country. The dataset should include specific types of data values as listed below.

- The latitude and longitude coordinates for each location are required.
- The order to connect various points such as day or date information, or manual order assigned for movement, or path order.
- A separate ID to identify each route.
- Adequate coordinates to trace each route and draw lines to visualize the route.

11.5.1 CASE STUDY

The Atlantic Hurricane dataset, designed from 1975 to 2021, provides information on hurricanes, including names, origins, and severity. This data can be downloaded from public data repositories such as *Kaggle* to create flow maps, as demonstrated in the case study using the CSV file for 1975–2021 hurricane details (Figure 11.19).

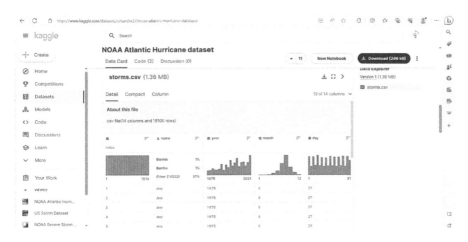

FIGURE 11.19 A view of the dataset.

The following are the steps to design a flow chart:

Step 1. Establish a connection to the storm dataset downloaded above and open a new worksheet.

Step 2. Double-click on the Lat and Lon fields to add these to the Rows and Columns shelves, respectively. Click on Lat and Lon added on the Rows and Column shelf to set these to Dimension (Figure 11.20).

FIGURE 11.20   Output.

Step 3. Drag Storm Name field "Name" from Dimensions to Detail on the Marks card. For each storm in the data source, a new data point is added to the map view (Figure 11.21).

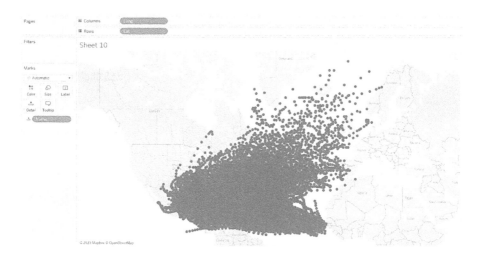

FIGURE 11.21   Output.

Step 4. Drag Year from Dimensions to the Filters shelf and choose the year 2020 alone to observe hurricanes in 2020 (Figure 11.22).

FIGURE 11.22   Output.

The map in the above illustration only shows the storms that happened in 2020.

Step 5. Drag Category to the Filters shelf from Dimensions. Select all categories in the dialog box that displays and then click OK (Figure 11.23).

FIGURE 11.23   Output.

Step 6. Select Line from the mark-type drop-down on the Marks card. The Marks card displays a Path button, and the map view changes to show a line linking each data point (Figure 11.24).

FIGURE 11.24   Output.

Step 7. Create a new Calculated field Date by combining separate columns for Day, Month, and Year using MAKEDATE() function. The function is given below:

MAKEDATE ([Year], [Month], [Day])

For this, click on the Analysis menu and select Create Calculated Field (Figure 11.25).

FIGURE 11.25   Output.

Step 8. Drag Date to Path on the Marks card from Dimensions. Right-click the YEAR(Date) box on the Marks card and choose Exact Date (Figure 11.26).

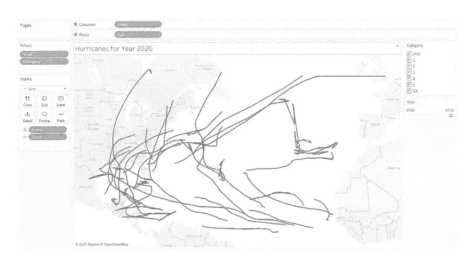

FIGURE 11.26 Output.

With each new date and time that is captured, a data point is added to the map view. The distinct storm paths are now visible.

Step 9. Drag the "Name" field from Dimensions to Color on the Marks card. The flow map is now complete after each storm path is given a color (Figure 11.27).

FIGURE 11.27 Output.

Step 10. Drag Wind Speed to Size on the Marks card from Measures. Each storm's path's various wind speeds are updated in the map view (Figure 11.28).

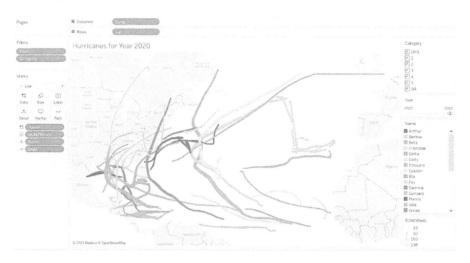

FIGURE 11.28   Output.

Conclusion:

- We can observe the paths for each hurricane storm in the year 2020.
- The thicker the path, the stronger winds accompanied the hurricane.

11.6   SPIDER MAPS (ORIGIN-DESTINATION MAPS)

Tableau Desktop allows users to create spider maps, also known as origin-destination maps, which depict the routes between starting and ending points [7, 8]. These maps are useful for hubs connecting multiple nearby locations and display connectivity between points. Spider maps can be created in various ways in Tableau. Some instances of using spider maps may include displaying airplane routes, train routes, or shipping routes to deliver products.

11.6.1   CASE STUDY

Let us consider the comprehensive data on metro stations in Delhi, the capital territory of India. This dataset is available for download from Kaggle repository. The data source contains station ID, name of station, distances, lines, and year of opening (Figure 11.29).

The steps to create an origin-destination spider map are given below:

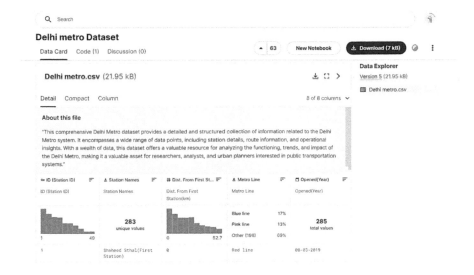

FIGURE 11.29 Dataset of metro routes.

Step 1. Connect to data source of metro stations as downloaded and open a new worksheet (Figure 11.30).

FIGURE 11.30 Output.

Step 2. Drag Longitude and Latitude to the Columns and Rows shelves, respectively, from the Measures section. Set both to type "Dimension" by clicking and setting (Figure 11.31).

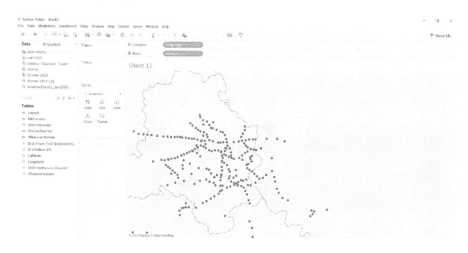

FIGURE 11.31   Output.

Step 3. Drag the Metro Line field to Detail on the Marks card now from the Data pane. Select Line from the Mark Type drop-down on the Marks card (Figure 11.32).

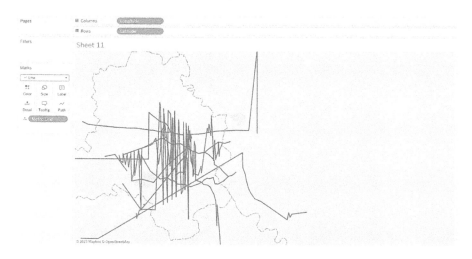

FIGURE 11.32   Output.

The revised map view with a line connecting all the spots is shown in the image above. On the Marks shelf, a Path button is seen to appear.

Step 4. Drag the dimension "Metro Line" to Color on the Marks shelf and ID(Station ID) field to the Detail card on the Marks shelf (Figure 11.33).

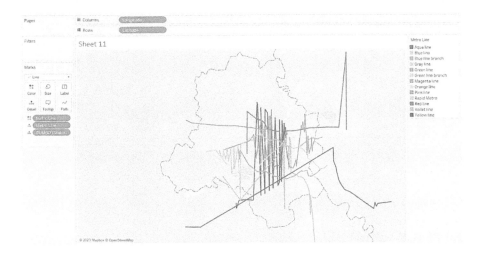

FIGURE 11.33 Output.

Step 5. Drag AVG(Longitude) to the Columns shelf to the right of the previous Longitude (Figure 11.34).

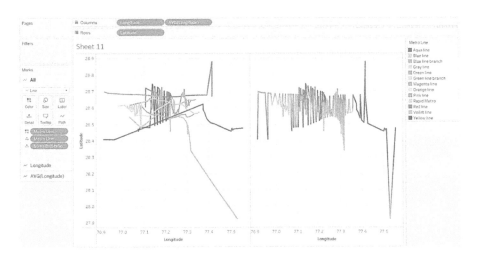

FIGURE 11.34 Output.

Step 6. Click the newly added AVG(Longitude) on the Columns shelf and select Dimension (Figure 11.35).

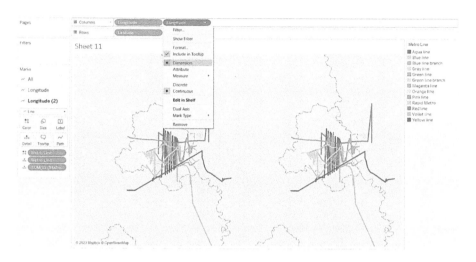

FIGURE 11.35   Output.

Step 7. Once more, click the Dual Axis option next to the second Longitude on the Columns shelf. Finally, choose Automatic from the Marks shelf's Longitude (2) or second Longitude section (Figure 11.36).

FIGURE 11.36   Output.

Step 8. Finally, drag Station Name to Label under the Marks shelf of second Longitude. Also, give a suitable title (Figure 11.37).

FIGURE 11.37   Output.

Conclusion:

- We can observe various metro lines with their path and station names.
  Note: The generated map may vary with differences in the dataset. The dataset used for the above examples is sample data. On applying data processing techniques or after removing spurious data (if any), the outputs may vary.

KEY NOTES

- Map charts in Tableau provide a dynamic and easy-to-understand approach for presenting demographic or geographic data.
- Maps can be used to resolve spatial queries, interpret numerical values, and display data points.
- A symbol map interprets numerical values over geographic locations, while filled maps display multiple regions colored based on measure or dimension, drawing a polygon around the entire border.
- Tableau Desktop offers advanced point distribution maps, which help identify visual clusters and demonstrate data point distribution.
- Flow maps or path maps depict paths over time, while spider maps, or origin-destination maps, depict routes between starting and ending points.

PRACTICE CASE STUDY

Covid-19 Global Investigation Dashboard

Download the COVID-19 global dataset for different countries worldwide from any public domain repository. Ensure to check the data for these fields: number of confirmed/infected cases, number of cases recovered, number of cases resulting in casualty, population vaccinated per country, etc. Use your imagination to create an interactive dashboard for representing different views across various countries.

TEST YOUR SKILLS

1. List some advantages of using maps over other graphs available in Tableau.
2. Differentiate between proportional symbol maps and filled maps with a case study example on a business-relevant dataset.
3. Generate a point distribution plot for observing Hailstorms in regions such as the United States or Pacific regions in recent years. Users can choose the datasets available in the public domain for download.
4. Develop a heat map for the global population data over the years from 2021 to 2023. Users can use the world population data available in the public domain for download.
5. Generate a spider chart for air flights in a region or country with the help of airports and flight coordinates datasets available in the public domain. With the help of spider charts, display the origin and destination route of each flight data.

REFERENCES

1. Milligan, Joshua N., and Guillevin, Tristan. *Tableau 10 Complete Reference: Transform Your Business with Rich Data Visualizations and Interactive Dashboards with Tableau 10*. United Kingdom, Packt Publishing, 2018.
2. Murray, Daniel G. *Tableau Your Data! Fast and Easy Visual Analysis with Tableau Software*. United Kingdom, Wiley, 2016.
3. Loth, Alexander. *Visual Analytics with Tableau*. United States, Wiley, 2019.
4. Dougherty, Jack, and Ilyankou, Ilya. *Hands-On Data Visualization*. United States, O'Reilly Media, 2021.
5. Sleeper, Ryan. *Innovative Tableau: 100 More Tips, Tutorials, and Strategies*. United States, O'Reilly Media, 2020.
6. Brown, Lorna. *Tableau Desktop Cookbook*. United States, O'Reilly Media, 2020.
7. Ohmann, Ashley, and Floyd, Matt. *Creating Data Stories with Tableau Public*. United Kingdom, Packt Publishing, 2015.
8. Ryan, Lindy. *Visual Data Storytelling with Tableau*. United Kingdom, Pearson Education, 2018.

12 Designing Stories through Data

12.1 INTRODUCTION TO STORYTELLING CONCEPTS

Tableau stories are visualizations that present information in a compelling way. They provide context, demonstrate the impact of decisions on results, make a persuasive argument, or tell a data story [1,2]. Stories can be created using the same techniques we use for worksheets and dashboards and can be organized in a particular order as "story points." Shared through Tableau Public, Server, or Cloud, users can interact with stories. By highlighting connections between data and showing how decisions impact outcomes, stories make our use case more engaging. We can present a story through presentations or sharing it online. Each story point can be supported by a unique view or dashboard, or the same visualization with various filters and annotations to narrate the entire story [3,4].

12.1.1 TYPES OF DATA STORIES WITH PURPOSE

Before constructing a story, it is crucial to consider the story's goal and the audience's journey. The type of narrative should be chosen, such as a simple narrative, a call to action, or a problem-solving initiative. When making a case, we must choose whether to provide the conclusion first and then the supporting evidence, or whether to show the supporting evidence first and then the conclusion at the final stage [2]. Outlining the story on paper or a whiteboard can help identify sequencing issues and ensure a successful presentation. We can use any of the seven different data story methodologies listed below, which are all illustrated with examples.

1. **Change Over Time**
   This can be useful to explain how data points collected can change over a temporal axis. A basic example of this is visualizing the rate change of something, for example, sea level change at different times of the day. Conclusions such as when the maximum and minimum point of a particular factor occurred can be drawn (Figure 12.1).

Story Type #1 - Change Over Time: World population growth

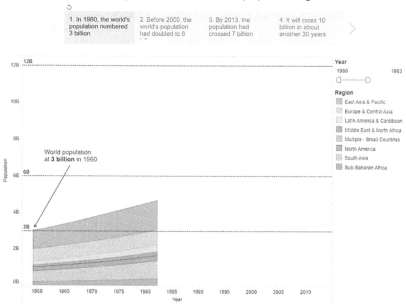

FIGURE 12.1   Illustration of change over time story.

2. **Drill-Down**

With the drill-down data story, we can look at the overall big picture of something and hone into a particular factor that is causing this within the data. For example, you can drill down into data from a particular region of the world by focusing on a particular country within that region and how much of an effect this country has on the data of the whole region (Figure 12.2).

Story Type #2 - Drill-down: The most populous region and country

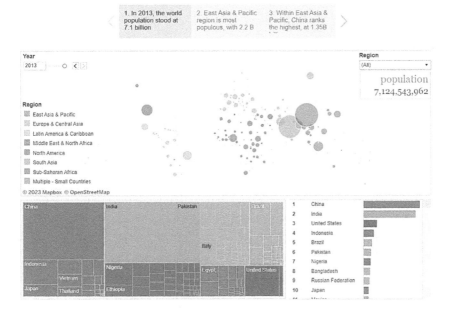

FIGURE 12.2   Illustration of drill-down story.

3. **Zoom Out**

   If we do the reverse of the drill-down story method, we have the next data story type: zoom out. This works by starting with a micro view and narrating the data in a way that you take a step back and take a more macro view (Figure 12.3).

Story Type # 3- **Zoom Out:** The most populous region and country

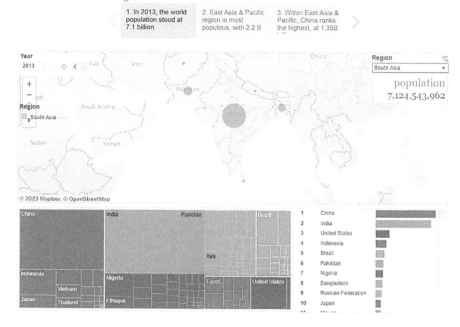

FIGURE 12.3   Illustration of zoom out story.

4. **Contrast**

With multiple datasets, you can compare them to push a particular narrative. This can help the audience to not only understand how two different data sets can be different but also similar. This method helps the brain to remember key points of the story you are presenting (Figure 12.4).

Story Type #4 - Contrast: Growing and shrinking countries

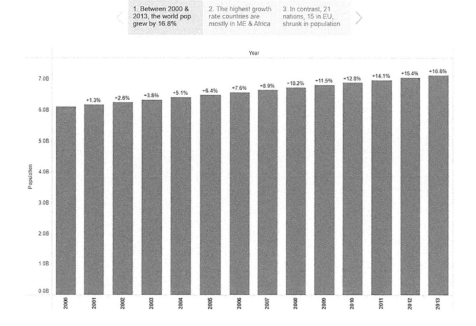

FIGURE 12.4 Illustration of contrast story.

5. Intersections

When two lines of data diverge and, in some cases, overlap, this can tell an interesting story of the data and in many cases can represent one variable overtaking another (Figure 12.5).

Story Type #5 - Intersections: Slow growth in Europe & Central Asia

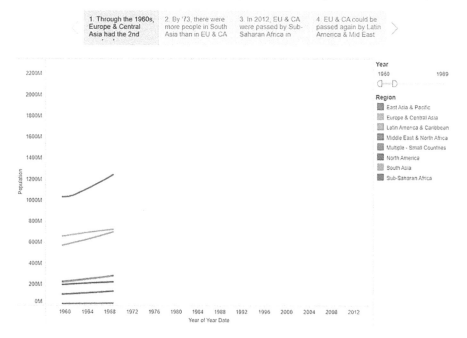

FIGURE 12.5   Illustration of intersections story.

6. **Factors**

A lot of times multiple factors can be used to represent one big story as these factors tend to have a relationship when added or multiplied together. When telling the story of economic growth, there are multiple factors that all combine to represent this. For instance, the entire storyline of economic growth might be represented by factors such as consumer spending, company investment, government spending, and net exports (Figure 12.6).

Story Type #6- Different Factors: Comparison of birth & death rates

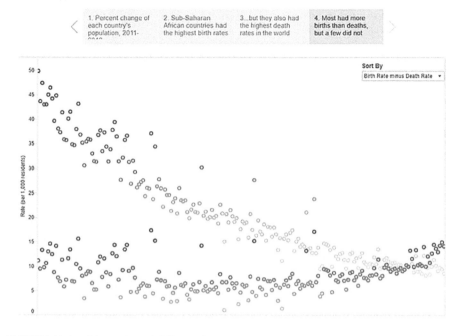

FIGURE 12.6   Illustration of different factors story.

7. **Outliers**

Outliers are plot points which fall outside the overall trend and can allow speculation as to why this value falls outside. This is important because this can skew the overall value of the dataset. When an outlier is highlighted, this can be focused on as what is affecting the dataset and possible steps can be taken to reduce the effect of this outlier (Figure 12.7).

Story Type #7 - Outliers & Trends: Population swings, 1960 - 2013

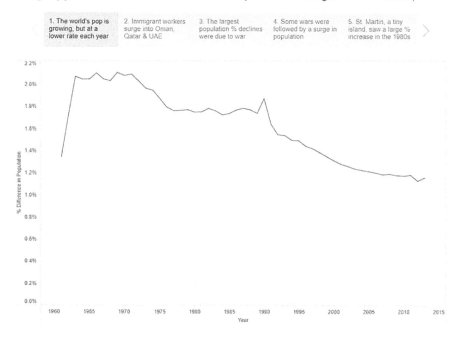

FIGURE 12.7   Illustration of outliers and trends story.

12.1.2 TABLEAU WORKBOOK, WORKSHEETS, DASHBOARD, AND STORY

Tableau uses a workbook and sheet file structure. A workbook has data connections, worksheets, views, dashboards, and stories [5]. A worksheet has a single view where you can build views of data by dragging and dropping fields and measures onto rows and columns. A dashboard is a collection of multiple worksheets and supporting data displayed together to compare and monitor information. A story is a sheet that contains a sequence of worksheets and dashboards that work together to convey related information. You can use stories to make your analysis more compelling by showing how facts are connected and how decisions impact outcomes. Story points, as their name suggests, focus on a story. We would normally utilize a story points presentation to tell a story that does not have a clear conclusion up front. The story would have a beginning, a middle, and a finish, and the audience would be guided through it step by step. This can be especially helpful for presentations or meetings conducted for stakeholders to break down the complete discussion in a step-by-step narrative.

Some useful tips while opting for workbooks, dashboards, and stories are listed below:

- When you have highlight filters that run through the charts, choose a dashboard.
- If you want to guide the audience through a step-by-step process or if you do not want them to see the solution right away, choose a story point.

- The most crucial piece of advice is that, although a story point typically has one worksheet per page, an entire dashboard can be dragged into the view to accommodate more charts on a single page.
- Your options for arranging titles and subtitles are limited because stories occupy some of the space at the top where the story point titles are located.
- Format every page of the story consistently.

12.2 COMPONENTS OF A BUSINESS STORY

Just like a novel or a movie, the business story also has several components such as a theme, a plot, several characters, some data, and visualizations that will help to give a better understanding of the entire story. These components are the building-blocks of a business story (Figure 12.8).

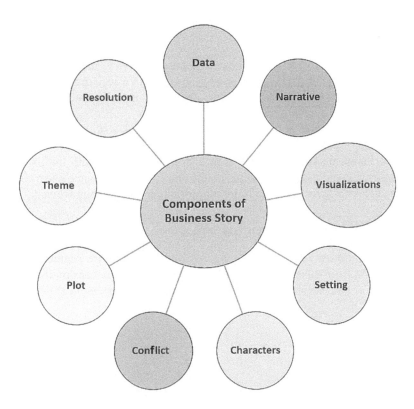

FIGURE 12.8 Various components of a business story.

Data storytelling is made up of the following nine essential elements:

1. **Data:** The core of your data story is a thorough study of correct, full data. You can gain a complete understanding of the data by analyzing it using descriptive, diagnostic, predictive, and prescriptive methods.

2. **Narrative:** A spoken or written narrative, also known as a tale, is used to convey insights drawn from data, the context surrounding it, and actions you advocate and hope to inspire in your audience.

3. **Visualizations:** Using visual representations of your facts and narrative can help you tell your message in a compelling and memorable way. These could take the form of diagrams, photos, videos, graphs, or charts.

4. **Setting:** This includes all the information needed to understand the situation, including the decision, the problem, the questions, and the data. The setting can be thought of in two pieces: the foreground and the background. The background includes the business' purpose, mission, goals, and culture. The foreground is the analytic context around the question and the data.

5. **Characters:** The audience or users are the protagonists in your story—they are the ones who must make the decision. Always design for the end-user or the audience, not for the data.

6. **Conflict:** The conflict is the business problem the users or audience are trying to solve. The most exciting scenes in stories are the ones that engage the conflict and drive the plot forward.

7. **Plot:** The plot is the flow from answer to answer, from visualization to visualization. A good data story plot links insights in a way that compels the user toward a specific response or a decision that is best supported with evidence.

8. **Theme:** The theme is the central message to the data story and should be apparent throughout. The theme is the decision plus all the evidence.

9. **Conclusion or Inference:** The conclusion should align with the topic or challenges addressed, providing a summary of the audience's learnings, strategies for achieving results, or suggestions for future improvement.

12.3　STORYTELLING PARTICIPANTS

Effective data stories require clear language and may require segmenting audiences based on their subject knowledge to ensure their comprehension [6, 7]. A list of players who possess a major role in the storytelling progression is given below (Figure 12.9):

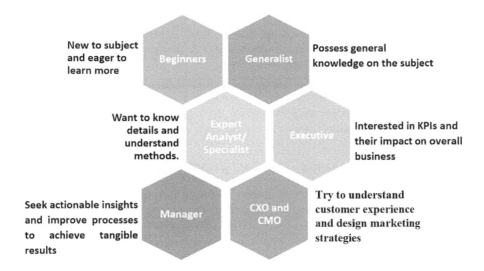

New to subject and eager to learn more — **Beginners**

Generalist — Possess general knowledge on the subject

Want to know details and understand methods. — **Expert Analyst/ Specialist**

Executive — Interested in KPIs and their impact on overall business

Seek actionable insights and improve processes to achieve tangible results — **Manager**

CXO and CMO — Try to understand customer experience and design marketing strategies

FIGURE 12.9 Various participants in a business story.

1. **Beginner:** Curious to gain a deeper understanding of the topic but new to it. And has an elementary understanding of the topic but requires further explanation.
2. **Generalist:** Significant topics and in-depth study are of the utmost interest. And knowledgeable on the topic but seeking a general perspective and key ideas.
3. **Manager:** He possesses a vast and useful understanding of challenges and correlation with data access. He seeks access to information as well as practical knowledge.
4. **Executive:** Recognizes only the significant outcomes of likely situations. They are time-bound participants who require initial assumptions and conclusions beforehand.
5. **Expert/Specialist:** Experts seek exploratory information with less story-driven data representation and more numbers, seeking detail and understanding of methodologies and may need to be convinced about the robustness of any in-house analysis.
6. **CXO and CMO:** A Chief Experience Officer (CXO) and Chief Marketing Officer (CMO) are high-level executives responsible for ensuring positive customer interactions. They aim to improve the customer experience by creating a customer journey map, which is a data-driven diagram of the customer's interaction stages. CXOs use data analytics teams to analyze communication and customer information, as well as social media management software. Executive dashboards and data stories are also crucial for monitoring resources and extracting customer insights.

   CMOs use data storytelling to manage the challenges of handling technology, analytics, and data. Incorporating data storytelling into content strategy allows marketing executives to create quality content that impacts, especially when people lack the skill or time to interpret complex dashboards. It also helps communicate insights to everyone, bridging the gap between obtaining and interpreting them.

We should be mindful of the fact we cannot satisfy everyone with one single story. To reach all our prospective audiences while working with data stories, we must be prepared to develop multiple stories or use different sets of data.

12.4 DECISION-MAKING STEPS IN STORYTELLING FRAMEWORK

Executives often struggle to structure their business narrative due to the lack of a proper framework. A well-designed storytelling framework serves as a foundation blueprint, ensuring that each component of the narrative is logically placed and easily understood by the audience [8]. The several decision-making steps involved in the storytelling framework are given below (Figure 12.10):

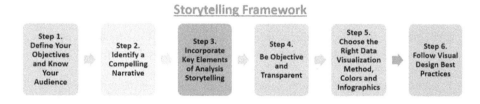

FIGURE 12.10   Steps in storytelling framework.

Step 1. Establish goals and recognize prospective audience.
- To effectively communicate data stories, it is crucial to define their purpose, identify trends, focus on specific data subsets, categorize information, demonstrate strategy effectiveness, and highlight product value.
- Different stories may be needed depending on audience priorities, such as marketing team vs. finance department, to cater to different audiences.

Step 2. Choose a powerful theme or storyline.
- Data storytelling with visualization techniques can be effective, starting with a question and building momentum to reach a solution.
- Five main data-driven narratives include trends, comparisons, tables/rank orders, statistical relationships, and infographics.
- Trend stories focus on data trends, comparisons, and broader context analysis. Tables/rank orders communicate hierarchy and predict the impact of factors.

- Statistical relationships explore correlations between datasets, while infographics capture attention and engage the audience.
- Overall, data storytelling is a powerful tool for conveying complex information.

Step 3. Combine key elements of effective storytelling.

- Include these essential components to create a persuasive data story:
    - Plan or plot of the story
    - Context settings and background work
    - Characters
    - Resolution (End)

Step 4. Be objective and transparent.

- Be objective when deciding which data to include in your data story; avoid discrete values when the data is continuous; be explicit about missing, outlier, or out-of-range values; and be open and honest when utilizing data ranges, capped values, volumes, or intervals.

Step 5. Pick the suitable color scheme and data visualization technique.

- The information can be displayed successfully to convey an argument by using a visualization technique and color scheme appropriate for the data at hand.
- Here are a few typical examples of data visualization:
- Maps, histograms, pie charts, line charts, bar charts, scatter plot, etc.

Step 6. Observe best practices for visual design.

- To effectively convey your message, choose a visualization method that is simple and clear.
- Use white space strategically to guide attention and eliminate unnecessary visual elements.
- Custom usage of bold colors to highlight key data in visualization report.

12.4.1 THE BUSINESS KPI STORY—A CASE STUDY

The story illustrates the key progress indicators (KPIs) of a sample superstore, a measurable value that demonstrates a company's effectiveness in achieving key business objectives. These KPIs, presented in various shapes and colors, aid stakeholders in easily interpreting crucial data, ensuring the success of the business. The procedure for creating KPIs requires the following steps:

- Design a worksheet that contains the fields or measurements we want to assess.
- Set a calculated field that specifies the threshold point separating profit from loss.
- To show which values fall over or below the threshold limit, use shape markings appropriate to the KPI.

To create a KPI story, we need to develop KPI dashboards for various roles in an organization. These dashboards can resolve management issues and monitor KPI progress status at different levels, as guidelines for different positions can vary and can be inconsistently handled. Here are some simple examples of departmental KPIs:

1. Marketing department KPIs:
   - Number of leads from the specific promotional source
   - Number of channels/partners for marketing
   - Number of marketing activities organized
2. Sales department KPIs:
   - Rate of conversion (to record the ratio of candidates who have completed a desired action out of the total number of candidates)
   - Overall value of business transactions
   - Value of sales booked at a given time interval
3. Finance department KPIs:
   - Total number of invoices issued per month
   - The average number of invoices issued per month each year
   - Number of payments received per month
   - Number of payments made per month
4. HR department KPIs:
   - Number of training days
   - Number of annual leaves taken
   - Number of medical leaves taken
   - Number of vacancies generated
5. Operation department KPIs:
   - Number of products delivered
   - Value of products delivered
   - Number of products returned or rejected
   - Number of complaints received
   - Number of grievances addressed

Below we create a story that considers the sales and profit KPIs and try to address the following questions:

- Does the current profit exceed the profit amount of the previous year?
- Do the current sales exceed the sales of the previous year?
- How many products reach the threshold of overall sales value (i.e., 30,000 in our case)?
- Is the sales trend varying for each category?
- Do the sales and profit vary greatly in different states?

The answers observed after analyzing different visualizations provide necessary insights.

12.4.2 CASE-1: SALES KPI DASHBOARD

Key performance indicators are now an essential component of analytics. KPIs may be readily created by Tableau users. The appropriate approach in this situation is to aggregate the metric we want to use to assess performance before choosing the threshold at which we decide if something is excellent or poor. Here, the KPI used for this case study is "Sales."

View 1: Sub-category Sales Performance for benchmark sales > 30,000.

A. *The field to be evaluated should be included in the view. In this instance, it is the sales field.*

Step 1. The first step is to connect to the Sample-Superstore data source and then create a new worksheet and label it "Sub-Category Sales Performance."

Step 2. Drag Sub-Category and Region from the Data window to the Rows and Columns, respectively. Also, drag Sales to Text on the Marks card (Figure 12.11).

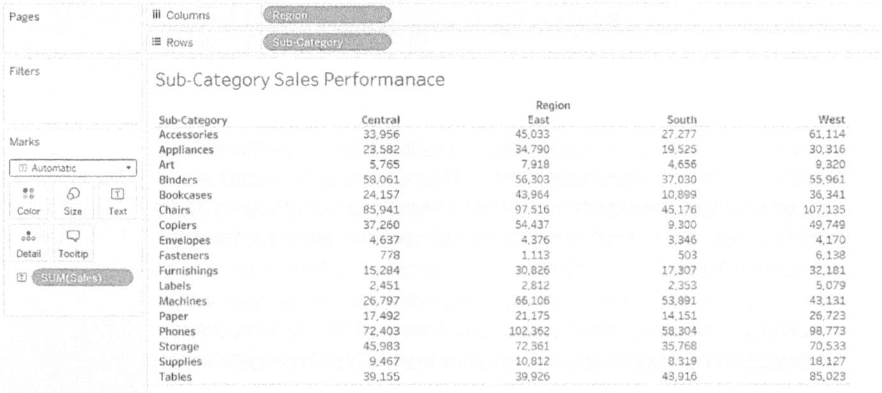

Pages		
iii Columns	Region	
≡ Rows	Sub-Category	

Filters

Sub-Category Sales Performanace

		Region		
Sub-Category	Central	East	South	West
Accessories	33,956	45,033	27,277	61,114
Appliances	23,582	34,790	19,525	30,316
Art	5,765	7,918	4,656	9,320
Binders	58,061	56,303	37,030	55,961
Bookcases	24,157	43,964	10,899	36,341
Chairs	85,941	97,516	45,176	107,135
Copiers	37,260	54,437	9,300	49,749
Envelopes	4,637	4,376	3,346	4,170
Fasteners	778	1,113	503	6,138
Furnishings	15,284	30,826	17,307	32,181
Labels	2,451	2,812	2,353	5,079
Machines	26,797	66,106	53,891	43,131
Paper	17,492	21,175	14,151	26,723
Phones	72,403	102,362	58,304	98,773
Storage	45,983	72,361	35,768	70,533
Supplies	9,467	10,812	8,319	18,127
Tables	39,155	39,926	43,916	85,023

Marks

☐ Automatic

Color Size Text

Detail Tooltip

SUM(Sales)

FIGURE 12.11 Output for sub-steps 1 and 2 in step A.

B. *Identify the threshold that separates success from failure and create a calculated field to reflect it.*

Step 1. Choose Create Calculated Field from the Analysis menu to launch the calculation editor. Name the calculation KPI "SalesThreshold" and enter the following formula in the formula box (Figure 12.12):

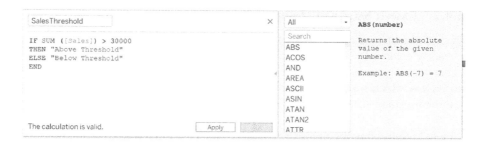

FIGURE 12.12   Output for sub-step 1 in step B.

$$IF\ SUM\left(\left[Sales\right]\right) > 25000$$

$$THEN\ \text{"Above Benchmark"}$$

$$ELSE\ \text{" Below Benchmark"}$$

$$END$$

Step 2. Then, click on "Apply" and "OK."

C. *To use KPI-specific shape markers, update the view.*

Step 1. From the drop-down selection, pick "Shape" on the Marks card (Figure 12.13).

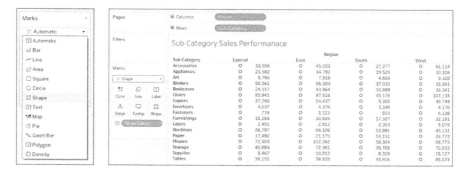

FIGURE 12.13   Output for sub-step 1 in step C.

Step 2. Drag "SalesThreshold" KPI field from the Measures section to the Shape card on the Marks shelf (Figure 12.14).

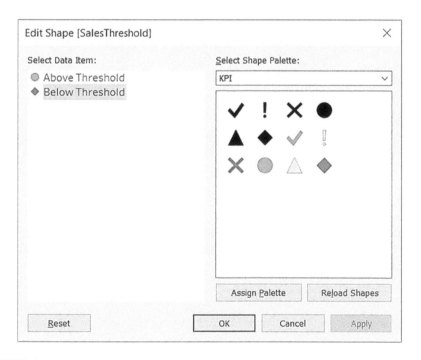

FIGURE 12.14 Output for sub-step 2 in step C.

Step 3. On the Marks shelf, select the "Shape" card. The Edit Shape dialog box is shown. Choose the desired shape for each data item by selecting the "KPI" kind of shape from the Select Shape Palette drop-down box (Figure 12.15).

FIGURE 12.15 Output for sub-step 3 in step C.

Step 4. Pick "Above Threshold" under "Select Data Item," and then click the green circle mark in the palette. Likewise, pick "Below Threshold" in the palette by clicking the red diamond. To close the Edit Shape dialog box, click OK (Figure 12.16).

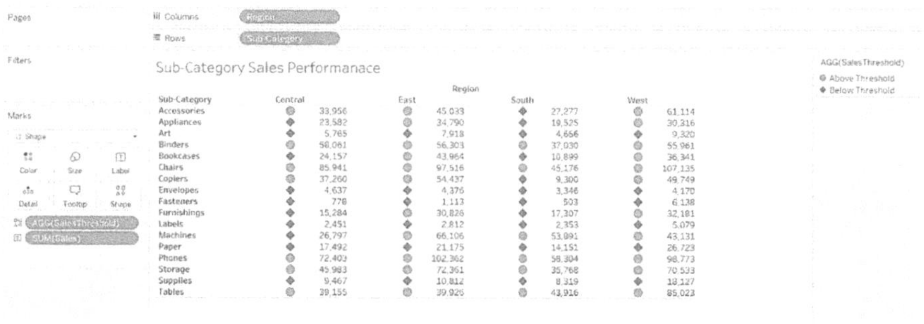

FIGURE 12.16　　Output for sub-step 4 in step C.

Step 5. On the Marks card, drag SUM(Sales) to Detail (Figure 12.17).

FIGURE 12.17　　Output for sub-step 5 in step C.

View 2: Forecast for Sales per Product Category

We can create simple line charts showing monthly sales for each product category along with linear trendline and forecast sales (Figure 12.18).

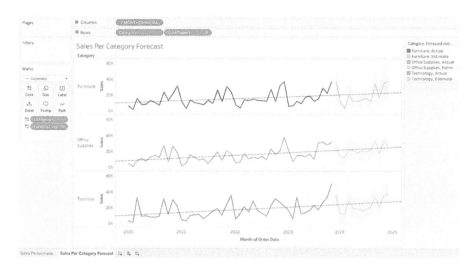

FIGURE 12.18   Output for view 2.

View 3: Tracking yearly count of orders

We create the worksheet to track the yearly count of orders per category (Figure 12.19).

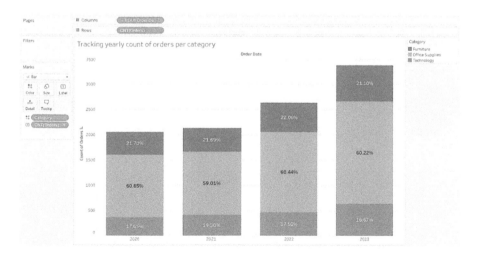

FIGURE 12.19   Output for view 3.

View 4: Plotting Trends and Forecasting Sales (Figure 12.20)

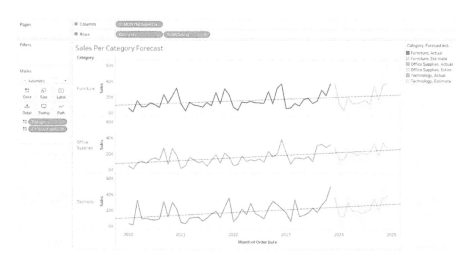

FIGURE 12.20 Output for view 4.

View 5: Sales Distribution across States (Figure 12.21)

FIGURE 12.21 Output for view 5.

12.4.3 Case-2: Profit KPI Dashboard

View 1: Category-wise Profit Summary Overall and Yearly (Figure 12.22)

FIGURE 12.22 Output for view 1.

View 2: Profit Distribution across States (Figure 12.23)

FIGURE 12.23 Output for view 2.

Dashboard 1: Sales KPI Dashboard (Figure 12.24)

FIGURE 12.24   Output for sales KPI dashboard.

Dashboard 2: Profit KPI Dashboard (Figure 12.25)

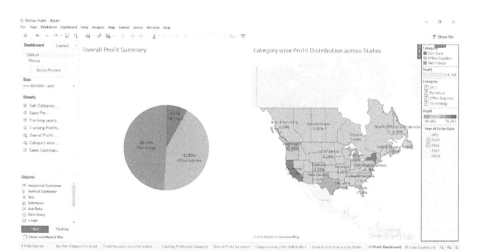

FIGURE 12.25   Output for profit KPI dashboard.

Story 1: Sales and Profit KPI Analysis

To add a new story point, click on the Blank button. Give a suitable title for each story point. We can change the size of the overall view, click on the Size section, and select the desired size. If not sure, then choose "Automatic" (Figure 12.26).

FIGURE 12.26 Output for sales and profit KPI analysis story.

We can design and arrange worksheets and dashboards in the story as per desired order.

12.5 DRAWING INSIGHTS FROM A STORY

Data insights are valuable information gained from studying relevant information sets. They aid in decision-making and reduce risks associated with traditional testing techniques. In the digital era, we have access to abundant data. However, the ability to extract useful information is key to gaining a competitive advantage (Figure 12.27).

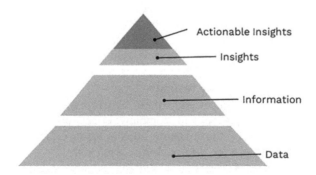

FIGURE 12.27 Progressing from data to insights.

12.5.1 DATA VS INSIGHTS

Data and insights are often used interchangeably, but they have significant differences. Data is information, typically numbers and text, while insights are the output of careful analysis. Industry-to-industry insights can vary significantly due to factors like access to data, dataset specifications, and the specific issue being addressed [8, 9]. Identifying metrics that provide useful information for your industry is crucial for gaining an advantage and setting you apart from competitors.

Some examples of data insights may include the following:

- Knowing the ideal staffing level for your store by examining recent shopping traffic trends is one example of data insight.
- Observing that your product or service is more in demand on some weekends of the year, allowing you to charge more during these times.
- Monitoring the performance statistics of your company's online advertising to identify which campaigns, target audiences, and ads are successful and which are not.

12.6 TYPES OF INSIGHTS

In general, there are two types of data insight categories that are often used by analysts to classify the inferences they obtain after careful data analysis. These are:

I. Actionable insights
II. Non-actionable insights

  A. **Actionable Insights**

   Actionable insights are inferences from data that can lead to a response or action, using structured or unstructured, quantitative, or qualitative data. These insights are catalysts for action, but people or processes are still needed to execute them. Raw data analysis by individuals yields actionable insights, while big data can provide actionable insights when large quantities of data are present. Further analysis may be needed to explain why an insight is actionable, focusing on the "why" rather than "what."

  Attributes of Actionable Insights

  Actionable data insights are simple conclusions that prompt action, enhancing customer value and company effectiveness. These insights should be based on specific attributes, such as value, effectiveness, and relevance, to determine if the information is applicable.

   1. **Relevance:** A dataset can provide valuable insights, but selecting measures relevant to our company's events is crucial to ensure meaningful actionable results.
   2. **Context:** Understanding the historical context of data analysis is crucial for practical insights.
   3. **Specificity:** Real actionable insights are focused, well-considered, and detailed enough to explain what happened and why it happened.

4. **Clarity:** Clarity enhances understanding of insights by providing specific, thorough information by using clear language and proper data labeling.
5. **Alignment:** An insight must align with your business objectives, such as key performance indicators (KPIs), to effectively communicate and relate to your audience, ensuring they can relate to the current story being discussed.

Use Cases for Actionable Insights

The following list showcases some real-time use cases for actionable insights.

- Produce targeted marketing campaigns that relate better with your audience.
- Based on sales data, determine the appropriate products to market in particular locations to boost profit volume.
- Analyze the supply chain process to identify maximum costs, optimize cost structure, and expand profit margins through actionable insights.
- Analyze financial data to classify loan borrowers who are highly likely to default and take appropriate actions.
- Analyze accounting data insights to identify error patterns or fraudulent behavior, preventing further loss.
- Using consumer traffic data, the work involves determining the right staff engagement ratio and taking the necessary steps to improve customer satisfaction and staff efficiency with their attendance.

B. **Non-Actionable Insights**

Recognizing actionable insights from non-actionable or non-insightful results is crucial for driving business results, as these findings are vague, impractical, or difficult to influence due to their lack of specificity. There are three major reasons that lead to classifying a data insight as non-actionable:

1. Insights may be too vague to act upon. In such cases, more research is the only plan we can consider.
2. Limited scope of the insight compared to the overall business picture.
3. Insights not related to company goals.

For example, employees may complain about poor leadership and team management without naming the manager, while university students may complain about circumstances outside their control like campus location or weather. In another scenario, a mobile app user may complain about a feature that was never planned due to its irrelevance. The common portion in all these examples is that no action can be taken to address any of these complaints. Please note that non-actionable feedback does not explain what is wrong or what worked for customers compared to our competitors. It may also contain irrelevant information that cannot be acted upon. All such instances may fall in the category of non-actionable insights since no action is logically or practically available to be applied to them.

KEY NOTES

- Business stories can be created using similar techniques as worksheets and dashboards, organized as "story points."
- A story consists of a theme, plot, characters, data, and visualizations for better understanding.
- Effective data stories require clear language and may require segmenting audiences based on subject knowledge.
- Data is information, while insights are the output of careful analysis.
- Actionable insights lead to responses or actions, while non-actionable findings are vague or impractical.

PRACTICE CASE STUDY

Customer Grievance Analysis Dashboard and Story Development

Download the sample of the financial complaint dataset for consumers as available on public data repositories such as Kaggle. Perform the necessary data preparation tasks using Prep. Use the cleaned data to analyze the different aspects of consumer grievances such as most complaints received from which region, maximum complaints against which product, number of settled vs unsettled grievances per state, etc. Create various dashboards for different features of grievance data. Finally, prepare a highlighting story for the audience.

TEST YOUR SKILLS

1. What is storytelling? How it creates an impact on the audience?
2. Discuss the different types of stories in relevance to business-oriented case studies.
3. Who are the different participants involved in the data storytelling progression?
4. Explain different components of a data story. Explain with a case study example.
5. Discuss the relevance of both actionable and non-actionable types of story insights in the decision-making process.

REFERENCES

1. Ryan, Lindy. *Visual Analytics Fundamentals: Creating Compelling Data Narratives with Tableau*. United Kingdom, Pearson Education, 2023.
2. Joshi, Prachi Manoj, and Mahalle, Parikshit Narendra. *Data Storytelling and Visualization with Tableau: A Hands-on Approach*. United Kingdom, CRC Press, 2022.
3. Ryan, Lindy. *Visual Data Storytelling with Tableau*. United Kingdom, Pearson Education, 2018.
4. Knaflic, Cole Nussbaumer. *Storytelling with Data: A Data Visualization Guide for Business Professionals*. Germany, Wiley, 2015.

5. Wexler, Steve, et al. *The Big Book of Dashboards: Visualizing Your Data Using Real-World Business Scenarios.* Germany, Wiley, 2017.
6. *Data-Driven Storytelling.* United States, CRC Press, 2018.
7. Milligan, Joshua N. *Learning Tableau: Leverage the Power of Tableau 9. 0 to Design Rich Data Visualizations and Build Fully Interactive Dashboards.* United Kingdom, Packt Publishing, 2015.
8. Loth, Alexander. *Visual Analytics with Tableau.* United States, Wiley, 2019.
9. Hwang, Jaejin, and Yoon, Youngjin. *Data Analytics and Visualization in Quality Analysis Using Tableau.* United Kingdom, CRC Press, 2021.

13 Exploratory Data Analysis (EDA) in Tableau

13.1 INTRODUCTION TO EXPLORATORY DATA ANALYSIS (EDA)

Exploratory data analysis, or EDA, is the technique of interpreting, understanding, and summarizing the data. Finding outliers or missing numbers in the data is helpful. EDA is typically used for understanding the properties of a variable and how they relate to other variables in the dataset [1,2]. Exploratory data analysis helps organizations understand their data better as they migrate to a more data-oriented approach.

The primary goals of exploratory data analysis (EDA) are:

- To improve understanding and interpreting data
- To acknowledge the importance of critical variables
- To help identify the outliers and missing values
- To formulate hypothesis
- To help formulate the data for modeling process

Tableau is a tool for data visualization that is mostly employed in business intelligence for decision-making. To gain insights, Tableau assists us in data analysis and dashboard creation. EDA is the first step in any procedure to acquaint ourselves with the data. Tableau stands out as a user-friendly and straightforward visualization tool. Tableau offers solutions for all types of data exploration, from quick, straightforward understanding of the data to connecting to various data sources and using custom SQL queries [3].

13.1.1 EDA FOR DESCRIPTIVE AND DIAGNOSTIC ANALYTICS

Data analysis is a broad term that encompasses several types of analysis, including descriptive, diagnostic, predictive, and prescriptive analysis. However, all types of data analysis begin with exploratory data analysis (EDA), which is also referred to as descriptive analysis. During EDA, hidden relationships and patterns in the available data are explored to better understand the data we are working with [3, 4]. This is achieved by summarizing the key features of the dataset using visual techniques such as bar and pie charts, histograms, boxplots, scatterplots, heat maps, and many more.

13.1.1.1 Descriptive Analysis

Descriptive analysis finds answers for: "What happened?" It is a numerical method of extracting information from data and helps to summarize or describe the characteristics of our dataset in a meaningful way [5].

 DOI: 10.1201/9781003429593-13

There are three primary categories of descriptive statistics:

A. **Frequency Distribution:** It reveals the number of occurrences of each value known as Frequency in the dataset.
B. **Central Tendency:** It measures and evaluates the median or average values in your dataset. The mean, median, and mode are statistical indicators of central tendency as described below:
   - **Mean:** It is the average of all the numbers in the list of numbers.
   - **Mode:** It is the number that appears the most often in the list of numbers.
   - **Median:** It is the midpoint of the provided set of numbers.
C. **Measures of Variability:** It enables users to assess the degree of variability or "spread" within the dataset, or the degree to which the values are dispersed. Range, standard deviation, and variance are measurements of variability as given below:
   - **Standard deviation:** Standard deviation is the amount by which the provided collection of values deviates from the mean value.
   - **Variance:** The term "variance" is used to refer to the square of standard deviation.
   - **Interquartile Range (IQR):** Values between the 25th and 75th percentiles of a list of numbers are known as the interquartile range or IQR.

13.1.1.2 Diagnostic Analysis

Diagnostic analysis is a type of data analytics that helps professionals determine the root cause of specific events. It takes a more detailed look at data to reveal why certain patterns occur, making it an excellent method for explaining anomalies [5, 6]. Diagnostic analytics examines trends and correlations between variables to determine why something happened. These methods can consist of the following:

1. **Identify Anomalies:** Trends and anomalies we discover during the descriptive analysis may not present the cause, so this requires diagnostics analysis to identify it.
2. **Data Mining:** This is the practice of searching through large data volumes to find patterns and relationships in them. It converts raw data into useful information.
3. **Data Drilling:** This method involves conducting a deeper analysis of the specific data layers or information we are analyzing. It reveals more details on the aspects of data that influence the trends in relational, tabular, and multi-dimensional data.
4. **Correlation Analysis:** Correlation is the relationship between the directional movement of two or more variables. They can have positive, negative, or no correlation. A positive correlation means an increase in one variable causes an increase in the other. A negative correlation occurs when the value of one item increases while the other decreases. It is important to note that correlation does not imply causation. Just because two variables have a relationship, it does not necessarily mean that one caused the other.

Finding correlations and associations between the variables in our data is made easier by exploratory data analysis. When describing data and offering estimates based on it, EDA uses descriptive statistical analysis. To uncover the causes of observed trends, patterns, and data correlations, it also employs diagnostic data analysis.

13.2 TYPES OF EXPLORATORY DATA ANALYSIS

EDA approaches come in two flavors: graphical and quantitative (non-graphical). While the quantitative method requires calculating summary statistics, the graphical method entails summarizing the data in a diagrammatic or visual fashion. Univariate and multivariate approaches are further subdivided into both categories (Figure 13.1).

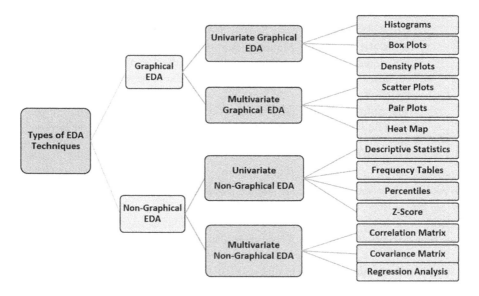

FIGURE 13.1 Types of exploratory data analysis (EDA) approaches.

Let us discuss each of these sub-types below:

13.2.1 UNIVARIATE APPROACH OF EDA

In univariate EDA, just one variable is examined at a time. We can analyze the distribution of the data and detect any outliers with the use of univariate EDA [7]. For instance, univariate data can be the weight of university students. Suppose that the weights of ten final-year university students are documented in Figure 13.2.

Weight (In Pounds)	112.9	136.4	153.0	144.2	123.3	114.1	139.9	124.0	141.8	155.3

FIGURE 13.2 Example of univariate data.

When analyzing this type of data, we can describe patterns by interpreting central tendency measures such as mean, median, and mode, as well as by evaluating data dispersion or spread through range, minimum, maximum, quartiles, variance, and standard deviation.

A. Graphical Univariate EDA

Charts and graphs are made using the univariate graphical EDA method to investigate a single variable. We use this approach to comprehend data distribution and spot outliers if any. Graphical univariate exploratory data analysis (EDA) involves visualizations to analyze each variable in a dataset individually. Here, the aim is to understand the distribution and characteristics of a single variable in the data. Some frequently used charts in univariate graphical EDA include:

- **Histograms:** By splitting the data into intervals (or bins) and counting the number of observations in each bin, a histogram illustrates the distribution of a single variable. These graphs may assist in determining the shape of the distribution and draw attention to skewness, outliers, and patterns in the data.
- **Box Plots:** By plotting the median, quartiles, and outliers in the data, a box plot (or box-and-whisker plot) visualizes the distribution of a single variable. It can show outliers and skewness in the data and offer a concise distribution summary.
- **Density Plots:** A smoothed histogram that calculates the probability density function of a single variable is called a density plot. These can be used to highlight the data's shape, including skewness and multi-modality, and to depict the distribution of the data.

B. Non-Graphical Univariate EDA

Utilizing statistical methods to investigate a single variable is a component of univariate non-graphical EDA. This may entail computing measures of central tendency (such as the mean or median), spread (such as the range or standard deviation), and form (such as skewness or kurtosis). Univariate non-graphical EDA frequently employs a variety of approaches, such as:

- **Descriptive Statistical Techniques:** To summarize the key features of the data by computing measures like mean, median, mode, standard deviation, quartiles, and range.
- **Frequency Tables:** This involves counting the number of occurrences of each unique value in a variable and creating a frequency table to summarize the data distribution.
- **Percentiles:** This involves dividing the data into 100 equal parts and calculating the value of each part, known as a percentile, which can be used to summarize the data distribution.
- **Z-Scores:** The formula for Z-score is shown in Figure 13.3:

$$Z\text{-}Score = (x - Mean) / Standard\ Deviation$$

FIGURE 13.3 Formula for Z-score calculation.

If a data point (x) has a z-score of more than 3, it is regarded as significantly distinct from the other data points. Such a data point can be an "Outlier." The farther away from zero (0) a data point is, the more likely it is that it is an outlier. Any Z-scores of more than 3 are normally categorized as "Extreme."

13.2.2 BIVARIATE APPROACH OF EDA

The term "bivariate analysis" refers to the study of bivariate data. To determine whether there is a relationship between two sets of numbers, one of the basic types of statistical analysis is performed. This sort of data analysis examines relationships and causes, and it seeks to understand how the two variables are related [7, 8]. Temperature and air conditioner sales throughout the summer are two examples of bivariate data. According to temperature, Table 13.1 displays air conditioner sales.

Bivariate data analysis involves studying two variables and their relationship. For example, temperature and air conditioner sales are directly proportional, with an increase in temperature leading to an increase in sales. To understand such data, we plot variables on a graph, with one independent and the other dependent.

- **Scatter Plots:** With scatter charts, we can plot marks or dots by mapping values on the x-axis and y-axis to depict the association between the two variables.
- **Regression Analysis:** In this method, a line or a curve is plotted using two variables. The plotted curve may be exponential, while the line can be linear. This technique is useful for determining a correlation coefficient utilized for regression analysis.
- **Correlation Coefficients:** In regression analysis, this method helps establish a correlation between two variables. If the coefficients have a value of zero, it means that the variables are independent of each other, and there is no correlation. For finding the correlation between two variables, these coefficients must have a non-zero value.

TABLE 13.1
Temperature and AC Sales Data

Temperature (in °C)	Air Conditioner Sales (in Units)
25	5
30	12
35	18
40	25
45	37

13.2.3 Multivariate Approach of EDA

Multivariate EDA involves looking at three or more variables in a single perspective. Multivariate EDA can help you understand the relationships between several variables and identify any complex patterns or outliers that might exist [8]. For example, predicting the weather of any month in a year based on factors such as season, pollution, humidity, and precipitation.

A. **Graphical Multivariate EDA**

Graphical multivariate exploratory data analysis (EDA) encompasses analyzing the relationship among multiple variables in a dataset using charts. The goal of multivariate graphical EDA is to understand how different variables in the data interact and influence one another and to identify patterns and relationships that can inform further analysis and modeling. Multivariate graphics can take various common forms, including:

- **Scatter Plots:** Scatter plots can be used to visualize the association between variables, including the strength, direction, and shape of the relationship, as well as the presence of outliers and skewness.
- **Pair Plots:** Pair plots can provide a comprehensive overview of the relationships between all variables in the data, including the presence of correlations, outliers, and skewness.
- **Heat Maps:** Heat maps can visualize the relationship between variables and identify patterns and correlations in the data.

B. **Non-Graphical Multivariate EDA**

Multivariate non-graphical EDA involves using statistical techniques to explore three or more variables at a time. This can include techniques like regression analysis or principal component analysis. Some common techniques used in multivariate non-graphical EDA include:

- **Correlation Matrix:** The correlation between each pair of variables in the data is displayed in a table called a correlation matrix.
- **Covariance Matrix:** A table displaying the covariance or join variability between each pair of variables in the data is known as a covariance matrix.
- **Regression Analysis:** In addition to forecasting future values based on historical data, regression analysis can also determine the strength and direction of relationships between variables.

13.3 EXPLANATORY DATA ANALYSIS

Explanatory analysis goes beyond exploratory analysis to focus on how and why things happen, and what should happen next [9]. Decision-makers and stakeholders need to be informed of the findings. For example, an analysis of product sales analytics data can identify why certain products sell well and how to increase goal completion. The steps for conducting an explanatory data analysis are outlined below:

Step 1. Define the research query.
Step 2. Frame a hypothesis.
Step 3. Collect data and plan a methodology.
Step 4. Examine collected data and maintain generated results.
Step 5. Infer results, improve understanding and motivation for future exploration.

Explanatory research explores why something happens with limited information. It helps increase understanding, predict future occurrences, and investigate patterns in existing data. It is a type of causal research that identifies a direct cause-and-effect relationship between variables (Figure 13.4).

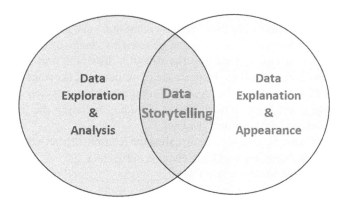

FIGURE 13.4   Relationship between data exploration, data explanation, and storytelling.

13.3.1 EXPLORATORY VS EXPLANATORY DATA ANALYSIS

Exploratory data analytics is the process of organizing and visualizing raw data to identify patterns, anomalies, and other factors. Explanatory data analytics determines the why and how of a given context and can be used to calculate outcomes. However, it may not always provide actionable insights for real-life scenarios. This type of analysis is often used in marketing to explain customer behavior and campaign success.

The notable points of difference between the exploratory and explanatory data analyses are given in Table 13.2.

TABLE 13.2

Differentiate between Exploratory and Explanatory Data Analyses

Exploratory Data Analysis	Explanatory Data Analysis
We utilize exploratory analysis to comprehend, investigate, and become familiar with our data and the current issue to produce helpful knowledge.	Explanatory study uses the limited knowledge that is available to investigate why something occurs.
Whether we begin with a hypothesis or query or analyze the data to see what might be interesting, the exploratory analysis focuses on creating connections between variables and detecting patterns and outliers.	It relates different ideas and concepts to understand the nature of cause-effect relationships to explain why certain events occur.
Exploratory analysis is conducted in the primary stage of data analysis.	Explanatory analysis is conducted after exploratory and descriptive analysis is complete.
As an outcome, it aids in the discovery of insights, improves the understanding of the data, and eliminates anomalies or irrelevant data.	The primary outcomes of explanatory analysis are insights, which, when used to inform choices and actions, develop into wisdom.

13.4 COMBINE EXPLORATORY AND EXPLANATORY ANALYSES FOR STORYTELLING

The question that arises now is whether we can combine exploratory and explanatory data analysis. The answer is "Yes." In real-world analysis, data explanation and data exploration can be combined for interactive data storytelling [4, 10] (Figure 13.5).

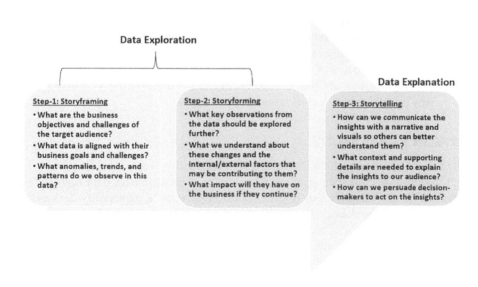

FIGURE 13.5 Combining data explanation and exploration for data storytelling phases.

There are three major steps in data storytelling. These are:

1. **Storyframing:** At this exploratory stage, frame data to identify key insights easily. No narrative yet. Prioritize areas that need attention and analysis, not entire dataset.
2. **Storyforming:** Storyforming involves analyzing and interpreting data to gain insights. Analyzing involves examining data closely while interpreting involves making sense of findings and concluding. Your analytical skills affect analysis quality, but data interpretation relies on your business knowledge. These steps are interdependent and iterative. Each conclusion informs the subsequent direction and focus of analysis until an insight is found.
3. **Storytelling:** After gaining insight, we must decide how to proceed. Data storytelling can help us refine and communicate the story in a way that incites action in others. A compelling data story will guide your audience through the numbers, enabling them to draw the same conclusions as us.

Here, the first two steps of Storyframing and Storyforming are steps of exploratory investigation. After we gain some insights that we want to share with others, we shift focus to data storytelling, which itself is an explanatory process.

KEY NOTES

- Exploratory data analysis, or EDA, is the technique of interpreting, understanding, and summarizing the data.
- EDA is typically used for understanding the properties of a variable and how they relate to other variables in the dataset.
- Descriptive analysis finds answers for: "What happened?" It is a numerical method of extracting information from data and helps to summarize or describe the characteristics of our dataset in a meaningful way.
- Diagnostic analysis is a type of data analytics that helps professionals determine the root cause of specific events.
- Explanatory analysis goes beyond exploratory analysis to focus on how and why things happen, and what should happen next.

PRACTICE CASE STUDY

Air Flight Fare Investigation Dashboard with Interactive Story

Download Airfare dataset available easily on public domain data repositories. Create different visualizations to perform different sorts of exploratory data analysis activities on the dataset. Carefully note the insights obtained. Plot tend lines to analyze the projection of ticket fares in the recent years. Also, forecast the fares for the coming 12–24 months. View the effects of seasonality and cyclic variations as well. Create interactive dashboards highlighting several aspects of Airfare data. Generate an interesting story highlighting noticeable insights that you obtained from this investigation.

TEST YOUR SKILLS

1. Define EDA. What visualization goals are satisfied using the EDA approach?
2. How descriptive analysis is different from the diagnostic analysis technique?
3. Elaborate various types of graphical and non-graphical EDA techniques with business-relevant case studies.
4. Differentiate between exploratory and explanatory data analyses with a few examples.
5. Discuss the association between exploratory and explanatory analyses to create interactive stories.

REFERENCES

[1] DuToit, S. H. C., et al. *Graphical Exploratory Data Analysis*. Switzerland, Springer New York, 2012.

[2] Bruce, Peter, and Bruce, Andrew. *Practical Statistics for Data Scientists: 50 Essential Concepts*. United States, O'Reilly Media, 2017.

[3] Theus, Martin, and Urbanek, Simon. *Interactive Graphics for Data Analysis: Principles and Examples*. United States, CRC Press, 2008.

[4] Knaflic, Cole Nussbaumer. *Storytelling with Data: A Data Visualization Guide for Business Professionals*. Germany, Wiley, 2015.

[5] Jones, Ben. *Communicating Data with Tableau: Designing, Developing, and Delivering Data Visualizations*. Germany, O'Reilly Media, 2014.

[6] Mukhiya, Suresh Kumar, and Ahmed, Usman. *Hands-On Exploratory Data Analysis with Python: Perform EDA Techniques to Understand, Summarize, and Investigate Your Data*. United Kingdom, Packt Publishing, 2020.

[7] Benoit, Gerald. *Introduction to Information Visualization: Transforming Data Into Meaningful Information*. United States, Rowman & Littlefield Publishers, 2019.

[8] *Data-Driven Storytelling*. United States, CRC Press, 2018.

[9] Murray, Daniel G. *Tableau Your Data! Fast and Easy Visual Analysis with Tableau Software*. Germany, Wiley, 2016.

[10] Monsey, Molly, and Sochan, Paul. *Tableau for Dummies*. Germany, Wiley, 2015.

14 Misleading Visualizations

14.1 INTRODUCING MISLEADING DATA VISUALIZATIONS

When presenting information through data visualization, it is common to focus on patterns and outliers. This can be an effective way to influence decision-making. However, it is important to exercise caution, as data visualization can also be used to misinform, either intentionally or unintentionally [1]. Data is often easy to understand immediately, which means that viewers may not take the time to delve further into the conclusions generated from the data. While data visualization can be a powerful tool for evaluating and presenting complex data, it is crucial to use it properly. If done incorrectly, data can be distorted or misrepresented, leading to incorrect conclusions [2,3]. Unfortunately, some people intentionally falsify data using data visualization to forward their agenda or viewpoint. Others create deceptive data visualizations due to errors or a lack of knowledge about portraying data. Regardless of the design's aesthetics, information must be communicated clearly and accurately. To understand how misleading visualizations work, let us consider a simple example. Imagine that company ABC presents a graph showing how its profits have evolved over 5 months (Figure 14.1).

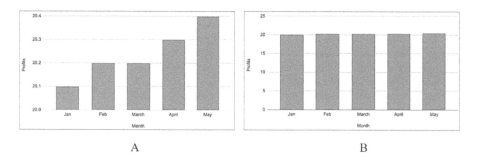

FIGURE 14.1   (a) Incorrect visualization of profits and (b) correct visualization of profits.

The company earned 20.1, 20.2, 20.3, and 20.4 million, respectively, in the first 5 months. However, the graph above is misleading as the y-axis starts at 20 rather than 0, making it seem like there has been a significant increase in profits. While the data is technically valid, it presents a false impression of growth which can deceive viewers and stakeholders into drawing inaccurate conclusions. This is a perfect example of how visualizing data inaccurately can change people's perceptions. Instead, the second graph with the y-axis starting at 0 provides a more accurate representation of the profit progress without exaggerating the data.

                    DOI: 10.1201/9781003429593-14

14.2 TYPES OF MISLEADING VISUALIZATIONS

In this section, we will discuss different types of common misleading visualizations that can lead to misinterpreting the real information and leading to wrong insights.

1. **Truncating the Scale of Bar Charts**

    Some of the most well-known examples of data visualization are bar charts. By comparing bar heights, it provides a rapid indication of relative size. Everyone can comprehend them, and they are simple to construct. In this illustration, a bar chart contrasts the net revenue ABC company received throughout the previous years. There are 48 billion units in the vertical scale. That makes sense and is accurate. The y-axis in the following example starts with 28 billion, which gives the revenue growth in the succeeding years the appearance of having skyrocketed (Figure 14.2).

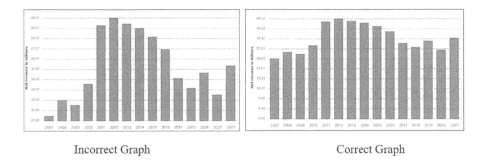

Incorrect Graph   Correct Graph

FIGURE 14.2 Incorrect and correct illustrations of bar graphs.

When a part of the vertical y-axis is truncated, it can make the differences in the size of the bars appear larger than they are [4]. Some people may use this technique to deceive others into thinking that there are larger differences in the data than there really are. This can lead to distorted data visualization and inaccurate marketing decisions.

2. **Skipping Information in Scatter Plot**

    Skipping certain data points can create false trends and overlook important details. Variable omission can change our interpretation of data [5]. Carefully evaluate the context and search for other variables that could impact the one being studied (Figure 14.3).

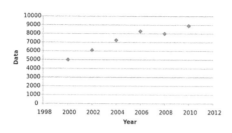 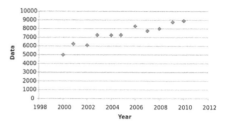

Scatter Plot with Missing Data Points   **Regular Scatter Plot**

FIGURE 14.3   Incorrect and correct illustrations of scatter plots.

Check out the scatter plot above as an illustration of what happens when we ignore certain data, whether we are doing it to intentionally produce a false data visualization or just to make our task easier. The chart, which would typically be packed with dips and spikes, seems much smoother and steadier when some data points are removed.

3. False Causation with Correlation

An important concept to understand is that "Correlation does not imply Causation" [4, 5]. In statistics and data analysis field, we frequently come across this concept which usually causes dilemma in the minds of young analysts. However, the fact is that, just because two trends or events seem to vary parallelly together with each other, it does not prove that one causes the other or that they are related to each other in a logical way (Figure 14.4).

Ice Cream Sales Vs Road Rage Cases in 2022

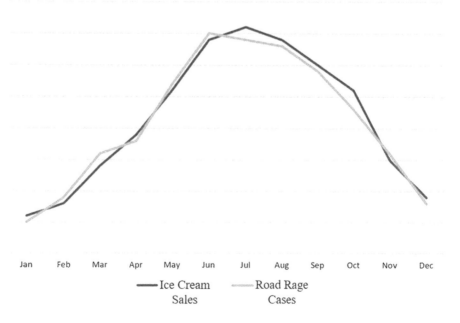

FIGURE 14.4   Line plots for ice cream sales and road accidents.

Observe the figure given above, which shows a line graph displaying trends of two different pieces of information. The first line graph in blue color depicts the initial increase with peak achievement and then a fall in ice cream sales. The second line plot in red color depicts a similar trend for road rage cases around the year. These two things have nothing to do with each other as both are unrelated quantities that appear to increase or decrease at the same rate over a similar time period.

4. Cherry-Picking in a Chart

Cherry-picking data is the act of selectively choosing facts and figures to support a particular viewpoint [6]. It could also mean presenting data in a way that is more favorable for creating the desired impression. To produce clear and consistent results that fit into a neat pattern, cherry-picked images are often employed. However, cherry-picking has the disadvantage of not providing an honest, unbiased picture, resulting in outcomes that are incorrect or exclude important areas of knowledge (Figure 14.5).

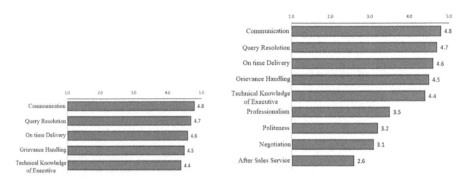

FIGURE 14.5   Demonstrating cherry-picking for a company survey.

Suppose an ABC company conducted a customer satisfaction survey where customers gave scores in the range of 1–5 based on their satisfaction level with the services provided by the company. The results obtained are presented to the management in the above given bar chart. It appears from the graph that the consumers are generally satisfied because all the scores are greater than 4, thus the average score is 4.6. Let us now look at a different graph or say the complete graph. Evidently, the survey included quite a few additional questions with substantially lower results. Your average mean score has dropped to 3.9, making your scenario appear less favorable. It is easy to make findings appear much better than they are by cherry-picking data and omitting the statements with the lowest scores. This may be done to fool the management or to influence their decision-making. Hence, cherry-picked visuals are more likely to influence decisions. We must ensure that the information we interpret from digital charts and graphs should be entirely objective and not merely cherry-picked.

5. Numbers Do Not Add up to the Total

Misleading pie charts are the most typical illustrations of poor data visualization. Pie charts, by their very nature proportionate, often display numbers that equal 100% (or the full pie slice). The purpose of a pie chart is to depict the components of a whole, not the distinction between groups. Pie charts should always add up to 100% neither below nor above (Figure 14.6).

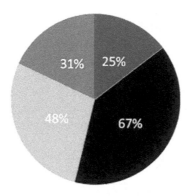

Percentages not adding up to 100%

FIGURE 14.6   Misleading pie chart not adding up to 100% composition.

6. Wrong Chart Type

We can use a wide variety of charts and graphs to visually depict data. Certain graphs and charts are effective in depicting specific types of information but not others. When we attempt to visualize data using an unsuitable format, problems may occur. The format of our visualization is typically determined by the type of data we are using. The most crucial factor is whether the data is qualitative (meaning it is categorical) or quantitative (i.e., it is measurable or numeric). Quantitative data is typically better represented in formats like scatter charts and histograms, while qualitative data is typically better suited to be presented in bar graphs and pie charts (Figure 14.7).

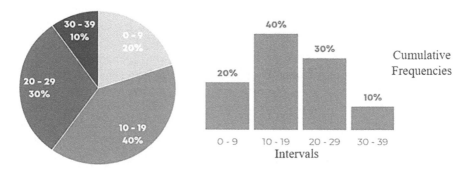

FIGURE 14.7   Demonstrating wrong graph choice for a given data.

For example: Suppose we have an ordinal or sequential data variable such as height, weight, or age intervals. In this case, although we can plot a pie chart, but histogram is a better alternative for representing and understanding ordinal or sequential sets of data. Let us summarize a set of guidelines while opting for pie charts to display our data:

a.   For negative numbers in a dataset, use column chart or bar chart instead of a pie chart.
b.   For an ordinal or sequential set of data, then use a histogram or scatter plot.
c.   To display patterns or trends over time, then use a time series chart or a line chart.
d.   If more than two or three categories are to be displayed, then use a bar chart.
e.   To display more than one pie chart or a group of pie charts at a time, use a stacked bar chart instead.

7. Too much Data to be Visualized

Data visualizations aim to tell a story effectively. To achieve this, we must include only relevant data and determine which variables are essential. The number of variables we choose to include will determine the structure of our visualization [6]. We must select the best visualization graph for clear understanding. If we include too many variables, it can be challenging to distinguish between values, potentially distracting or confusing the user from the main point we are attempting to convey (Figure 14.8).

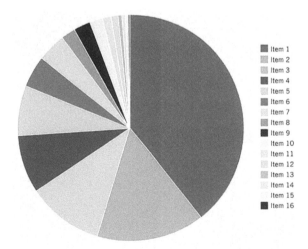

Pie chart with so many categories

FIGURE 14.8   Too many variables depicted in pie chart.

8. Bad Color Choice

Using appropriate colors not only make our visualization attractive but also help the viewer to easily understand the information we are trying to convey. However, when too many colors are used incorrectly, it can make the visualization messed up leading to confusion [7]. Therefore, we must wisely choose colors for our visualization charts and graphs. Some common issues that must be addressed while applying colors to our visualization are given below:

- If too many colors of indistinct shades are used together, it makes it difficult for the viewer to quickly understand the visualization or differentiate the details.
- We must use familiar colors for relevant contexts. For example, in a pie chart, use red color for displaying percentage of customers ordering non-vegetarian dishes and green for those ordering vegetarian dishes.
- Avoid using similar colors. We must ensure that contrasting colors are used for clarity and differentiating categories of information.
- We must avoid using tones or shades that are likely to confuse color-blind people (Figure 14.9).

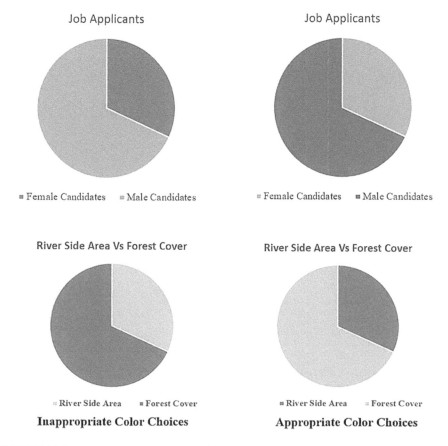

FIGURE 14.9 Inappropriate and appropriate color choice examples.

9. Three-Dimensional Charts Leading to Distortion

A 3D graph looks more interesting and appealing compared to simple and boring 2D graphs. However, a 3D chart can distort the bars making differences appear larger compared to a corresponding 2D chart. Also, a 3D graph can hide or superimpose certain parts of a graph data by blocking them because a 3D graph adds a new dimension and imitates natural space. Apart from this, distortion is another issue related to 3D data visualizations. Distortion is the result of foreshortening in images since objects closer to us appear larger than the ones far away. However, in visualization charts, this poses an issue of giving the wrong impression of hierarchies that do not exist and skews data relationships (Figure 14.10).

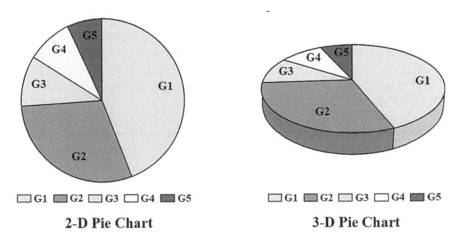

2-D Pie Chart   **3-D Pie Chart**

FIGURE 14.10   Comparison of 2D and 3D pie charts for a sample data.

The 3D pie chart on the right side displays G1 and G2 values to look much larger while G3, G4, and G5 look much smaller than they are. This is because pie slices that are visually closer or in front of the viewer will always appear oversized than those far from the user. This demonstrates how common it is for 3D pie charts to misrepresent angles (Figure 14.11).

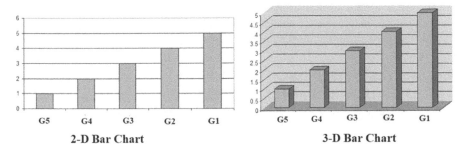

2-D Bar Chart   **3-D Bar Chart**

FIGURE 14.11   Comparison of 2D and 3-D bar charts for a sample data.

Similarly, we find it quite challenging to compare the bar heights in the 3D chart (on the right) due to perspective distortion while in the 2D chart (to the left), that task is simple.

14.3 IMPACT OF MISLEADING VISUALIZATIONS

Misleading data visualization could result in incorrect conclusions and bad business decisions that could not be in the best interests of the firm and that might have an impact on your company [7]. Some effects of deceptive data visualization include the ones listed below:

1. **Incorrect Decision-Making due to Misleading Information**
   A misleading and inaccurate graph (or dashboard) that displays exaggerated advertising efforts with respect to annual revenue may result in the organization spending a lot of money and effort in promoting in a region where there are not enough potential customers who could use their products or services. Thus, incorrect decisions due to misleading visualizations not only wastes time and effort but also degrades the overall financial performance of the organization.
2. **Low Prospects for Improvement**
   It may be hard to identify issues and come up with resolutions and ideas if we rely on misleading data for our business needs. For instance, certain conventional marketing methods may not generate the desired results but we may not be aware of this scenario due to the misleading data affecting our understanding. This leads to wastage of time, money, effort, and resources on useless marketing strategies.
3. **Missing Out the Latest Trends**
   Using wrong data visualization techniques might cause the decision-makers to make erroneous conclusions, which can cause the organization to miss out on latest industry trends that could have been essential for the development of the company.
4. **Reduced Trust in Management**
   Use of deceptive graphics by management while giving a crucial presentation to their team will generate more questions than it will resolve. If they keep giving false information to the coworkers, this can make them soon lose their faith in management's decisions.
5. **Legal and Compliance Issues**
   In the worst-case scenario, poorly created charts and misleading information may result in compliance challenges as well as legal issues. This could affect the business, resulting in increased expenses and decreased customer loyalty.

14.4 MISTAKES TO BE AVOIDED DURING VISUALIZATION AND STORYTELLING

Data visualizations can be effective storytelling and communication tools, but if not done properly, they can also be boring, confusing, or deceptive. Let us discuss about some of the most prevalent mistakes to avoid while designing data visualizations for narrative purposes, as well as how to strengthen our presentation skills.

1. **Choose the Right Chart Type:** One of the primary decisions while creating a data visualization is choosing the type of chart for use. Each chart type has its own set of strengths and weaknesses, and they can convey different messages with appeal. Thus, it is vital to choose the chart type that best suits our data, your audience, and your story.
2. **Employ Clear and Consistent Labels:** Making sure that your axes, titles, legends, and annotations are labeled clearly and consistently is another crucial step in developing a data visualization. Labels assist our audience in understanding the subject matter of our data, the variables we are employing, and the key insights we are emphasizing. Labels must reflect the tone and style of your article and be brief, accurate, and informative.
3. **Prevent Clutter and Noise:** Making the graph excessively cluttered and noisy with extra grid lines, borders, backdrops, colors, fonts, or effects is a common mistake when producing a data visualization. The viewers may become distracted from the primary idea by clutter and noise, which can also make the chart difficult to read and understand and lessen the visual appeal of the visualization. One should only utilize things that improve your story and data and adhere to the principles of simplicity and minimalism to prevent clutter and noise.
4. **Pick the Right Colors and Scales:** Choosing the appropriate colors and scales for the chart is another important step in producing a data visualization. Scales and colors can express meaning and emotion as well as significantly influence how the audience interprets and responds to what we are presenting.
5. **Portray a Compelling Story:** Telling a compelling story with data at hand is the first and most crucial step in developing a data visualization. A story can be used to engage an audience, explain data, and deliver a message rather than just being a collection of facts and figures. A story ought to have a distinct outline, a logical progression, and an engaging storyline.

KEY NOTES

- Data is often easy to understand immediately, which means that viewers may not take the time to delve further into the conclusions generated from the data.
- While data visualization can be a powerful tool for evaluating and presenting complex data, it is crucial to use it properly. If done incorrectly, data can be distorted or misrepresented, leading to incorrect conclusions.
- Misleading data visualization could result in incorrect conclusions and bad business decisions that could not be in the best interests of the firm and that might have an impact on your company.

TEST YOUR SKILLS

1. How misleading graphics can impact stakeholders' decision-making? Discuss with a business-relevant case study.
2. What are the different types of misleading visualizations? Give examples.

3. Discuss the scenarios where pie charts can be deceptive and confusing.
4. Give an example of a misleading bar chart leading to delusion of information.
5. Which common mistakes are made by designers while creating interactive visualizations? How can these mistakes be avoided?
6. Why it is generally suggested that 3D graphs should be avoided and replaced by corresponding 2D graphs?
7. Have you ever come across any misleading graphics on social media platforms, news channels, newspapers, magazines, etc.? Discuss and examine it for learning purposes.

REFERENCES

[1] Schwabish, Jonathan. *Better Data Visualizations: A Guide for Scholars, Researchers, and Wonks.* United States, Columbia University Press, 2021.
[2] Ranganathan, Kavitha. *Impactful Data Visualization: Hide and Seek with Graphs.* India, Penguin Random House India Private Limited, 2023.
[3] Cairo, Alberto. *How Charts Lie: Getting Smarter about Visual Information.* United Kingdom, WW Norton, 2020.
[4] Brooks-Young, Susan. *The Media-Savvy Middle School Classroom: Strategies for Teaching against Disinformation.* United Kingdom, Taylor & Francis, 2020.
[5] Dougherty, Jack, and Ilyankou, Ilya. *Hands-On Data Visualization.* United States, O'Reilly Media, 2021.
[6] Wilke, Claus. *Fundamentals of Data Visualization: A Primer on Making Informative and Compelling Figures.* Taiwan, O'Reilly Media, 2019.
[7] Milligan, Joshua N. *Learning Tableau: Leverage the Power of Tableau 9. 0 to Design Rich Data Visualizations and Build Fully Interactive Dashboards.* United Kingdom, Packt Publishing, 2015.

Index

actionable insight 434
additive model 200, 201
aggregation 67, 82, 120, 202
ANOVA 231–232
attribute 37–38, 232

bar chart 4–7, 143–144, 164–169
bimodal 252
bivariate analysis 442
blending 14, 29, 41–46
box plot 152, 250, 302–305
bubble chart 276–279
bullet chart 338, 365–366

calculated sorting 47
candidate key 38
cardinality 37
causation 439, 450
cherry-picking 451
choropleth map 388, 393
column chart 8, 164, 172
column shelf 93, 99, 211
comparison chart 164, 171, 194
condition filter 88, 99
context filter 88, 97, 138
continuous area plot 332
contrast 414
correlation 439–442
crosstab 141
cyclic variations 198–199, 248

dashboard 418–419
data cleaning 22, 50
data extract 15, 20, 26
data storytelling 321, 327, 330
dates filter 88, 93, 108
degree 32, 56, 178
density map 122, 178, 303
descriptive analysis 438, 445
diagnostic analysis 439, 446–447
dimensions 41, 75, 77
dimension filter 88, 91, 138
discrete area plots 332
distribution chart 141, 201, 250
distribution map 399, 409
donut chart 317, 319, 321
drill-down 412
dynamic composition 331, 335

explanatory analysis 443, 445, 446
exploratory data analysis 438, 440, 443

exponential trend 216, 217
extract filter 88, 94, 138

filled map 142, 388, 393
flow map 399
forecasts 201, 209
foreign key 38, 41
frequency table 346
full outer join 33

Gantt chart 149, 338
gauge chart 338–339

heat map 140–141, 298–299
highlight table 141, 151
histogram 148, 250–256

inner join 38, 40
insight 8, 434–435
intersection 415

joins 38–40

key progress indicator (KPI) 423

left outer join 38
line chart 3, 116, 117
linear trend 197, 210–211
logarithmic trend 212–214
lollipop chart 164, 187–189

manual sorting 47, 112, 116
measures 77, 109
measures filter 72, 74
metrics 164, 339
misleading graphics 456–457
multiplicative model 200–201
multimodal 252–253
multivariate EDA 443

noise 199–200, 457
non-actionable insight 434–435
NULL 37–39

operator 67, 71
origin-destination map 388, 404–406
outer join 38–39
outlier 199–200

page shelf 1, 2
Pareto chart 378–379, 380–385

459

Milton Keynes UK
Ingram Content Group UK Ltd.
UKHW031125141024
449569UK00006B/442